BESTSELLING
BOOK SERIES

The Ancient Egyptians For Dummies®

Cheat Sheet

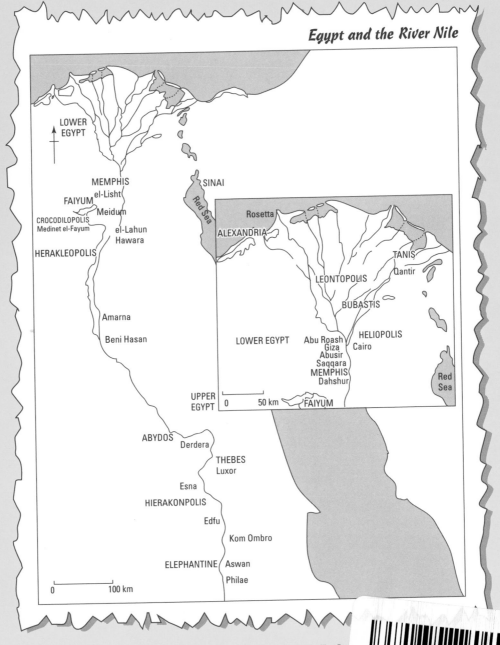

Egypt and the River Nile

LOWER EGYPT

MEMPHIS
el-Lisht
FAIYUM
Meidum
CROCODILOPOLIS
Medinet el-Fayum   el-Lahun
Hawara
HERAKLEOPOLIS

SINAI

Red Sea

Rosetta

ALEXANDRIA

TANIS
Qantir

LEONTOPOLIS

BUBASTIS

LOWER EGYPT   Abu Roash   HELIOPOLIS
Giza   Cairo
Abusir
Saqqara
MEMPHIS
Dahshur

Red Sea

UPPER EGYPT   0   50 km   FAIYUM

Amarna

Beni Hasan

ABYDOS
Derdera

THEBES
Luxor

Esna

HIERAKONPOLIS

Edfu

Kom Ombro

ELEPHANTINE   Aswan
Philae

0   100 km

D1205357

For Dummies: Bestselling Book Series for Beginners

The Ancient Egyptians For Dummies®

Egypt and the Ancient Near East

Periods of Egyptian History

You can see from this timeline that some of the dates and dynasties overlap in ancient Egyptian history, especially during the Intermediate Periods, because different kings ruled different parts of Egypt at the same time — all holding the title of king.

Predynastic Period

The Badarian period: 4400–4000 BC
Maadian period: 4000–3300 BC
The Amratian period: 4000–3500 BC
The Gerzean period: 3500–3200 BC
The Negada III period: 3200–3050 BC

Early Dynastic Period

Dynasty 0: 3150–3050 BC
Dynasty 1: 3050–2890 BC
Dynasty 2: 2890–2686 BC

Old Kingdom

Dynasty 3: 2686–2613 BC
Dynasty 4: 2613–2500 BC
Dynasty 5: 2498–2345 BC
Dynasty 6: 2345–2333 BC

First Intermediate Period

Dynasties 7 and 8: 2180–2160 BC

Dynasties 9 and 10: 2160–2040 BC

Middle Kingdom

Dynasty 11: 2134–1991 BC
Dynasty 12: 1991–1782 BC

Second Intermediate Period

Dynasty 13: 1782–1650 BC
Dynasty 14: Dates unknown. This dynasty is characterised by a few chieftains ruling one town, calling themselves kings.
Dynasty 15: 1663–1555 BC
Dynasty 16: 1663–1555 BC
Dynasty 17: 1663–1570 BC

New Kingdom

Dynasty 18: 1570–1293 BC
Dynasty 19: 1293–1185 BC
Dynasty 20: 1185–1070 BC

Third Intermediate Period

High Priests (Thebes): 1080–945 BC
Dynasty 21 (Tanis): 1069–945 BC
Dynasty 22 (Tanis): 945–715 BC
Dynasty 23 (Leontopolis): 818–715 BC
Dynasty 24 (Sais): 727–715 BC
Dynasty 25 (Nubians): 747–656 BC
Dynasty 26 (Sais): 664–525 BC

Late Period

Dynasty 27 (Persian): 525–404 BC
Dynasty 28: 404–399 BC
Dynasty 29: 399–380 BC
Dynasty 30: 380–343 BC
Dynasty 31: 343–332 BC

Graeco-Roman Period

Macedonian Kings: 332–305 BC
Ptolemaic Period: 305–30 BC

The Ancient Egyptians

FOR

DUMMIES®

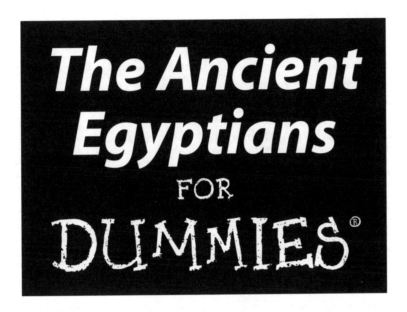

The Ancient Egyptians FOR DUMMIES®

by Charlotte Booth

1807
WILEY
2007

John Wiley & Sons, Ltd

The Ancient Egyptians For Dummies®

Published by
John Wiley & Sons, Ltd
The Atrium
Southern Gate
Chichester
West Sussex
PO19 8SQ
England

E-mail (for orders and customer service enquires): cs-books@wiley.co.uk

Visit our Home Page on www.wiley.com

For general information on our other products and services, please contact our Customer Care Department within the U.S. at 800-762-2974, outside the U.S. at 317-572-3993, or fax 317-572-4002.

For technical support, please visit www.wiley.com/techsupport.

Wiley also publishes its books in a variety of electronic formats. Some content that appears in print may not be available in electronic books.

British Library Cataloguing in Publication Data: A catalogue record for this book is available from the British Library

ISBN: 978-0-470-06544-0

Printed and bound in Great Britain by Bell and Bain Ltd, Glasgow.

Translations by James Henry Bressted, B. Brier, J. and R. Janssen, Barbara S. Lesko, M. Lichtheim, C. El Mahdy, C. Nims, R. Partridge, James B. Pritchard.

With thanks to C. Banks, W. Frostick, D. Thompson, and G. Webb for their kind permission to reproduce the photographs in this book.

WILEY

About the Author

Charlotte Booth is a freelance Egyptologist who started her education at Birkbeck, University of London, with a Diploma in Egyptology. From there she went to University College London and gained a degree and a Masters in Egyptian Archaeology. She is currently studying at the University of Wales, Swansea, for a PhD, and has written a number of articles and books on Egyptology. Charlotte teaches archaeology and Egyptology in various adult education institutions including the Workers' Educational Association and Birkbeck. She is the founder of the Essex Egyptology Group.

Charlotte has worked in Egypt on the Egyptian Antiquities Information System (EAIS) project (part of the Supreme Council of Antiquities) as an Archaeological Researcher. Closer to home, she appeared on *The New Paul O'Grady Show* as the mummification expert!

Author's Acknowledgements

Over the years many people have inspired me to continue researching and writing. I would like to thank my mum for giving me the all-important first break, the good education, and for her support over the years. Thanks to my fiancé, Wayne Frostick, who knows when to offer advice and when to go and watch the football. Various Egyptologists over the years have also inspired me, including Rosalind Janssen and the late Dominic Montserrat; both were inspirational and memorable teachers. My students also help a great deal by letting me know exactly what is interesting and what is not. Apparently I get the two confused sometimes. Let's hope I have got the right blend in this book. If I have got it right, this is due to the guidance of the *For Dummies* team: Sam Clapp, Rachael Chilvers, and Brian Kramer.

Publisher's Acknowledgements

We're proud of this book; please send us your comments through our Dummies online registration form located at www.dummies.com/register/.

Some of the people who helped bring this book to market include the following:

Acquisitions, Editorial, and Media Development

Project Editor: Rachael Chilvers

Development Editor: Brian Kramer

Content Editor: Steve Edwards

Commissioning Editor: Samantha Clapp

Copy Editor: Sally Lansdell

Proofreader: Mary White

Executive Editor: Jason Dunne

Executive Project Editor: Martin Tribe

Cover Photos: © Trip/Alamy

Cartoons: Rich Tennant
(www.the5thwave.com)

Composition Services

Project Coordinator: Jennifer Theriot

Layout and Graphics: Claudia Bell, Shane Johnson, Barbara Moore, Heather Ryan, Alicia B. South, Christine Williams

Proofreaders: Laura Albert, Susan Moritz

Indexer: Aptara

Brand Reviewer: Jennifer Bingham

Publishing and Editorial for Consumer Dummies

Diane Graves Steele, Vice President and Publisher, Consumer Dummies

Joyce Pepple, Acquisitions Director, Consumer Dummies

Kristin A. Cocks, Product Development Director, Consumer Dummies

Michael Spring, Vice President and Publisher, Travel

Kelly Regan, Editorial Director, Travel

Publishing for Technology Dummies

Andy Cummings, Vice President and Publisher, Dummies Technology/General User

Composition Services

Gerry Fahey, Vice President of Production Services

Debbie Stailey, Director of Composition Services

Contents at a Glance

Table of Contents

Introduction

As a 5-year-old child, I only ever wanted to spend my Saturdays at the British Museum looking at the mummies – until my own mummy started to think I was odd. But nothing is odd about mummies (the ancient Egyptian or the parental kind). The Egyptian mummy was a fundamental part – albeit a small part – of Egyptian funerary beliefs and culture. The mummy has now become an iconic image of Egypt, and many horror films have given it a bad name. Other than questions about mummies, the first thing anyone ever asks me as an Egyptologist is 'So who built the pyramids?' or 'Was Tutankhamun murdered?' As valid as these questions are, *Egyptology* (the study of ancient Egypt) offers so many more interesting things to discover and explore than these age-old queries. (And while others have answered these questions frequently and well, I offer my plain-English answers too in this book.)

In my opinion, some smaller pieces of research in Egypt are far more impressive than the pyramids, such as examining clay objects that still bear the fingerprints of ancient craftsmen, discovering the specific diseases an individual suffered from prior to being mummified, or reading a note from a woman to her dressmaker stating she 'has nothing to wear' (we've all been there). These small insights into the lives of the people who make up a history that is now world famous better answer the question 'Who were the Egyptians?' After you know *who* the ancient Egyptians were, figuring out *how* they built the pyramids doesn't seem like such a monumental question.

The ancient Egyptians were just like modern humans: They wanted to build pyramids, so they used all their available resources and did it. No mystery. In fact, I'm sure the ancient Egyptians would have loved a book entitled *Westerners of the 21st Century AD For Dummies*, so they could learn about this futuristic society that is so primitive it can't even build pyramids!

I think it essential to stop thinking of the ancient Egyptians as some bizarre civilisation so far removed from modern life that the people are undecipherable. They were amazingly similar to us, with the same drives, motivations, emotions, and weaknesses. I hope this book goes some way to helping you make a connection with this fascinating culture and the colourful individuals who created it.

About This Book

Egyptian history has been described as a jigsaw with half the pieces missing, no picture, and no indication of how many pieces there are – it is a daunting task to try to recreate a history that makes sense. Every year, new excavations uncover information that changes or adds another dimension to the available history of this culture. What this means in regard to this book is that I present the history of Egypt *as it stands today*. In ten years' time, it may look different due to new discoveries and new interpretations of the evidence – and this book would need to be updated.

The Nile Valley (a romantic way of saying Egypt) was relatively small and only covered about a mile on each side of the Nile river, but its people achieved so much. Generals waged numerous battles and went on expeditions, priests honoured a pantheon of gods numbering nearly 1,000, and hundreds of kings with what appear to be unpronounceable names (many of them the same – for example, there are eleven King Ramses) produced great architectural feats. In addition to the pyramids, the most iconic image of Egypt, ancient Egypt featured an array of temples, palaces, villages, and subterranean tombs, all with religious elements and iconic imagery, built and added to over hundreds of years.

Hundreds of texts are available from ancient Egypt that help explain the lives and beliefs of the kings, the priests, and even the ordinary people. This book weaves together all these stories to create a complicated but beautiful tapestry of the lives of the Egyptians.

If you think you'll mispronounce all those odd names, confuse the religious practices, and get your dynasties in a diddle, relax. This book presents more than 3,000 years of history as a straightforward outline of eras and periods. To the basic sketch, I then add clusters of intriguing details about ancient Egyptian lifestyle, culture, religion, and beliefs. Further chapters layer on insights about the incredible art and buildings produced by the ancient Egyptians. It's a fascinating journey, and you're going to love it.

Conventions Used in This Book

The dating system used in ancient Egypt was complicated. Surviving records use regnal years (for example, 'year 16 of Ramses II') rather than a centralised calendar ('1450 BC'). However, the Greek traveller Manetho divided ancient Egypt's 3,000-year history into 30 dynasties, and his system is still applied today. This is what this book uses.

Ascertaining exact dates for these dynasties is difficult, but I have added accepted chronological dates to give an idea of when events happened, although I also refer to general eras such as the 18th dynasty, 19th dynasty and so on. All dates are BC (before Christ) unless otherwise stated. Many people prefer BCE (before the Common Era), but I opt for BC because it's more traditional.

The names of kings are often spelt differently from publication to publication, sometimes with Greek versions of the name being used (Cheops instead of the Egyptian Khufu, for example). As an Egyptologist, I use the Egyptian version of the name that the people themselves would recognise, except when the Greek is the better known (for example, I use Thebes rather than Waset for modern Luxor).

Foolish Assumptions

I assume, perhaps wrongly, that you:

- ✔ Are interested in Egyptology through watching popular television shows, going to movies, and visiting museums
- ✔ Know a little about pyramids, Tutankhamun, and Cleopatra, but do not know how these flashy topics and figures fit into the wider history of ancient Egypt
- ✔ Find general books on Egypt and history dry, confusing, and uninviting
- ✔ Want to find out more – as long as the journey is interesting

How This Book Is Organised

You can either read this book from cover to cover, or you can dip in and out if you prefer. You can jump from chapter to chapter as their contents interest you. You can even skip around in each chapter, because each subsection offers information on a specific, selected topic. I also provide numerous cross-references between sections and chapters so you can easily jump from topic to topic and quickly locate the parts of the book that cover the specific aspects of Egyptology that you find most captivating.

The following information gives you an idea of what you can find in each part of the book.

Part I: Introducing the Ancient Egyptians

The landscape and ecology of Egypt were fundamental to the formation of the civilisation and are essential to understanding the culture, government, and even religion that developed along the Nile river. This part looks at the foundations of the ancient Egyptian culture, including its villages, careers, and social arrangements (marriage, divorce, and more). The social structure of Egyptian civilisation was particularly important, with the king at the top and everyone else beneath him, as this part details.

Part II: Stepping Back in Time

This part is the true story behind all the monuments. It covers the personalities who built them, fought for them, and later dismantled them. I take you on a chronological journey through more than 3,000 years of history, starting at the very beginning of Egyptian civilisation in the pre-dynastic period, and travelling down the timeline to the Roman invasion at the death of Cleopatra in 30 BC. This history is pitted with battles, especially in the period known as the New Kingdom, when Egypt had its first permanent army. This part investigates the life of a soldier, including the gruesome battle techniques, the victories, and the near misses.

It also considers the role of Egypt's women – including notable queens as well as working-class wives and mothers. This part ends with the collapse of the Egyptian civilisation after a period of constant invasion and divided rule – the sobering end to a dynamic culture.

Part III: Living Life to the Full: Culture and Beliefs

The Egyptians loved life – partying, hunting, eating, dancing, and chatting with their friends. Compare the intricacies of your own social life with that of the Egyptians and be amazed at the similarities. Sadly a part of life, now and then, is disease and illness, and the Egyptians suffered many of the same ailments as modern humans – although I wouldn't recommend their cures!

When the cures didn't work, death often followed and involved a great number of funerary beliefs and practices. Nowadays, mummification is synonymous with ancient Egypt, although the Egyptians were not the only culture to practise it. Mummification practices were slow in developing, but quickly became an essential part of the afterlife of the deceased, because without a body, the afterlife is pretty dull. To further prevent boredom, all the deceased's belongings were dumped in tombs for use after rebirth.

The Egyptians loved life so much they wanted it to continue for as long as possible. However, mummification and funerary practices are not the only religious beliefs covered in this part. The temples in Egypt were closed to the public, so the Egyptians developed two forms of religion – a complex state religion with the king as a direct communicator with the gods, and an equally rich household religion with a completely new set of gods to help with specific aspects of life, such as health, fertility, and childbirth.

Part IV: Interpreting Egyptian Art and Architecture

Part IV starts with the deciphering of the Egyptian hieroglyphic language, one of the most fundamental discoveries of Egyptology. Artwork is also a substantial part of any document (and of architectural remains), and being able to 'read' artwork is as important as reading the texts. This part explains some of the fundamental characteristics of Egyptian art.

This part also includes a study of the monumental structures of the Egyptians, including temples, tombs, and pyramids. The Egyptians did nothing randomly or because it looked nice (but it has to be said it all looks nice as well). Instead, a religious ideology influences every ancient Egyptian architectural element. So as I explore these incredible structures, I also introduce you to the inspiration behind them.

Part V: The Part of Tens

This part gives you easy-in, easy-out information, including a list of ten famous Egyptologists and ten critical discoveries and milestones in the discipline of Egyptology. You meet ten Egyptian personalities who helped the culture develop, as well as examples of the top achievements of this culture. I also present my list of ten great places to visit in Egypt.

Icons Used in This Book

Egyptology gets people thinking and coming up with their own interpretations of a complex history and culture. I use a number of icons to help highlight some of the points you may be thinking about.

We're lucky to have so many written records from ancient Egypt. Where you see this icon, you know you're reading the words of the ancients.

Many beliefs about ancient Egypt aren't true or are misinterpreted. Where you see this symbol, these myths are explained away.

This icon pinpoints important information that's essential for understanding future information.

There are many aspects of Egyptian history that get the response 'No way! You're making it up!' This icon shows that the information is true, no matter how bizarre.

These are intricate details that aren't essential for understanding the section. Skip these as you wish or absorb them so you can be the nerd at the party!

Where to Go from Here

Well, tradition says start at the beginning and continue until the end; but the thing about traditions is that someone years ago made them up because they seemed good ideas at the time. New traditions can be created right here! Simply jump in and out of the following pages and read them in whatever order you like. All the information is fun and interesting (I promise!), so does it matter what order you read it in?

If you're interested in the pyramids, dash to Chapter 14, or if you want to join the troops in the military, march to Chapter 3. If you want the gruesome details of mummification, flip to Chapter 10. But if you're a stickler for tradition and want to build your understanding of the roots of this intriguing culture, simply turn to the next page.

Part I
Introducing the Ancient Egyptians

The 5th Wave   By Rich Tennant

"Living on the Nile is wonderful. It brings us water, it brings us mud for bricks, it brings us fish, it brings us green pastures..."

In this part . . .

The ancient Egyptians are famous throughout the world for their pyramids and lashings of gold jewellery. However, this is only part of the story. The Egyptians were part of a large, intricate society, with the king at the top and the unskilled workers at the bottom. Rather like a pyramid, in fact.

Luckily, the Egyptians left loads of information regarding their everyday lives. This part explores the houses they lived in and with whom, their education system, and their social arrangements concerning marriage, divorce, adultery, childbirth, and the elderly.

Chapter 1

Getting Grounded: The Geography and History of Ancient Egypt

The ancient Egyptians have gripped the imagination for centuries. Ever since Egyptologists deciphered hieroglyphs in the early 19th century, this wonderful civilisation has been opened to historians, archaeologists, and curious laypeople.

Information abounds about the ancient Egyptians, including fascinating facts on virtually every aspect of their lives – everything from the role of women, sexuality, and cosmetics, to fishing, hunting, and warfare.

The lives of the ancient Egyptians can easily be categorised and pigeonholed. Like any good historian, you need to view the civilisation as a whole, and the best starting point is the origin of these amazing people.

So who were the ancient Egyptians? Where did they come from? This chapter answers these questions and begins to paint a picture of the intricately organised culture that developed, flourished, and finally fell along the banks of the Nile river.

Splashing in the Source of Life: The Nile

The ancient Egyptian civilisation would never have developed if it weren't for the Nile. The Nile was – and still is – the only source of water in this region of north Africa. Without it, no life could be supported.

Ancient Egypt is often called the *Nile valley*. This collective term refers to the fertile land situated along the banks of the river, covering an area of 34,000 square kilometres. This overall area has not altered much during the last 5,000 years, although the course of the river Nile itself has changed, and with artificial irrigation the fertile land has been increased a little. See the Cheat Sheet for a map of Egypt.

In de-Nile: Size and scope

The Nile is the longest river in the world, running 6,741 kilometres from eastern Africa to the Mediterranean. Six *cataracts*, or rapids, caused by rock outcrops on the riverbed, separate the southern section of the Nile between Aswan and Khartoum. The first cataract at Aswan created a natural boundary for Egypt until the New Kingdom (1550 BC), when the ancient Egyptians began travelling further and further south in the hunt for gold and areas to build up their empire. (See Chapters 3 and 4 for more information about this era of ancient Egyptian history.)

The Nile flows from south to north – from the interior of Africa to the Mediterranean Sea. Southern Egypt is called *Upper Egypt* because it is closest to the source of the Nile, and northern Egypt is called *Lower Egypt*.

The northern part of the Nile fans out into a series of canals, all leading to the Mediterranean. This area of northern Egypt is known as the Delta and is primarily marshland. The zone is particularly fertile – papyrus (on which many surviving ancient Egyptian records were written) grew in abundance here.

The failing flood

During the reign of Djoser in the third dynasty (refer to the Cheat Sheet for a timeline), Egypt is said to have experienced seven years of famine because of particularly low annual floods. The king was held responsible for the situation because he was an intermediary between the people and the gods, and the famine was seen as punishment from the gods for the king not doing his job. On the Island of Sehel in the south of Egypt, Ptolemy V (204–181 BC) commissioned a stela recording this famine and Djoser's actions:

I was in mourning on my throne. Those of the palace were in grief . . . because Happy [the flood] had failed to come in time. In a period of seven years, grain was scant, kernels were dried up . . . Every man robbed his twin . . . Children cried . . . The hearts of the old were needy . . . Temples were shut, Shrines covered with dust, Everyone was in distress . . . I consulted one of the staff, the Chief lector-priest of Imhotep . . . He departed, he returned to me quickly.

Imhotep, the builder of the step pyramid (see Chapter 14), traced the source of the Nile to the island of Elephantine and the caves of Khnum. He assured Djoser that renewed worship of Khnum would start the floods again. Khnum then appeared to Djoser in a dream:

> When I was asleep . . . I found the god standing. I caused him pleasure by worshipping and adoring him. He made himself known to me and said: 'I am Khnum, your creator, my arms are around you, to steady your body, to safeguard your limbs . . . For I am the master who makes, I am he who makes himself exalted in Nun [primeval waters], who first came forth, Happy who hurries at will; fashioner of everybody, guide of each man to their hour. The two caves are in a trench [?] below me. It is up to me to let loose the well. I know the Nile, urge him to the field, I urge him, life appears in every nose . . . I will make the Nile swell for you, without there being a year of lack and exhaustion in the whole land, so the plants will flourish, bending under their fruit . . . The land of Egypt is beginning to stir again, the shores are shining wonderfully, and wealth and well-being [?] dwell with them, as it had been before.

Djoser awoke and was pleased at the message. He passed a decree of an increase of taxes to be paid to the temple of Khnum:

> All the peasants working their fields with their labourers and bringing water to their new and high-lying lands, their harvest shall be stored in your granary in excess of the part that used to be your due. All fishermen and trappers and hunters on the water and lion catchers in the desert, I impose on them a duty of one tenth of their catch. Every calf born by the cows on your land shall be given to the stables as a burnt offering and a remaining daily offering. Moreover one tenth of the gold and ivory and the wood and minerals and every tree stem and all things which the Nubians . . . bring to Egypt shall be handed over together with every man who comes with them. No vizier shall give orders in these places and levy a tax on them, diminishing what is being delivered to your temple.

Once these gifts had been given to the temple of Khnum, the floods would once again reach the appropriate level, restore Egypt to the agricultural haven it once was, and re-inspire the people's faith in king Djoser.

However, because this stela was written more than 2,000 years after the date of the event, historians have difficulty assessing its accuracy as a historical document. Some scholars believe the stela is a copy of an Old Kingdom example erected by Djoser; others believe it was created in the Ptolemaic period as a means of justifying new goodies for the temple of Khnum. The truth may never be known.

The inundation: Surviving and thriving

Every year for the months between July and October the Nile flooded, covering the land on both banks with as much as 2 feet of water. When the water receded, very fertile black silt covered the land. Because of this, the Egyptians called their country Kemet, which means 'the black land'. Through careful crop management and intricate irrigation canals, the Nile valley became a major agricultural area.

Although the inundation of the Nile was essential for the agricultural success of the ancient Egyptian civilisation, a risk always existed of the Nile flooding too much or not enough. Either situation resulted in crop failure, famine, and death.

Since 1830 AD, a series of dams and sluices at the southern end of the Nile have checked the floods. In 1960 AD, the Egyptians built the High Dam at Aswan, which has stopped the Nile flooding altogether. Although these new technologies create a more stable environment for the modern Egyptians to farm, the steady nature of the present-day Nile makes imagining the up-and-down aspects of ancient Egyptian life more difficult.

Meeting the Ancient Egyptians

The ancient people who lived in the Nile valley were a melting pot of many ethnic groups, with many different origins. Prior to 5000 BC, the Nile valley did not have any settled people, because the surrounding area was rich in vegetation and was inhabited by a number of nomadic hunter-gatherer tribes, which followed large animals such as lions, giraffes, and ostriches as a source of food.

However, due to climatic change in approximately 5000 BC, the area surrounding the Nile valley began to dry out and was no longer able to sustain the large animals. This climate shift meant that the nomadic tribes all converged on the Nile valley because the river was slowly becoming the only source of water in the region.

As a result, the first Egyptian population was a collection of different nomadic tribes, which slowly integrated with each other and created a new society:

- **In the south of Egypt,** the origins of the people were closer to Nubia, resulting in a darker people.
- **In the north of Egypt,** the origins of the people were more in the Near East, creating a paler people.

By 3100 BC and the start of the pharaonic period of Egyptian history, a brand new culture – the Egyptian culture recognised today – had developed from this collection of different people, cultures and languages.

Dating the ancients

One of the most confusing aspects of Egyptian history is applying specific dates to eras, reigns, and even recorded battles and ceremonies. Also, the history of ancient Egypt spans more than 3,000 years, which is a lot to get your head around.

Making matters more difficult, the Egyptians themselves did not have a centralised dating system such as the one used today (for example, BC and AD). Instead, they referred to dates in regnal years of the current king. For example year 5 of Ramses II or year 16 of Akhenaten.

This system probably worked well in ancient times, but it doesn't help modern Egyptologists a great deal – especially when a number of kings are missing from the records or the exact length of some reigns is uncertain. So, for example, dating something from year 4 of Ramses II to year 2 of Merenptah made perfect sense to an Egyptian, but if you don't know how long Ramses II ruled and you don't know whether another king came between Ramses II and Merenptah (the king historians believe followed Ramses II), ascertaining true periods is very difficult.

A passion for all things Egyptian

For centuries – millennia, in fact – people have been fascinated by ancient Egyptian culture, including its language, history, politics, religion, burial practices, architecture, and art. Indeed, even the Greeks and Romans (ancient cultures themselves by any historian's account) were intrigued by the people of the Nile, arranged sight-seeing excursions to the area, and ended up transporting Egyptian treasures back to their homelands.

Modern *Egyptology*, a discipline that blends rigorous study of ancient history and archaeology with touches of sociology, art history, political science, economics, and more, began in earnest in 1823 when Jean-François Champollion was the first to decipher hieroglyphs, which led historians to begin deconstructing the many myths and misunderstandings of the ancient Egyptians.

Check out Chapter 19 for ten profiles of noteworthy Egyptologists, including Champollion.

Today, Egyptology is bigger than ever. Many universities now offer degrees in Egyptology or Egyptian archaeology. However, the work available for professional Egyptologists is scarce, with limited opportunitites to teach in universities or excavate in Egypt. Many museums employ volunteers instead of paid staff, therefore hundreds of applicants often seek the few paid positions. Furthermore, excavating in Egypt is particularly difficult because Egyptian researchers are favoured over westerners. Many Egyptologists therefore work in other jobs and write books and articles on Egyptology or conduct field work on a part-time basis. Hard work, but someone's gotta do it.

Manetho to the rescue

Modern Egyptologists weren't the only ones who thought that the Egyptian dating system was confusing. Manetho, an Egyptian historian and priest from the third century BC, devised the *dynastic system* of dating that is still used today.

In the dynastic system, a dynasty change was introduced whenever a change occurred in the ruling family, geography, or any other continuity issue in the succession of kings. Manetho divided the kings of Egypt into 31 dynasties, subdivided into three main kingdoms with turbulent 'intermediate' periods between them.

- **Early dynastic period:** Dynasty 0–2, around 3150–2686 BC
- **Old Kingdom:** Third to sixth dynasties, around 2686–2181 BC
- **First intermediate period:** Seventh to tenth dynasties, around 2181–2040 BC
- **Middle Kingdom:** 11th to 12th dynasties, around 2040–1782 BC
- **Second intermediate period:** 13th to 17th dynasties, around 1782–1570 BC
- **The New Kingdom:** 18th to 20th dynasties, around 1570–1070 BC
- **Third intermediate period:** 21st to 26th dynasties, around 1080–525 BC
- **Late period:** 27th to 30th dynasties, around 525–332 BC

This dating system has been very useful, and Egyptologists have been able to add chronological dates to the dynasties. However, these dates do not match from publication to publication, and this discrepancy can be very confusing for beginners. For this reason, referring to dynasties rather than dates is often easier. The dates I use in this book are based on Peter Clayton's *Chronicle of the Pharaohs* (Thames and Hudson Press), a widely accepted general chronology.

Unifying the Two Lands

Despite some quirks in their dating system, the ancient Egyptians were a very organised civilisation. This is particularly obvious in their division of the country. The most important division politically was the north–south divide. This division, into Upper (southern) and Lower (northern) Egypt produced what was referred to as the Two Lands – a concept that dominated kingship ideology from the reign of the first king, Narmer (3100 BC), to the final days of Cleopatra VII (30 BC).

The Narmer Palette, a flat stone plaque about 64 centimetres tall, shows King Narmer unifying the country – the earliest recorded battle in Egyptian history. It depicts Narmer dominating Lower Egypt to become the king of the Two Lands.

From this period on, any king needed to rule both Upper and Lower Egypt in order to be recognised as a true king of Egypt. The Egyptians considered this concept such a fundamental part of kingship that they incorporated the title 'king of Upper and Lower Egypt' into two of the five traditional names that the king received at his coronation.

These names describe certain elements of the king's rule. The traditional order of these names was:

- ✔ Horus name
- ✔ He of the two ladies (under the protection of the vulture goddess of Upper Egypt and the cobra goddess of Lower Egypt)
- ✔ Golden Horus name
- ✔ He of the sedge and the bee (under the protection of the sedge of Upper Egypt and the bee of Lower Egypt)
- ✔ Son of Ra

Representing the Two Lands

In addition to the king's titles, a number of symbols and hieroglyphs in Egyptian records highlight the importance of the unity of the Two Lands. Important imagery in kingship regalia included:

- ✔ The white crown of Upper Egypt
- ✔ The red crown of Lower Egypt
- ✔ The double crown of Upper and Lower Egypt
- ✔ The sedge of Upper Egypt
- ✔ The bee of Lower Egypt
- ✔ Nekhbet the vulture goddess of Upper Egypt
- ✔ Wadjet the cobra goddess of Lower Egypt

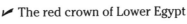

Additionally, the following images frequently appear in architecture, especially on pillars and as temple decoration (see Chapter 12). Although these images do not represent kingship specifically, they often define the region of rule of a particular king or, if both are shown, the unity.

✔ Papyrus of Lower Egypt

✔ Lotus of Upper Egypt

✔ The lotus and papyrus plants tied around symbolic 'heart and lungs' of Egypt, which indicates a unified Egypt

Uniting east and west

Although the Upper and Lower Egypt division was the most important (at least where kingship was concerned), Egypt was further divided into east and west. The Nile formed the dividing line between the two sides.

✔ **The east bank of the Nile** was used primarily for the construction of the cult temples (see Chapter 12) and settlements. The ancient Egyptians considered the east bank to be the Land of the Living because the sun rose each morning in the east, giving hope and bringing new life.

✔ **The west bank of the Nile** was home to cemeteries and funerary temples and was referred to as the Land of the Dead. West was where the sun set in the evening, starting the nocturnal journey into the afterlife until rebirth in the east.

However, exceptions to these divisions existed. Some settlements were built on the west bank, while some cemeteries existed in the east.

Subdividing further

If the divisions of Upper/Lower and eastern/western Egypt weren't enough, the whole of Egypt was further divided into 42 provinces, currently known as *nomes*. In Upper Egypt, 22 nomes were present from the start of the dynastic period; the 20 nomes in Lower Egypt developed later.

Each nome (or *sepat* as the ancient Egyptians called them) was governed by a *nomarch* or mayor who answered to the vizier and ultimately the king. Ideally, only one vizier monitored the government, but many kings split the role into two – a vizier of Upper Egypt and a vizier of Lower Egypt. Each nome had a capital city and a local temple for the worship of the local deity, complete with individual religious taboos, practices, and rituals.

Each nome was represented by a *standard*, consisting of a staff bearing the statue of its local deity and a regional animal or plant. The animals and plants are often represented in offering scenes, which highlight the crops of a particular region. Nomes often took their names based on their regional animal or plant, such as the ibis nome and the hare nome.

Following the Floating Capital

Although the Egyptians were very organised with a well-established system of governmental divisions, they were not as strict about the location of their capital city. In fact, Egyptologists have identified numerous royal residences and royal burial sites in cities throughout Egypt, which indicates that the capital moved according to the whim of the reigning king. In some reigns, rulers had two capitals: a religious capital and an administrative capital.

Pre-dynastic capitals

The Egyptian civilisation had not developed in the pre-dynastic period (prior to 3100 BC), so a capital city as such did not exist.

Instead, three sites that included settlements and large cemeteries seem to dominate (see Cheat Sheet for locations):

- **Naqada** was one of the largest pre-dynastic sites, situated on the west bank of the Nile approximately 26 kilometres north of Luxor. Archaeologists have discovered two large cemeteries here with more than 2,000 graves, a number of which belong to the elite and royalty.

- **Hierakonpolis** was also used as a royal cemetery and was the base for the funerary cult of the second-dynasty king Khasekhemwy. The most famous finds from this site are the Narmer Palette (see the section 'Unifying the Two Lands', earlier in this chapter), the Narmer Mace Head and the Scorpion Mace Head. These last two items are both on display in the Ashmolean Museum, Oxford, and depict the early development of Egypt's kingship ideology.

- **Abydos** was a major site during the pre-dynastic period and remained prominent for most of the pharaonic period. The earliest settlement here dates to 4000–3500 BC, although most of the current remains are from the 19th and 20th dynasties. Abydos was a major religious centre with monuments of all the first-dynasty kings and two of the second-dynasty kings.

Moving to Memphis

The three pre-dynastic centres were abandoned as capital cities during the Old Kingdom (around 2686–2333 BC), and Memphis, near modern Cairo, became the new administrative capital. The location of Memphis provided easy access and control over both the Delta region and the Nile valley, ensuring that trade through this region was firmly under royal control.

The royal cemeteries of the Old Kingdom were also very close to Memphis, with pyramid fields at Giza, Saqqara, Dahshur, Abusir, and Abu-Roash (see Chapter 14) covering an area of approximately 35 square kilometres.

Memphis remained important throughout the New Kingdom as well. During the reigns of Sety I (1291–1278 BC) and Ramses II (1279–1212 BC), the royal harem (see Chapter 5) was located at Memphis, which shows the continuity of the city as a royal residence.

Settling in Thebes

During the New Kingdom, the major royal and religious capital was Thebes (modern-day Luxor), which was home to the powerful cult of the god Amun. This region includes the temples of Karnak and Luxor, as well as the New Kingdom funerary temples and the royal burials in the Valley of the Kings and Queens (see Chapter 13).

For the majority of the New Kingdom, Thebes was the religious capital and Memphis in the north was the administrative capital, ensuring that the king had control over both Upper and Lower Egypt.

Noting other short-lived settlements

Although Memphis and Thebes were important settlements for much of the pharaonic period, some rulers chose to have their capital elsewhere, although these locations did not maintain this important status for long:

  ✔ **Avaris:** The Hyksos rulers of the second intermediate period (1663–1555 BC) built their capital in the Delta. The settlement shows an interesting juxtaposition between two cultures: Egyptian and Palestinian (the latter where the Hyksos are thought to have originated). For more information, see Chapter 3.

✔ **Amarna:** This was the new capital city built by Akhenaten of the 18th dynasty (1350–1334 BC) and dedicated to the solar disc, the Aten. (Turn to Chapter 4 for more on this period of Egyptian history.) Amarna was situated half way between Memphis and Thebes in Middle Egypt and included a number of temples, palaces, an extensive settlement, and a cemetery. (Check out Chapter 18 for what you can see today.)

✔ **Pi-Rameses:** This city in the Delta, very close to Avaris, was built originally by Sety I (1291–1278 BC) as a harbour town and was important in controlling the transportation of goods from the Mediterranean into the Nile valley. Ramses II of the 19th dynasty (1279–1212 BC) greatly expanded the city and named it Pi-Rameses to serve as a rival to Thebes.

✔ **Tanis:** This was another capital in the Delta during the 21st dynasty, under king Psusennes I (1039–991 BC). Most of the city was built with reused blocks from Pi-Rameses.

These cities all had very limited lives. At the end of most of the kings' reigns, these sites declined in importance, and Thebes and Memphis were re-established as the capitals.

Populating the Nile Valley

From approximately 5000 BC, settled communities inhabited the Nile valley in an area of approximately 34,000 square kilometres. However, the population of this region was never recorded until the Roman administration of Egypt, which began in 30 BC.

Egyptologists have estimated population data based on the available area of agricultural land and the number of people it was able to support:

✔ Late pre-dynastic period: 100,000–200,000 people

✔ Early dynastic period: 2 million people

✔ Old Kingdom: 1–1.5 million people

✔ New Kingdom: 2.9–4.5 million people

✔ Ptolemaic period: 7–7.5 million people

The population fluctuated throughout the pharaonic period, with a marked rise during the Ptolemaic period due to an increased area of agricultural land, plus an influx of foreigners into Egypt after Alexander the Great (see Chapter 6).

TECHNICAL STUFF

Estimating the population of a warrior nation

More accurate population estimates can be calculated for specific periods of Egypt history. For example, in the period between the Saite dynasties (727–525 BC) and the time of Herodotus (fifth to fourth century BC), records state that Egypt had 410,000 warriors. Egyptologists assume that each soldier was part of a family of four, so the soldiers and their families during this time would have constituted around 1,640,000 people.

However, each soldier was given 12 *arouras* of land (1,200 square cubits or 0.63 square kilometres), a total of 4,920,000 arouras (3,099,600 square kilometres) of land for all the soldiers. This land constituted half of the agricultural land in Egypt at the time. Therefore, assuming that the other half of the agricultural land sustained the same number of people, the estimated population is $1{,}640{,}000 \times 2 = 3{,}280{,}000$ people.

Furthermore, historians believe that 2 arouras of land was able to sustain one person, so each soldier had enough land to sustain six people. This means that the population may have been higher: $3{,}280{,}000 \div 4 \times 6 = 4{,}920{,}000$ people.

Climbing the Egyptian Social Ladder

Egyptian society was greatly stratified. However, most evidence available today is only from the upper levels of society – royalty and the elite – because these individuals were able to afford to leave behind stone monuments and elaborate tombs.

REMEMBER

The social structure of ancient Egyptian society from the Old Kingdom on was rather like a pyramid (how appropriate!). The king was perched at the top, followed by the small band of priests drawn from the elite, a slightly larger group of the ruling elite, and then the working class (including skilled trades and unskilled labour), which comprised the rest of the population.

Obviously, the majority of the population were working class. They were responsible for working on the agricultural land and producing food for the elite classes and priests. Unfortunately, Egyptologists do not know the exact number of the elite – and very little information about the working class exists in written records.

The following sections discuss the experiences of individuals at each level of ancient Egypt's social pyramid.

Being king of the heap

The most powerful person in ancient Egyptian society was the king. He was born into the position, and ideally he was the son of the previous king – although on several occasions the king was a usurper who nicked the throne from the rightful heir.

As head of state, the king had a number of functions and roles that he needed to maintain, including

- High priest of all temples in the country
- Head of the army (in the New Kingdom especially)
- International diplomat for trade and peace treaties
- Intermediary between the people and the gods

The king was considered to be an incarnation of the god Horus on earth – and therefore a god in his own right. This divine status meant that he was able to converse directly with the gods on behalf of the population of Egypt. Keeping the gods happy was also his job. If Egypt were afflicted with disease, famine, high floods, or war, Egyptians believed that the king was being punished and that it was his fault for not keeping his people happy. That's a lot of pressure for one man!

Serving the gods

The priesthood was a very powerful occupation, especially in its upper echelons (see Chapter 2 for more details). The priests worked for the temple and were able to gain honours, wealth, and titles.

The priests were privileged enough to be in the presence of the gods every day, and many people made gifts to the priests (some say bribes) to put a good word in with the gods or to ask for something on their behalf. Even the king was not immune to this gift-giving, often bestowing land, titles, and rewards on the priests. These gifts eventually helped the high priests to become very wealthy. And with wealth comes power. For example:

- The Priesthood of Amun at Karnak was the richest and most powerful in Egypt. During the reign of Ramses III, this group owned 1,448 square kilometres of agricultural land, vineyards, quarries, and mines, in addition to riverboats and sea-faring vessels. Most of this agricultural land was rented to the peasants, who paid a third of their harvest to the temple as rent.

✔ The *daily* income of the mortuary temple of Ramses III at Medinet Habu from its associated land was 2,222 loaves of bread, 154 jars of beer, 8,000 litres of grain, plus meat and other commodities – enough to feed 600 families.

Throughout Egyptian history, the kings felt that appeasing the priests was essential because the priests worked on the king's behalf, keeping the gods happy and keeping Egypt safe. Hardly surprising that gradually the king's presents increased and the priesthood's power grew and grew, until it rivalled that of the king.

Powering the elite

In order to alleviate some of the pressure, the king had a large number of advisers and officials who helped in decisions and activities. Royal sons who were not destined for the throne were appointed by the king to fill many of the top official positions.

The easiest role to delegate was that of high priest. Obviously the king wasn't able to carry out all the rituals expected of him as high priest in every temple in Egypt. Even though the king was a god, he wasn't Superman!

Nomarchs, get set

In the Old and Middle Kingdoms, much of the power of the king was in fact delegated to local *nomarchs*, or mayors. They were in charge of their *nome*, or province, and controlled the economy, taxes, and employment of the people living there. The nomarchs ultimately relied on the generosity of the king and needed to make regular reports and payments to the king on behalf of their nomes.

Egypt's standing army

During the New Kingdom, the king did not have to rely so heavily on the nomarchs to conscript men for war or trade, because Egypt had a permanent standing army at the beck and call of the king.

Two generals led the New Kingdom army – one for the army of Upper Egypt and one for the army of Lower Egypt. This clever ploy by the king limited how much of the army one general controlled and prevented a military coup to usurp the throne. It clearly helped if the king was a little paranoid.

Many generals in the New Kingdom army were royal princes. Some were given the title when they were small children, indicating that this was an honorary title that gave the young princes something to do – playing with a sword and chariot – as well as keeping such powerful positions within the royal family.

My word is law

The tomb of the 18th-dynasty vizier Rekhmire includes one of the few inscriptions describing in full the role of the vizier, which was rich and varied and was clearly a position of great power.

The vizierate is not to show respect of princes and councillors; it is not to make for himself slaves of any people.

Behold, when a petitioner comes from Upper or Lower Egypt, even the whole land, see to it that everything is done in accordance with law, that everything is done according to custom, giving every man his right. A petitioner who had been adjudged shall not say: 'My right has not been given to me!'

Beware of that which is said of the vizier Kheti. It is said that he discriminated against some of the people of his own kin in favour of strangers, for fear lest it should be said of him that he favoured his kin dishonestly. When one of them appealed against the judgement which he thought to make him, he persisted in his discrimination. Now

that is not justice. It is an abomination of the god to show partiality.

Cause yourself to be feared. Let men be afraid of you. A vizier is an office of whom one is afraid. Behold, the dread of a vizier is that he does justice. But indeed, if a man cause himself to be feared a multitude of times, there is something wrong in him in the opinion of the people. They do not say of him: 'He is a man indeed.' Behold, this fear of a vizier deters the liar, when the vizier proceeds according to the dread one has of him. Clearly the vizierate was such a powerful position that the population feared corruption and lack of justice. (In fact, records indicate a number of instances where the viziers were accused of this.) Rekhmire himself had a mysterious end to his life: He was never buried in his tomb, and many of the images in his tomb were intentionally damaged, perhaps to prevent him from having an afterlife. Was this vandalism due to his corrupt activities? Historians may never know, but it does make you think.

However, the king also relied on these nomarchs, especially in times of war or foreign expeditions. Before the New Kingdom saw the start of the full-time militia (see Chapter 4), the nomarchs were responsible for conscripting and training fit young men from their provinces to fight for Egypt or to accompany the king on foreign expeditions, either for trade or mining purposes.

Therefore the king had to keep the nomarchs on his side through payments and gifts. Otherwise these fit young men may be conscripted to march *against* the king and potentially steal the throne.

Vizier arising

The responsibilities of the vizier were varied and made him the second most powerful man in Egypt after the king.

The *vizier* was basically a personal assistant and secretary of state to the king and compiled a weekly or monthly report on all the key information for the whole of Egypt, based on daily reports from workshops and lesser officials. At times, the vizier acted as king by proxy, distributing land and the spoils of war to nomarchs or as rewards for loyalty.

Additionally, the vizier was responsible for hiring policemen and received reports from all the guard posts throughout Egypt regarding movements of enemy armies or other threatening activities. The vizier also presided over the court, dealing with the daily petitions of the ordinary people, including crimes and minor offences.

May the priest be with you

The most prominent power struggle in ancient Egyptian history took place during the reign of Ramses XI between the royal family and the high priests of Amun. At this time, the power of the throne was so diminished that a civil war broke out in order to decide who was to take over Ramses XI's throne – while he was still on it!

Throughout the first 12 years of Ramses XI's reign, the high priests of Amun held virtually the same power as Ramses and had his support because he was a particularly pious sovereign. However, the one difference between the high priests and Ramses XI is that the king had the military under his control, which gave him the edge.

However, at some point prior to year 12, one of Ramses's administrative officials – Panehsy, the Viceroy of Nubia, who was based in Thebes – came into conflict with the high priest of Amun, Amenhotep. This conflict denied Amenhotep his position for nine months, until he eventually turned to Ramses XI for help. Ramses commanded his army to destroy Panehsy, who was exiled to Nubia, and Amenhotep got his position back.

A few years later, Amenhotep was replaced by Herihor, whom the king also bestowed with the military titles that Panehsy held. For the first time in Egyptian history, one man held the top religious and military titles, making Herihor more powerful than Ramses. One gift too many, indeed!

Ramses was in a very weak position and was king in name only, while Herihor effectively ruled Egypt. Herihor showed his revered position by placing his name and high priest title in a cartouche in the manner of a king.

On the death of Herihor, his position passed to his son-in-law Piankhy, who ruled alongside Ramses in the same way as his father. At the death of Ramses, Piankhy continued to rule Thebes, while Lower Egypt was ruled by King Smendes from Tanis, who legitimised his claim to the throne by marrying a daughter of Ramses XI.

This started a period of divided rule and a dynasty (the 21st) of Theban high priests, all successors of Piankhy who held military and religious titles. Just goes to show you really shouldn't put all your eggs in one basket.

Shifting power

Although the king was the top dog in Egypt, at times lower-ranking officials such as the vizier, the military, or priests surpassed him in power. A prime example is that of Ramses XI of the 20th dynasty who was succeeded to the throne by the high priest of Amun. In fact, even throughout Ramses XI's reign, the high priests held equal or more power than he did. See the sidebar 'May the priest be with you' for more information.

The vizierate was often used as a stepping stone to the role of king, with Ay in the 18th dynasty becoming king, and Bay in the 19th dynasty being the power behind the puppet king Siptah. In fact, the 19th dynasty itself started due to a shift in power between the royal family (ending with Ay, the uncle of Tutankhamun) and the military (with Horemheb, an army general who took over the throne). Horemheb then passed the throne to his general, Ramses I, and started a new military era in Egypt.

Other lesser officials grew in wealth – and therefore power – until they overshadowed the king. Of course, this wealth came from the king in the first place, in the form of titles, land, and gifts. So at some point the king obviously gave one gift too many. This imbalance of wealth is on clear display in the tombs and pyramids at the end of the Old Kingdom. The tombs of officials were expensively carved and decorated in stone, while the royal pyramids were small and built with desert rubble.

Even historians have difficulty identifying whether various new dynasties started due to the usurpation of power by a wealthy official or a natural change when the king lacked a male heir.

During periods of political instability, when the throne did not follow the traditional line of succession, the whole of Egypt was affected, especially the economy. Any battle over the throne resulted in neglect of international trade (albeit briefly), as well as increased spending on military action, resulting in further economic problems, such as the distribution of food and the abandonment of tomb-building projects (especially in the 21st dynasty and later).

One such problem occurred in year 29 of Ramses III's reign. The workmen at Deir el Medina had not been paid for six months and went on strike, protesting before the funerary temples of Thutmosis III, Ramses II, and Sety I, which stored the grain used for their wages. The strike worked, and they were paid. But later that year when payment was again late, Djhutymose, a scribe from Deir el Medina, decided strikes were not as effective as initially thought and went with two bailiffs to collect the grain himself from the local farmers and the temples. A true vigilante.

The vast working class: Producing the essentials

Although the officials and the military were essential to the safety and stability of Egypt, those in the working classes were essential to its success. Tragically, most of the information on these people is lost. Because they were mostly poor and often illiterate, the working class did not leave stone tombs, stelae (the plural of *stela*, a round-topped stone monument), or statues. (Chapter 2 pieces together a portrait of these individuals.)

Farmers: Salt of the earth

The majority of the working classes were agricultural workers, because farming and food production were essential for survival and for Egypt to participate in trade.

While no written evidence exists from farmers themselves, some tombs of members of the elite mention farmers who worked their land, thus preserving these farmers' names for eternity. One such farmer worked for the scribe Ramose from Deir el Medina. According to tomb records, the farmer's name was Ptahsaankh, and he ploughed the land with two cows called 'West' and 'Beautiful Flood'.

Most land was owned by the state or the temples and was only rented to the farmers. As employees of the state, farmers were expected to give a specific amount of their grain yields to the landowners, plus rent and tax (tax is always there). Farmers' earnings were whatever was left. The poor were clearly working for free.

Labourers: Serving the state

During the annual flood of the Nile, many thousands of farmers were virtually unemployed because they were able to do little while their land was under 3 feet of water. In these periods, the state often conscripted farmers to work as labourers on large monumental building projects, such as the pyramids.

Commentators often say that slaves built these monuments, but in reality this wasn't the case. While working for the state, unskilled labourers were well paid and provided with housing near the building site. After the flood waters started to recede in October, workers returned to their villages to work on their farms.

Hard manual labour, such as working in the quarries or mines, was done by prisoners of war or criminals. Because this work was punishment, these people were fed, but were probably not given any spare food with which to trade. While their work was dangerous, many of these individuals probably died simply as a result of trudging through the hot desert, thirst, or encountering violent nomadic tribes.

Craftsmen: Whittling away

The only existing evidence regarding craftsmen comes from special settlements built for specific work forces, including

- **Giza,** built for the workmen who built the Giza pyramids
- **Kahun,** which housed the workmen who built the Lahun pyramid
- **Amarna,** which housed the workmen who built the Amarnan royal tombs
- **Deir el Medina,** which was home to the workmen who built the Valley of the Kings

The workmen's villages of Amarna and Deir el Medina (where most available information about craftsmen and ordinary Egyptians comes from) housed extremely privileged workmen who worked directly for the king. They were not from the ordinary working class.

Although the information from Amarna and Deir el Medina is valuable and interesting (go to Chapter 2 to find out how interesting), it only describes the experience of elite workers – not the common, non-literate members of society. No doubt many craftsmen worked throughout Egypt on non-royal projects, but sadly information about them is lacking.

Chapter 2

Examining the Lives of the Everyday Egyptians

*T*he tombs provide a wealth of information about the upper classes and the elite, but they also paint a remarkably detailed portrait of the day-to-day lives of the Egyptian masses. For instance, tomb records provide names and job titles, while mummies detail diseases and general health. Additional artefacts and remains from ancient villages give an insight into family life, religion, childhood, and old age. Given all this information, we can truly trace the lives of the Egyptians from the cradle to the grave.

One of the most important features of everyday Egyptian life is that these ancient people had the same motivations, interests, and problems as people today. From establishing homes to choosing careers, from getting married to growing old, this chapter covers the ins and outs of living as an Egyptian.

Appreciating Village Life

Most information about ancient Egypt comes from research and exploration of tombs and temples. Although these structures and the treasures they hold are truly fascinating, examining only tombs, mummies, and treasures gives a biased view of the Egyptians as a morbid nation that was obsessed with death.

Although dying was immensely important to the Egyptians, so was living! To fully understand these people, you need to look at their villages – the centres of their regular, everyday life.

Although the tombs were built of stone and meant to last forever, the villages were made of mud-brick and were not intended to last. Fortunately, researchers have identified several villages that somehow endured, providing valuable information about the Egyptian lifestyle. Unfortunately, these villages are mainly special settlements inhabited by the elite; as such they don't necessarily give an accurate overview of the life of all Egyptians, rich and poor.

The most important villages are:

- **Deir el Medina** on the west bank of the Nile at Thebes in the south of Egypt. Amenhotep I of the 18th dynasty built Deir el Medina to house the workmen who constructed the royal tombs in the Valley of the Kings. The village was occupied until the late 20th dynasty. Today the foundations of the village are still visible, including staircases, cellars, ovens, and elaborately decorated tombs, some virtually complete with mummies and treasures.

- **Kahun** in the Faiyum region dates to the Middle Kingdom and was built to accommodate the workmen who built the pyramid of Senwosret III, although it was inhabited for a number of years after the death of the king. The remains at the site are quite substantial, with three-quarters of the settlement foundations surviving, showing three styles of houses: mansions, large houses, and the equivalent of small terraces.

- **Pi-Rameses** is situated in the eastern Delta region and was the capital city of Ramses II of the 19th dynasty. The village covered an area of approximately 5 kilometres, and excavations at the site have uncovered a number of temples, palaces, and houses for the elite and their servants. The remains are very fragmentary because many building blocks were reused in later periods.

- **Avaris,** located very close to Pi-Rameses in the Delta, was the capital of the Hyksos kings from the second intermediate period (see Chapter 3). Many Asiatics (primarily from the Palestine, Syria, and Canaan region) lived at this site, which the village's style of temples and houses reflected.

- **Amarna,** about halfway between Cairo and Luxor, was the home of Akhenaten from the 18th dynasty. The village stretches for a distance of approximately 7 kilometres and included a number of palaces and temples as well as army barracks, two settlement districts, and a workmen's village similar to Deir el Medina. So many archaeological remains have been found at this site that it is often used as a blueprint for all Egyptian settlements.

You can visit Deir el Medina on the west bank at Luxor and see the layout of the whole settlement. The more adventurous tourist can visit Amarna in Middle Egypt. The archaeologists have reconstructed some sample buildings to give the gist of what it may have looked like.

Planning a village

The layout of each surviving village differs depending on whether it was built as a single project (for example, to house tomb builders) or whether it was allowed to develop naturally. Most villages needed to be near the Nile or a canal to provide a water source, and have agricultural land for food, although in the case of Deir el Medina, the state brought in water and food basics for the villagers.

Planners for single-project sites (like Deir el Medina and Amarna) built the most important building, either the temple or the palace, first, and then the elite houses were constructed around this structure. In the pre-planned villages, the streets are evenly laid out and houses arranged in neat rows. But as these towns expanded and developed, houses were extended, and new smaller houses were built among the larger mansions, destroying the grid layout.

Naturally developing settlements aren't half as tidy as planned villages. No grids divide the settlement, and the general appearance is more haphazard. Planned villages have a uniformity of house style and size, whereas in naturally developing villages the house styles are irregular because people built according to taste and need.

Housing

Houses in Egyptian villages were generally very basic. Although some were larger than others (depending on the wealth and status of the owner), the average house at Deir el Medina, Gurob, and Amarna consisted of four rooms (see Figure 2-1):

- A **front room** leading from the street, which may have been used as a meeting place for guests.
- A **living room** where the household shrine was situated. (See Chapter 9 for more on household religious practices.) The family would worship their personal gods or ancestors here.
- A **living space,** probably used as a sleeping area, with a staircase to a flat roof or upper floor.
- A **kitchen** at the rear of the house, which was open to the sky to prevent the room from filling with smoke.

Cellars underneath the rear rooms were used as storage for foodstuffs. Houses were small so each room was multi-purpose.

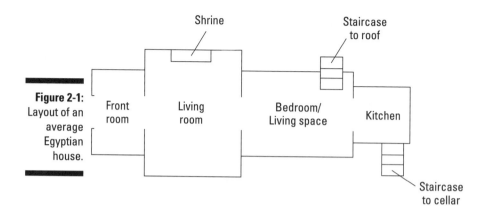

Figure 2-1:
Layout of an average Egyptian house.

The houses of the elite, more appropriately described as mansions, followed a similar layout to the small houses, although they consisted of a number of small suites of rooms joined by interlinking corridors, as shown in Figure 2-2. These gave the elite owners the privilege of separating the public from the private family quarters. Many mansions also contained

- An audience chamber in which to greet visitors.

- An office in which to conduct business.

- A bathroom with built-in shower area (essentially a stone slab and a servant with a jug of water) and toilet (a horseshoe-shaped wooden seat over a bowl of sand). Some homes at Pi-Rameses also had sunken baths open to the sky – to catch some rays while bathing.

- Women's quarters, for privacy rather than confinement. These quarters provided living, dressing, and sleeping areas from the rest of the household.

All houses in ancient Egypt were nearly bursting at the seams with people. The mansions were run like estates. In addition to the owner and his family, a plethora of employees, administrators, and servants lived in these larger homes.

Small homes were even more crowded. An Egyptian couple may have had up to 15 children, all living in a single four-roomed house. When men married, their wives moved into the home as well; and when the wives had children, the children potentially also lived in the house. It was not unusual for three or four generations – as many as 20 people, mostly children – to be living in these small houses. The Egyptians truly knew the meaning of no privacy and no space.

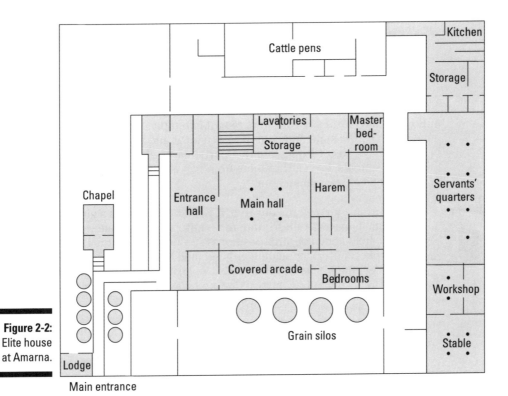

Figure 2-2: Elite house at Amarna.

Main entrance

Growing Up Egyptian

Preparing for – and sometimes choosing – a career was a major part of the early lives of most Egyptians, particularly boys. The following sections consider the schooling, careers, and working conditions of the vast majority of ancient Egyptians.

Educating the young

Today, most people's earliest memories are from school, and in ancient Egypt it was probably no different.

Although not every child was lucky enough to have a formal education, the oldest son in most families followed in his father's footsteps in his career choice, so he began learning his father's trade from as young as 5 years old (whether farming, sculpting, or administration). Other sons needed to be trained in a career; this inspired some elite families to educate their children.

School's out

School as you know it didn't exist in ancient Egypt, but for want of a better word I have to use the term. Egyptian schools didn't include large buildings, complete with classrooms and playing fields. There was no smell of chalk and there were definitely no uniforms.

Royalty and the upper elite were taught in temple or palace schools, which were run by the state and consisted of a tutor and a small group of hand-chosen boys. Records indicate that particularly gifted boys were accepted into the schools, even if they were from non-elite families – so the lower classes had at least some hope.

Although some girls were educated, it wasn't the norm. If a girl did receive an education, it wasn't in these state-run institutions. Because women were unable to hold administrative positions (see 'Considering the Lives of Women', later in this chapter), educating girls seemed like a pointless task to many ancient Egyptians. One Egyptian called Ankhsheshonq immortalised this idea with the following quote: 'Instructing a woman is like having a sack of sand whose side is split open.' Charming!

Some of these formal temple and palace schools taught specific trades and only accepted boys from families of certain occupations, such as scribes or magistrates. Children leaving these schools were then employed in the central government.

For boys not accepted into the elite educational institutions, local alternatives existed. Boys in most villages learned only basic literacy skills if their father was a scribe – normally in preparation for taking his place as a scribe. Village scribes also occasionally decided to teach groups of village children reading and writing as a means of boosting income.

House of Life

Although schools as you know them today did not exist, the *House of Life* was an institution that provided some education and training for a select few. A House of Life was attached to most temples. Each stored a number of texts relevant to that particular temple. The term is often mistranslated as a school, university, library, or archive. However, it was a strange institution that was all of these things and yet did not fit any of the descriptions particularly well.

Although shrouded (intentionally) in mystery, the following is known about this institution:

✔ **The House of Life stored a number of religious texts,** which were used for training priests and medical professionals (see Chapter 8 for more on the role of doctors). Being educated here was a great privilege, available to only a chosen few. However, how students were chosen remains unknown.

✔ **The priests in charge of the House of Life were responsible for conserving, copying, and storing religious texts.** The texts stored here were world famous. Later, Greek and Roman authors praised the wisdom recorded in these texts. The texts are said to include information about medicine, medical herbs, geography, geometry, astronomy, and the history of kings.

✔ **The institution was not open to the public.** The extremely restricted access only enhanced its aura of mystery. Many literary tales refer to texts stored in the House of Life that have information on how to speak the language of all animals, birds, and fish in the world, as well as a text that enables the reader to see the sun god. Powerful stuff, indeed!

School days

A number of teaching materials have survived and tell a great deal about the day-to-day education that children received. An Egyptian child typically entered school at about 5 years old and started with the three Rs: reading, writing, and arithmetic.

In Egypt, two different types of written language exist – hieroglyphs (go to Chapter 11 for more on these pretty pictures) and *hieratic* script, a shorthand version of hieroglyphs. Modern students of Egyptian history typically learn hieroglyphs first and then progress to hieratic writing, but the ancient Egyptians did things the other way round:

✔ A tutor dictated hieratic phrases and sentences.

✔ A student learned these phrases by heart.

✔ The student then wrote these phrases onto a wipe-clean wooden board through dictation and later from memory.

✔ The tutor made corrections.

✔ The board was wiped clean, and the process began again.

This intensive curriculum lasted until children were 9 years old, when they made a decision about their careers. Whatever career they chose then resulted in apprenticeships, which lasted for about ten years. Apprentices worked alongside professionals and learned the trade on the job, earning a wage (see the following section 'Checking the Balance: Wages and Values in Ancient Egypt', later in this chapter).

The ancient Egyptian proverb 'A boy's ear is on his back; he hears when he is beaten' gives an indication of how education was administered in ancient Egypt. It certainly puts my school days into a much better light!

Choosing a career

Trying to choose a career as a modern adult is difficult enough, but having to do it at 9 years old seems unreal. (At 9, I wanted to be a princess – and no amount of education can help there!) However, Egyptian 9-year-olds made this monumental decision.

In the New Kingdom, the military and the scribal profession were intense rivals for Egypt's best and brightest. For many boys, the life of a soldier seemed more glamorous than any other lifestyle. Soldiers were promised glory, foreign trips, and acknowledgement by the king, whereas the scribal profession offered knowledge, wealth, and a peaceful life with no physical strain.

In fact, one text called *The Miscellanies* appealed to the weaker, non-sporty boys who wished to join the army, but were not physically suitable, by stating:

> *Be a scribe! Your body will be sleek, your hand will be soft. You will not flicker like a flame, like those whose body is feeble. For there is no bone of a man in you. You are tall and thin. If you lifted a load to carry it, you would stagger. Your feet would drag terribly, you are lacking in strength. You are weak in all of your limbs, poor in body. Set your sights on being a scribe, a fine profession that suits you.*

Many careers were open to Egyptian children. A great text called *Satire of the Trades* lists the many occupations – and the downsides to each. As this text outlined, careers fell into four main categories: manual, administration, priesthood, and military.

Obviously some people were limited by status and wealth in what career they pursued. But on the plus side, no unemployment existed as farming and building work always needed doing.

Scribes: Leading the administration

Being a scribe was the most lucrative occupation. Scribes had many opportunities for promotion, and scribes who showed particular talent and skill could even rise to the position of *vizier*, which was second only to that of the king. If the king was weak, the vizierate could be a stepping stone to the throne.

The vizier's role was powerful and diverse; the entire palace and its internal operations was under the vizier's control. The vizier was also responsible for the safety of the king and the security of Egypt, which meant the police force was also under the vizier's control. In addition, the vizier presided over the legal court (*kenbet*) and dealt with the daily petitions of the people, normally concerning petty crimes or offences. In legal matters, the vizier acted as judge, sentencing and administering punishments on behalf of the king.

Scribes with less ambition or power were still busy because only 1–5 per cent of the ancient Egyptian population was literate. At some point, most people needed the service of a scribe for personal or legal letters, accounts, or legal petitions. Scribes were essentially civil servants and were well paid for their work.

Satire of the Trades

The *Satire of the Trades* was written by a man called Duaf for his son Khety. He is trying to encourage his son to work hard at his studies to become a good scribe. As an incentive, he describes the pitfalls of all other professions in graphic detail:

I will make you love scribedom more than your mother, I'll make its beauties stand before you; It is the greatest of all callings. There is none like it in the land.

I have never saw a sculptor as envoy, not is a goldsmith ever sent; but I have seen the smith at work at the opening of his furnace; with fingers like claws of a crocodile he stinks more than fish roe.

The jewel-maker bores with his chisel in hard stone of all kinds; when he has finished the inlay of the eye, his arms are spent, he's weary, sitting down when the sun goes down, his knees and back are cramped.

The barber barbers until nightfall, he takes himself to town, he sets himself up in his corner, he moves from street to street,

looking for someone to barber. He strains his arms to fill his belly like the bee that eats as it works.

I'll describe to you also the mason: his loins give him pain; though he is out in the wind, he works without a cloak; his loincloth is a twisted rope and a string in the rear. His arms are spent from exertion, having mixed all kinds of dirt; when he eats bread with his fingers, he has washed at the same time.

The bird-catcher suffers much, as he watches out for birds; when the swarms pass over him, he keeps saying 'Had I a net!' But the god grants it not, and he is angry with his lot. I'll speak of the fisherman also, his is the worst of all the hobs. He labours on the river, mingling with the crocodiles. When the time of reckoning comes, he is full of lamentations; He does not say 'there's a crocodile': Fear has made him blind. Coming from the flowing water he says 'Mighty God.'

Look, there is no profession without a boss, except for the scribe – he is the boss.

Most scribes were established in the village where they lived and gave their services to anyone who asked. They charged a set rate for services or a waived rate depending on the wealth of his client. Agreements were oral, so historians don't know what the fees and charges were. There could have been one scribe per village or a few scribes undercutting each other with their service charges.

The priesthood: Servants of the god

The priesthood was open to all – literate or not – although the positions given reflected the skills held. Obviously, temple scribes were literate and many worked in the House of Life, archiving, copying, and reading the numerous texts stored there.

Many priests worked on a part-time basis, only working one month in three in the temple and then returning to their villages. This arrangement was like National Service when people were called on to work for a short period.

Because many of the priests were part time, they weren't expected to be celibate. In fact the priesthood was traditionally passed down from father to son, so families were actively encouraged. Joining the priesthood was therefore not a spiritual calling, but an inheritance.

The nature of the Egyptian priesthood was very different from, say, the Christian or Hindu priesthood. Egyptian priests had virtually no contact with the population in their role as priest. They did not preach, offer advice, or try to convert people to their particular cult. The Egyptian title *Hem-Netjer* means 'servant of the god', and that is what they were. They served the god, ensuring the prayers, offerings, and incantations were carried out correctly.

A distinct hierarchy existed within the priesthood with the *first prophet* being the top dog or high priest, followed by the second, third, fourth, and fifth prophets, who all hoped at some point to have the first prophet's job. Ideally, the king was responsible for hiring the first prophet, although more often than not the king allowed the priest to name his own heir.

The lowest-ranking priests were the *wab priests* or 'purification priests', who were responsible for many of the purification rituals in the temple, carrying the *sacred barks* (small sacred boats that were used to parade statues of the gods on festival days), supervising the painters and draftsmen, and looking after other general tasks around the temple.

Military men: Dreaming of victory

Prior to the New Kingdom, no army existed, so every little boy's dream of being a soldier had to remain unfulfilled. In the earlier periods, if an army was needed, local mayors gathered likely lads from their regions and conscripted them for the duration of the expedition or campaign.

Purifying the priests

A number of purification rituals had to be performed before a priest could enter a temple. A priest anointed his hands and feet in water and then plunged into the sacred lake, which was present at every temple and represented the pure waters of the time before creation. This ritual ensured the priest was clean before entering into the presence of the god.

The Greek historian Herodotus records that Egyptian priests shaved off all (and yes, I mean *all*) their body hair to prevent lice. Some priests may even have gone so far as to pluck out their eyebrows and eyelashes just to make sure they were 100 per cent clean. They carried out this hair removal every other day. In the Ptolemaic period, any priest who forgot to shave was fined 1,000 drachmas.

Sexual intercourse was banned in the temple (quite right, too!), and priests carried out specific cleansing rituals before entering the temple after sex. In fact, it was expected that a priest about to start his working month in the temple should abstain from any contact with women for several days before entering temple service, just in case he was contaminated with menstrual blood or bodily fluids.

In the New Kingdom (go to Chapter 3 for more details), a permanent army was set up, enabling career soldiers to exist. Many autobiographies found in tombs chronicle long military careers. In fact, some soldiers rose to positions of great power; the generals Horemheb and Ramses I both became king, proving that the vizierate was not the only path to the throne.

As with all careers in ancient Egypt, soldiers started their training in basic skills, stamina, and strength young – even as young as 5 or 6.

Tomb images at Beni Hasan from the Middle Kingdom show how temporary soldiers were trained, and no doubt the training was similar for the permanent army. Training included

- ✔ Stick fighting
- ✔ Wrestling
- ✔ Weightlifting with bags of sand
- ✔ Chariot riding (although not until the New Kingdom)
- ✔ Archery
- ✔ Use of spears

A soldier's skills dictated which regiment he entered – charioteers, spearmen, or infantry.

Scribes were also an essential part of the army entourage (they get everywhere!). Scribes recorded campaign events and are often depicted in battle scenes calmly standing at the rear, recording the action. They also listed the booty gathered by the soldiers.

One particularly gruesome task of the military scribe was counting the enemy dead, which were identified by amputated right hands or penises (if they were uncircumcised). Soldiers left piles of these body parts on the battle field for the scribes to count serenely.

Manual labour

Working conditions were relatively good for the craftsmen of Deir el Medina, who were at the top of their careers and built the tombs in the Valley of the Kings, but maybe less good for the not-so-privileged members of society. These craftsmen worked long weeks with eight-hour days and only officially received one in every ten days off. Farmers and other lower class people had no days off.

However, in addition to their weekend, workers at Deir el Medina were able to take as many days off (within reason) as they needed. Surviving records from the site, known as the 'Absentee records', list an incredible range of excuses for skiving off work. Things haven't changed much in 3,500 years, as one of the most common excuses is a hangover.

The first industrial action in history?

The workmen of Deir el Medina were supposed to get paid on the 28th day of each month, and most of the time this worked fine. But on some occasions, payments were late or even non-existent.

During the reign of Ramses III, the villagers did not get paid for six months, which resulted in the workmen going on strike. Workers protested at the funerary temples of Thutmosis III, Ramses II, and Sety I, where the grain stores providing their rations were situated. Whether they had placards and chanted 'What do we want? When do we want it?' is unknown, but records describe the event as follows:

It is because of hunger and because of thirst that we come here. There is no clothing, no

ointment, no fish, no vegetables. Send to Pharaoh our good Lord about it and send to the vizier, our superior so that sustenance may be made for us.

I think this message – as a slogan on a placard – is a tad long, but it does get the point across. On this particular occasion, the workers received their rations.

However, later the same year, pay was again delayed. A village scribe named Djhutymose left out the middle man (the temple) and went with two bailiffs, no doubt with large sticks, to collect the grain rations directly from the local farmers. Luckily, Djhutymose was successful, and the villagers were able to eat again.

Other excuses included

- ✔ Wrapping a deceased family member
- ✔ Burying a deceased family member
- ✔ Making libations for the deceased
- ✔ Being ill (they didn't always elaborate on this)
- ✔ Being bitten by a scorpion
- ✔ Having an argument with the wife (this one intrigues me)
- ✔ Female family members menstruating

The villagers of Deir el Medina had a resident doctor, paid by the state, which ensured that not too many days were taken off with illness or injuries. For a description of the types of medical treatments that these unfortunate villagers endured, skip to Chapter 8.

Although the ancient Egyptians have a reputation for slave labour, promoted by the Bible and Hollywood movies, the evidence shows a very positive employment programme with health care, a bonus scheme, and opportunities to earn extra income after working hours, ensuring the workmen were well fed and able to accumulate wealth.

Artists: Creating beauty

Men with artistic talent could become artists, carpenters, or sculptors and were well paid whether they had a formal education or not. Unlike artists in the modern world, ancient Egyptians did not sign their work, so identifying the work of a particular painter or sculptor is very difficult. (For more information on art, see Chapter 11.)

Most artists worked as part of a team and were responsible for one aspect of the production of a tomb or temple scene – even if they were proficient in all aspects – and would work on this skill, making it their speciality. For example:

- ✔ Plasterers prepared walls for painting.
- ✔ Stone masons prepared walls for carving.
- ✔ Outline scribes drew the outlines on the walls.
- ✔ Sculptors carved the outlines.
- ✔ Artists painted the images.
- ✔ Overseers double-checked all work and made corrections throughout the process.

The village of Deir el Medina consisted almost exclusively of artists. Although their daily jobs were to provide a tomb and goods for the king, they also used their talents to earn income outside their regular jobs. A number of working contracts survive, showing prices and services including:

- ✔ The scribe Harshire inscribed three coffins for a songstress of Amun and was paid 329 *deben* (30 kilos) of copper.
- ✔ The workman Bekenwernero made some coffins, beds, chairs, boxes, and tables and received 91 deben (more than 8 kilos) of copper.

Farmers: Working the land

With less than 1 per cent of the Egyptian population literate, many uneducated people worked at jobs that didn't require formal education. The most important of these was farming.

A large proportion of the population of Egypt worked on the land, producing food. This was hard work and essentially one of the most important jobs, because if the farmer didn't work hard, the rest of Egypt didn't eat. The state – either the temple or the king – owned the majority of agricultural land and rented it to the farmers. If farmers didn't produce the specified grain quotas, they were beaten.

The ancient Egyptians grew various crops and typically rotated their plantings each year. The following grains formed the staple of the Egyptian diet:

- ✔ Barley
- ✔ Emmer wheat (a low-yielding wheat, first domesticated in the Near East)
- ✔ Einkorn wheat (a hulled wheat with a tough husk)
- ✔ Spelt (similar to common wheat)

Many families also kept vegetable plots, and no doubt farmers grew vegetables on a large scale. Vegetables formed a large proportion of the Egyptian diet, and included the following:

- ✔ Onions
- ✔ Garlic
- ✔ Peas
- ✔ Lentils
- ✔ Beans
- ✔ Radishes

> ✔ Cabbage
>
> ✔ Cucumbers
>
> ✔ Lettuces

Many farmers also grew sesame and castor (used for oil), flax (used for the production of linen), dates (for beer flavouring and to be eaten as a fruit), and trees (fibres used in basket and rope production).

Despite the importance of the farmers' job, they were the poorest paid workers in ancient Egyptian society. Technically they didn't get paid at all! Farmers gave a grain quota to the land owner, with the addition of rent and tax (also paid in grain). Whatever they produced in excess of this they kept or sold. This arrangement worked sufficiently well for the head of a family or head farmer, but field hands were paid a pittance and no doubt couldn't feed their families well or have any excess for purchasing other goods.

Laundrymen: Airing dirty linen

One of the worst careers described in the *Satire of the Trades* is that of laundryman.

In ancient Egypt, men were always the professional launderers. They traipsed from village to village collecting the washing, which they took to the Nile. Records from Deir el Medina show that the laundrymen were allocated certain houses to collect laundry from and they were constantly moaning about the workload. Nothing's new.

After collecting the laundry, the laundryman left a 'receipt' in the form of an *ostracon* (stone flake used as note paper) with images of the clothes that he had taken. This note ensured that the household got the right stuff back – nothing's worse than someone else's loincloth being delivered among your own laundry.

The washing was done in the Nile using *natron* (hydrous sodium carbonate) and lime as soap. The clothes were crushed against stones to get the stains off, and then left in the sun to bleach and to dry.

Working in the Nile was dangerous, because of the number of crocodiles living there. A laundryman concentrating on a stubborn loincloth stain might easily disregard the log with eyes – until he had been dragged off. And if the crocs weren't dangerous enough, the Nile and its canals were rife with parasitic worms and biting insects, which could prove fatal.

Considering the Lives of Women

Although the experience of Egyptian women was not equal to that of their male counterparts, female Egyptians enjoyed a surprisingly high level of opportunity, responsibility, and empowerment.

Appreciating women's rights

Royal women had very little freedom, were used as political pawns, and were locked away from the world in the harem (see Chapter 5 for more details).

Ordinary women were much luckier. They had more freedom than most women in other contemporary societies. For example:

✔ Women were able to walk around unchaperoned. Although this is something most women today take for granted, such freedom was unusual in ancient times.

✔ Although many of the larger houses included women's quarters, women were not confined to these areas. Instead, these rooms offered privacy during childbirth, child weaning, and menstruation.

✔ Women held the same legal rights as men from the same class. Specifically, a woman could

- Own property; she could also manage her land in any way she wanted without assistance from a man

- Inherit property

- Bequeath property; in fact, landed property was passed down from mother to daughter

- Loan property and earn interest

- Bring an action of law against another person, including a man

- Bear witness to a legal document

- Be an equal partner in legal contracts; for example, in the Ptolemaic period, she could sign her own marriage contract

Furthermore, a woman did not lose her legal rights after she married and she retained her property during the marriage. While married, she could own, inherit, and sell any of her property with the same freedom as if she were single. When drawing up her will, a woman could distribute her property any way she wanted and had no legal obligation to leave anything to her children.

Taming of the shrewd

From the numerous surviving records, many clever Egyptian women are known today. One such woman was Tay-Hetem from 249 BC, who decided to help her hubbie out when he had a few financial problems. From a contract she drew up herself (all very official!), scholars know that Tay-Hetem loaned her husband 3 *deben* of silver (273 grams) from her personal store and charged him a rate of interest of 30 per cent, which was the standard interest rate of the time. She specified that the loan was to be paid back within three years.

Although it is unknown whether her husband made the payments, it would be interesting to know how far Tay-Hetem went to get her repayments. Beat him with a rolling pin? Send the boys round? Take him to court? Hopefully, he paid in time, so he never found out how far she would go.

An Egyptian widow was automatically entitled to a third of her husband's property as well as keeping all she entered the marriage with, in addition to all she accumulated throughout the marriage. (The remaining two-thirds of her husband's property was divided between his children and his siblings.) By making gifts to his wife during his life, a husband could prevent distribution of his property after death, because his wife already owned everything. Now that is my kind of arrangement!

Working women

Sure, men in ancient Egyptian society had varied opportunities and a chance of a lucrative career. But what of the women? Most women, whether married or single, spent a lot of time in the home – raising children, helping to produce family meals, or working.

Women within farming communities were also expected to help in the field during harvest time. Women are often depicted in tomb scenes helping with the winnowing of crops, grinding grain into flour, and making beer (see Chapter 7 for how).

In their spare time – although it doesn't sound like they had much! – women were able to earn money by selling the fruits of various home-making skills. Goods produced in the home, such as beer, bread, vegetables, linen, baskets, and clay vessels, were all sold at market.

Stitch in time

The linen trade was one that started in the home, but expanded to large workshops attached to the temples and even the royal harem. Flax processing and linen production was important as a cottage industry. These workshops were dominated by female workers and supervisors and produced linen for royalty and the religious cults, as well as to trade.

Royal women in the harem workshops were responsible for training and supervising the textile workers. Royal women probably carried out the delicate embroidery work themselves to pass the time.

Management positions: Ruling the roost

Although married and unmarried woman could work without social stigma, tight restrictions applied to the occupations they could actually hold.

The tightest restrictions were on bureaucratic or administrative positions, especially working for the state, although in private households women were permitted to hold positions such as:

- Treasurer
- Major doma (a female 'butler')
- Superintendent of the dining room
- Steward of the storehouse
- Steward of the food supply
- Sealbearer (a very important role, responsible for the sealing of boxes, letters and rooms)

All these positions fall under the modern title of housekeeper – ensuring the cupboards are full, meals are prepared on time, and the family's wealth remains intact.

In royal households, the bureaucratic positions held by women were all in connection with the female-oriented aspects of the royal household. These positions included:

- Overseer of the singers
- Overseer of amusements
- Mistress of the royal harem
- Overseer of the house of weavers
- Overseer of the wig shop

Whatever the administrative position, women were never in charge of the work of men, although some women held quite important positions. Indeed, the sixth dynasty included a female vizier. The Suffragette movement would have been proud.

Midwifery and wet nursing

Most girls were taught skills related to children and childbirth, and some women chose to make these skills into lucrative careers as midwives.

Most women in ancient Egypt gave birth to at least five children, so midwifery skills were often learned by helping the village women through their pregnancy and deliveries. Although the vast majority of midwives simply learned by assisting, some chose to have formal training. For example, records show that a school of midwifery existed at the Temple of Neith in Sais. Formal training enabled midwives to work for the palace or the elite members of society, thus increasing their potential incomes.

After midwives safely delivered babies, the elite and the royal family commonly employed wet nurses to help care for children. A wet nurse was viewed as a status symbol; no family worth its salt was without such a woman. Wet nurses were normally women who had just given birth to their own child and were able to feed their employers' baby alongside their own.

Market day

Ancient Egyptian market day was certainly different from a weekly trip to Tesco.

A physical market place as such did not exist, although merchants at various Egyptian port sites set up stalls to sell their goods to sailors and foreign merchants. The rest of the population had some means of selling and buying goods, possibly meeting in public squares or on the river bank, or visiting houses of people in the village and offering a service or product.

Negotiating over price is where things get complicated. Coins were not used in Egypt until Alexander came in 332 BC, so prior to this people swapped goods for goods. Relative prices in weights of copper or silver existed, and people would have been aware of these. But objects are only valuable if someone wants to buy them, and the value depends on *how* much someone wants them.

Imagine the uproar of bartering: Perhaps an Egyptian woman wants to buy some clothes for her family, but only has four unruly goats and a bad-tempered donkey to exchange! She has to traipse around until she locates a dressmaker, only to discover that the seamstress has no interest in goats or donkeys and will only exchange for a necklace. Now the poor home-maker has to look for someone with a necklace who wants one of her unruly goats and then return to the dressmaker, only to find she has already sold that must-have loincloth and kilt ensemble with the matching sandals. Blimey! Shopping would take all day – and you may have to return home with unruly goats and a bad-tempered donkey.

Infants were normally nursed for three years. Breastfeeding acted as a safeguard against pregnancy (because it is a natural – if unreliable! – contraceptive) and was a way of ensuring uncontaminated food during the most vulnerable years of the child's life.

Entertaining the masses

Some women, who were probably unmarried, chose to go into the entertainment business. The general belief is that it was unbecoming for an elite woman to perform in public. Although women sang, danced, or played instruments in private, engaging in any of these activities in public was taboo. In fact, the only time an elite woman was permitted to perform in public was if she was in the priesthood, participating in religious ceremonies and processions.

For the lower classes, however, being a performer was a respectable, lucrative career. Troupes of women and sometimes men were hired to entertain at banquets, performing with groups of same-sex dancers, singers, or musicians (see Chapter 7 for more details).

Turning tricks

Very little evidence of prostitution in ancient Egypt exists, but as 'the oldest profession in the world', prostitution was no doubt common.

Scholars have suggested that some banquet entertainers may have made a little extra income at gatherings. Records show that a particular group of dancers known as *Hn-mwt* did offer sexual favours for financial reimbursement. However, most of the evidence of prostitutes comes from the Graeco-Roman period, when prostitution was taxed and records were kept.

Some small details are also recorded about prostitutes' practices. For example, many prostitutes had alluring messages, such as 'follow me', incised into the soles of their sandals so that they left an imprint in the mud with every step. Think of it as the ancient equivalent of cards in phone boxes.

A prostitute, like a midwife, was never unemployed in ancient Egypt. Some scholars believe that most young, rich men may have visited a prostitute before marriage in order to gain some experience. But the poorer men left in the villages, who couldn't afford high-class prostitutes, had sex with each other or the farm animals.

Serving the goddesses

Many middle-class, upper-class, and royal women chose to join the priesthood, the most prestigious profession for women.

For the upper classes, the priesthood was a convenient way of occupying unmarried women – although, like their male counterparts, woman who wanted to serve the gods did not have to be celibate, and many were in fact married.

STRANGE BUT TRUE

Mourning the dead

Women were regularly involved in the funerals of the elite – although not often as priestesses. Professional mourners were hired to wail, throw dust over their heads, rend their clothes, and scratch their cheeks. Such behaviour would have been unseemly for the women of the deceased's family to display.

Many non-royal tombs depict these professional mourners. Among the women are often small girls emulating their moves, which indicates that mourners were trained on the job. This profession, like many others, was probably passed down from mother to daughter.

Additionally, as with the male priesthood, the role of priestess was often passed from mother to daughter, and it may have been served on a part-time basis, one month in three.

Women were mostly employed in the priesthood of the cults of a goddess such as Isis, Neith, or Hathor – although they could hold roles in most cults of both gods and goddesses. Priestesses were primarily musicians, singers, or dancers for temple rituals and processions.

Checking the Balance: Wages and Payment in Ancient Egypt

As today, everyone in ancient Egypt worked to sustain their family and to increase personal wealth – so all looked forward to pay day. Records from Deir el Medina show that the workers were paid on the 28th day of every month, although unlike modern payday it was not in cash.

Because a monetary system was not introduced until Alexander the Great in 332 BC, wages were paid in produce or services. Quantities of grain were specified for various levels of workers. Wages depended on the position, and those in positions of responsibility were paid more than lower positions. A higher salary was approximately 422.5 litres of grain per month, which was enough to feed a family of 10–15. If an employee had a smaller family, he would have grain left over for shopping.

In addition to wages, the state gave workmen working for the king all the essentials of daily life, such as housing, firewood, fish, vegetables, water, and oil. At Deir el Medina, the workmen were often given extra rations by the state during religious festivals, or as an incentive if the king was pleased with progress on the royal tomb.

50 Part I: Introducing the Ancient Egyptians

When buying and selling items, all goods had a relative value, which everyone was aware of. These relative values were based on a fairly complex system of weights, volumes, and measures:

- *Khar*: Used to measure grain; 1 *khar* was equivalent to 76.8 litres.
- *Deben*: Used as a general value for many items; 1 *deben* was equivalent to 91 grams of copper.
- *Kite*: A weight of silver; 1 *kite* was equivalent to 0.6 *deben* of copper.
- *Hin*: Used to measure liquids; 1 *hin* was equivalent to 0.48 litres and worth 1 *deben*.
- *Medket*: Used for larger quantities of liquids; 1 *medket* was worth 50 *hin*.

A number of transaction records survive from Deir el Medina, offering a good snapshot of the relative values of various goods:

- A simple wooden chair: 11 *deben*
- A bed: 25 *deben*
- A table: 15 *deben*
- A bull: 95–120 *deben* (depending on size and condition)
- A cow: 4–50 *deben* (depending on size and condition)
- A young servant girl: 410 *deben*

Christmas comes early

During the reign of Merenptah (1212–1202 BC) in the New Kingdom, the king provided a large amount of extra rations for the Deir el Medina workmen. Think of this gift as the equivalent of a nice Christmas bonus in your pay packet.

One of the village scribes, Anupenheb, recorded an inventory of the gifts: In addition to their ordinary wages, workers received extra rations consisting of 150 donkey loads of provisions, including 9,000 fish, salt for drying, ten oxen ready for slaughter, four donkey loads of beans and sweet oils, eight donkey loads of barley malt (enough for four pints of beer per person), 9,000 loaves of bread (enough for 150 per household), and eight donkey loads of natron used for soap.

The ensuing village feast no doubt produced an interesting array of aromas as the ox were slaughtered and roasted and the 9,000 fish were simultaneously gutted and dried in salt on the roofs. If the villagers did not consume all that the king provided on this occasion, they could sell any excess at market.

Tying the Knot: Marriage

A particularly important aspect of Egyptian life was marriage. Remaining unmarried was considered unusual because everyone was expected to have children.

Ancient Egyptians married young – girls sometimes as young as 10. As soon as a girl started her menstruation cycle, she was a woman and of marriageable age. Boys also married as young as 10, although a man could remain unmarried until later life (30–40 years old), especially if he had been working his way through a career.

Most people probably chose their spouses, but arranged marriages weren't unheard of, especially if the families were wealthy or important.

Exposing the truth of incestuous relationships

The Egyptians are well known for their brother-sister marriages, but this is actually a misconception. Throughout the whole pharaonic period, the practice was completely taboo for the ordinary population. Only the deities and the royal family participated in this practice – as a means of ensuring the safety of the royal line.

Unmarried princesses were dangerous because ambitious men could corrupt them. However, princesses were unable to marry outside the royal family without express permission from the king, which was rarely given. These restrictions meant that more often than not, princesses married their brothers, fathers, and even grandfathers. Sometimes these arrangements were marriages in the true sense of the word and produced children.

Evidence shows that full brother-sister marriages took place in Roman Egypt so that the marriage could take place earlier than normal and a dowry was not required, keeping family property intact.

If these marriages broke down, the couple often remained living in the same house with their parents. Evidence of this weird family set-up comes from the town of Arsinoe. A man married his sister and had two children with her before getting divorced. They remained in the same household with their two children. When the man married again, his new wife moved in to the house, and this second marriage produced two daughters. Can you imagine the tension?

Skipping formality

Although the Egyptians placed much importance on marriage, no legal cere-monies were performed, nor were any records of marriages kept. As marriage was a social event organised by the families, the ancient Egyptians had no need to formalise things.

After a couple decided to get married, the most important part was to move in together. The transport of the new wife to her husband's house may have been ceremonial, accompanied by a procession and a party, but no records of this exist.

The only records that survive involve dowries and property and what should happen in the event of a divorce. These records, however, were unusual and should not be viewed as the norm. Most marriages were between people of similar wealth and rank, with no need for pre-nuptial agreements.

Divorcing

Divorce was generally as informal as the wedding, with no formal written docu-mentation unless financial considerations existed, such as a dowry to return or property to deal with. A man or a woman could divorce a spouse by simply stat-ing 'I divorce you'. The woman typically then moved back to her family home.

Divorcees, both male and female, were allowed to remarry, although women over 30 did not often remarry. This was either because the women were financially self-sufficient or past their child-bearing years and thus not con-sidered good marriage material.

Much information is missing regarding what happened to children in cases of divorce. Children may have stayed with the father or left the home with the mother. The records have not been found, but may emerge in the future.

Considering adultery

One common ground for divorce was adultery.

The penalties for adultery were harsher for women than men. For example, during the pharaonic period, divorce was the normal punishment for adul-tery, but some literary tales suggest that a woman could lose her life for com-mitting adultery. Later, in Roman Egypt, a man having an affair with a married woman would be condemned to have 1,000 lashes, while the woman was mutilated by nose amputation.

Contractual arrangements

Many marriage contracts have survived, although they're from later periods when there may have been less distinction between the classes. The marriage contract of a couple called Heraclides and Demetria, from 311 BC, states:

> In the seventh year of the reign of Alexander son of Alexander . . . Marriage contract of Heraclides and Demetria. Heraclides takes as his lawful wife Demetria . . . both being freeborn, from her father Leptines, . . . and her mother Philotis, bringing clothing and ornaments to the value of 1,000 drachmae, and Heraclides shall supply to Demetria all that is proper for a freeborn wife, and we shall live together wherever it seems best to Leptines and Heraclides consulting in common. If Demetria is discovered doing any evil to the shame of her husband Heraclides, she shall be deprived of all that she brought, but Heraclides shall prove whatever he alleges against Demetria before three men whom they both accept.

> It shall not be lawful for Heraclides to bring home another wife in insult of Demetria nor to have children by another woman nor to do any evil against Demetria on any pretext. If Heraclides is discovered doing any of these things and Demetria proves it before three men whom they both accept, Heraclides shall give back to Demetria the dowry of 1,000 drachmae which she brought and shall moreover forfeit 1,000 drachmae of the silver coinage of Alexander. Demetria and those aiding Demetria to exact payment shall have the right of execution, as if derived from a legally decided action, upon the person of Heraclides and upon all the property of Heraclides both on land and on water.

> This contract shall be valid in every respect, wherever Heraclides may produce it against Demetria, or Demetria and those aiding Demetria to exact payment may produce it against Heraclides, as if the agreement had been made in that place. Heraclides and Demetria shall have the right to keep the contracts severally in their own custody and to produce them against each other.

> Witnesses Cleon, Gelan; Anticrates, Temnian; Lysis, Temnian; Dionysius, Temnian; Aristomachus, Cyrenaean; Aristodicus, Coan.

This contract shows that even in the time of Alexander the Great, the women of Egypt were legally active and able to divorce their husbands as long as they could produce the same evidence and proof as they would have to in a similar situation today.

Although adultery was not approved of, it was acceptable for a man to have a *concubine*, a woman brought into the house to live alongside his wife and children. Having a concubine was considered a status symbol, as it reflected the man's wealth. Whether the concubine's role was purely sexual is unknown, and the difference between a wife and a concubine are not clearly defined from the ancient texts, apart from the difference in their status.

Monogamy or monotony?

Records show that a young man from Deir el Medina called Nesamenemope had been having a long-term affair with a woman in the village. Nesamenemope was married and the young woman was not. One evening an angry mob arrived at the woman's home to beat up her and her family. Luckily officials calmed the angry mob and Nesamenemope was instructed to divorce his wife and provide for his mistress before continuing with the affair.

If he didn't get divorced and still continued with the affair, the officials stated that they wouldn't prevent the crowd from beating the woman up next time, and Nesamenemope would have his nose and ears amputated before being sent to Nubia for hard labour.

Nesamenemope couldn't live without his mistress and continued the affair; although whether the threat to send him to Nubian quarries or mines was ever carried out is unknown.

Caring for the Elderly

The average age of death in Egypt was 30–35, but many people lived much longer. In surviving texts, the ideal old age is recorded as 110, although it is unlikely that many people reached this ripe old age.

Children were expected to care for their parents in old age. Girls in particular were obliged to care for their parents, whereas boys were not, presumably because a man had to care for his wife and her parents.

If a couple were childless, they quite often adopted children for the sole purpose of providing care later in life. Little is known about the adoption process, but it was normally an informal affair. However, if the adopting couple were wealthy, they sometimes signed a document before witnesses.

From Deir el Medina, limited evidence suggests that the state provided a sort of pension for the widows of the workmen still residing at the village. The records are rare and indicate that the rations distributed to widows were not enough to live on – but these did supplement the care their children provided.

Military records show that the state provided a better pension for soldiers in the form of land and *gold of honour* – jewellery and honorary priestly titles, which included a further pension.

Other than the Deir el Medina workmen and the military, no one else received a state pension. Elderly and widowed Egyptians relied solely on the kindness of friends and family.

Part II
Stepping Back in Time

The 5th Wave   By Rich Tennant

"Remember, he's known as the 'Catfish King',
but never call him that to his face."

In this part . . .

The history of the ancient Egyptians is varied and colourful, and this part takes you on a chronological journey from the very beginning of the Egyptian civilisation in the pre-dynastic period to its collapse at the death of Cleopatra.

In this part I cover the battles of Thutmosis III, which were nearly lost due to the army plundering when they should have been fighting, and the spectacular stalemate of Ramses II at Kadesh that he chose to record as a great victory.

All of the military kings were supported by a great number of women, including wives, mothers, and daughters, some of whom made history in their own right such as Hatshepsut and Cleopatra who ruled Egypt without the assistance of the king. You'll find out about them in this part.

Sadly, due to constant invasions, and economic and ecological disasters, Egyptian civilisation suffered a slow decline until it was engulfed by the Romans and eventually disappeared altogether in the fourth century AD.

Chapter 3

Building a Civilisation with Military Might

*I*n order to summarise more than 3,000 years of ancient Egyptian history, a chronology of rulers and events is necessary. One seemingly sensible place to look for this sequence is in Egyptian records of kings and their achievements.

A number of kings produced *king lists* (Egyptologists never come up with imaginative names.) These lists record the names and titles of the kings in order, in addition to reign length and major events or achievements that occurred during each reign.

Unfortunately, these lists were created to connect the king to previous rulers and therefore are selective, only listing the 'good' kings. Anyone who upset the equilibrium, was disliked, or ruled a divided Egypt was omitted from the lists. Also, the Egyptians did not have a centralised calendar. The dates chronicled on king lists are based on the years of rule of the current king (for example, year 12 of Ramses II). This is accurate unless you have no idea how long the king ruled for and when he ruled.

This chapter follows the ups and downs of centuries of Egyptian rule and change, breaking the course of civilisation into handy periods and eras. It also explores the development of a permanent Egyptian army, which had an enormous impact on the later history of ancient Egypt.

Tracing the Course of Egyptian Civilisation

Based on king lists and other historical documents and artefacts, historians organise ancient Egyptian history into the following major periods:

- Pre-dynastic period
- Early dynastic period, or archaic period
- Old Kingdom
- First intermediate period
- Middle Kingdom
- Second intermediate period
- New Kingdom
- Third intermediate period
- Late period
- Graeco-Roman period

The following sections cover Egyptian history from the pre-dynastic period through to the second intermediate period. Chapter 4 explores the New Kingdom, one of Ancient Egypt's most dynamic eras. Check the Cheat Sheet timeline so see how the periods all slot together.

Pre-dynastic period

The pre-dynastic period dates from approximately 5500 BC to 3100 BC and ends with the unification of Egypt.

During this period, Egypt was divided into two very distinct cultures: one in Upper Egypt and the other in Lower Egypt. Archaeologically speaking, cemetery sites are located primarily in Upper Egypt and settlement sites in Lower Egypt.

Comparing and contrasting Upper and Lower Egypt

For many years, archaeologists thought that the cultures of Upper and Lower Egypt were completely separate from the later Egyptian culture. Flinders Petrie (see Chapter 19) even suggested that the pre-dynastic cultures were completely foreign cultures created by an Asiatic invasion. More recent research now shows a slow progression from these contrasting cultural elements to the better-known Egyptian civilisation.

Existing king lists

Most of the existing king lists are recorded in religious or funerary contexts (although few of these lists are located in tombs and temples). Most of the lists are simply a list of royal names written in cartouches on monumental stone blocks or temple walls. The kings who commissioned them were trying to show that their lineage was an ancient one. The known king lists include:

✔ Royal List of Thutmosis III from Karnak, now in the Louvre in Paris

✔ Royal List of Sety I at Abydos

✔ Abydos King List of Ramses II, now in the British Museum in London

✔ Saqqara Tablet from the tomb of Tenroy, which lists 57 rulers

✔ Turin Royal Canon from the 19th dynasty

✔ The Palermo Stone from the fifth dynasty

✔ Graffiti from the quarries in the Wadi Hammamat, which include very short lists

Egyptologists use king lists in combination with each other, other historical records, and archaeological evidence because the lists aren't reliable on their own – they omit disliked rulers, portions of the text are damaged, or the lists only go up to a certain period.

The cultures of both areas are very different from the more traditional culture that most people associate with ancient Egypt. However, several commonalities that continued through to the Graeco-Roman period appear in the art of these earliest Egyptian cultures, including:

✔ **Smiting scenes,** or images in which the king is depicted hitting his enemy. The earliest known example comes from tomb 100 at Hierakonpolis and is dated to 3500–3200 BC.

✔ **Images of a cattle cult,** which eventually developed into the cult of the goddess Hathor (see Chapter 9).

✔ **The red crown of Lower Egypt,** which symbolised royal power in this region. The earliest image of the red crown of Lower Egypt is dated to approximately 3500 BC from a potsherd currently in the Ashmolean Museum, Oxford.

Uniting the land of Egypt

The Egyptian civilisation as it is known today started during the reign of King Narmer (dynasty 0) in approximately 3100 BC. At the start of King Narmer's reign, Egypt was divided into locally governed regions, but at some point Narmer was instrumental in unifying these regions to be governed by one man – himself.

Historians are uncertain whether this unification of Egypt was achieved by a number of small battles or one major battle, although the former is more likely.

The unification is recorded on the Narmer Palette, a ceremonial slate palette found at Hierakonpolis and now in the Cairo Museum. The palette includes the earliest battle scene from ancient Egypt as well as a number of images that continued to be used for the next 3,000 years, including

- ✔ The king hitting an enemy over the head with a mace
- ✔ The king wearing the crown of Upper and Lower Egypt
- ✔ The king as a bull trampling on captured enemies

The symbolism on the palette reinforces the idea that the king was the undisputed head of a single state. The imagery is the beginning of the kingship ideology prescribing that Egypt should never be divided. From this point on, all kings tried to maintain this ideal and all strived to rule a united Egypt.

Early dynastic period

The early dynastic period, sometimes referred to as the archaic period, covers only the first two dynasties. This period is a kind of transition between the culture of the pre-dynastic period and the Old Kingdom. Some historians contend that Narmer unified Egypt and commenced Egypt's earliest dynastic period, while others believe that the process was slow and evolutionary.

The earliest evidence of writing comes from this period in the form of

- ✔ Stone stelae (stone slabs with a curved top used in monumental inscriptions)
- ✔ Wooden and ivory labels (probably attached to grave goods in tombs)
- ✔ Pottery jars
- ✔ Clay cylinder seals (used to seal boxes, doors, and possibly accounts or correspondence)

By the end of the early dynastic period, the state was fully formed, and the kings had begun to build large subterranean tombs (see Chapter 13) with elaborate and expensive funerary goods to show the wealth they had amassed.

Old Kingdom

The Old Kingdom (2686–2333 BC) was primarily a time of royal affluence and economic strength and included the third to the sixth dynasties. The period is best known for pyramid building, which peaked during this period.

The first stone building and the first pyramid to be built was the third dynasty Step Pyramid at Saqqara (see Chapter 13 for details). King Djoser built this structure as an extension to a traditional tomb and stepped monument. The evolution of pyramids continued throughout the Old Kingdom until the culmination of the structure, the Great Pyramid of King Khufu at Giza, constructed between 2589 and 2566 BC. (For further pyramid facts, skip to Chapter 14.)

Towards the end of the Old Kingdom (the fifth dynasty), the *Pyramid Texts* were introduced. These provided some of the earliest information about the funerary beliefs of the ancient Egyptians. These texts, coupled with the biographical texts in the tombs, give historians loads of information about the bureaucracy and officialdom of the Old Kingdom.

The sixth dynasty saw a change in the economy of Egypt, with the nobility becoming increasingly more powerful and eventually growing richer than the kings. This wealth and power disparity is reflected in tombs of sixth dynasty royals and nobles; the nobles' tombs are far more elaborate. Ironically, this power swap may have been due to one too many tax exemptions granted by the king to his favoured courtiers.

The collapse of the Old Kingdom was due to a number of factors, of which the most important were a series of floods resulting in small harvest yields, famine, and eventually disease.

First intermediate period

The first intermediate period (2180–2140 BC) was a time of political unrest following the end of the Old Kingdom.

Introducing the wheel

Strangely, the Egyptians didn't really use the wheel for transportation until the New Kingdom and the introduction of the chariot. However, this is not to say that they didn't have wheels. Wheeled vehicles and carts simply weren't particularly practical forms of transportation on agricultural or desert terrain. Instead, the Egyptians of the Old Kingdom used donkeys, oxen, and boats as means of getting about.

The earliest representation of the wheel in use comes from the Old Kingdom, in the tomb of Kaemhesit at Saqqara. The image shows a scaling ladder being pushed up against a wall. The ladder has very distinct solid wooden wheels to manoeuvre it into place. The soldiers climbing the ladder are using axes to help pull themselves further up the wall. Other soldiers are blocking the wheels with a lump of wood to prevent the ladder moving and injuring those climbing up.

After the Old Kingdom collapsed (probably due to a series of bad floods and a resulting famine), the poor, who were hit worst by famine and disease, rose up against their rulers and the upper class. These uprisings are described in a long text called the 'Admonitions of Ipuwer':

> *The wealthy are in mourning. The poor man is full of joy. Every town says: let us suppress the powerful among us. The door-keepers say, 'Let us go out and plunder.' A man looks upon his son as his enemy. The wrongdoer is everywhere . . . the plunderer is everywhere. The robber is a possessor of riches, the rich man is become a plunderer. The bird-catchers have drawn up in line of battle and the farmers go out to plough with his shield.*

This text paints a picture of a horrible environment in which to live – one in which anarchy reigned and people were in constant fear for their lives. The first intermediate period seems to be proof of the saying that any civilisation is only three meals away from anarchy.

The administration of Egypt became divided again, with the eighth dynasty ruling in the Memphite region, although its power was limited to the local area. Petty chieftains who had gained control of local towns and provinces ruled the rest of Egypt.

At the collapse of the eighth dynasty, the ninth dynasty took control of Herakleopolis. This dynasty might have controlled the whole of Egypt for a short while at least, although its hold did not last long. The tenth dynasty saw a divide in Egypt again, with the dynasty ruling from the Herakleopolis area, and the trend continued with the 11th dynasty ruling from Thebes.

Losing oneself in the labyrinth

In the Faiyum, a pyramid complex built by Amenemhat III (12th dynasty) has a reputation for containing a labyrinth. Herodotus visited the site, called Hawara, and recorded that the labyrinth had a total of 3,000 rooms connected by winding passages. Based on Herodotus's description, the site of Hawara became a major tourist attraction for the Romans and Greeks visiting Egypt.

The complex was in fact relatively straightforward by Egyptian standards, with a pyramid in the north and the mortuary temple (the labyrinth) to the south. Sadly, very little remains of the mortuary temple, but enough exists to show that it was a substantial building. The mortuary temple was probably similar to the Step Pyramid complex at Saqqara, with a number of chambers, shrines, and pillared courts.

However, the temple probably consisted of far fewer rooms than Herodotus mentions; he may have been confused by numerous subterranean tomb chambers in the area. You can't blame poor old Herodotus for getting confused over the differences between an elaborate mortuary complex and a Greek-style labyrinth.

Middle Kingdom

The 11th dynasty eventually managed to take control of all of Egypt, reuniting it and starting the period called the Middle Kingdom. The unification took place during the reign of the fourth king, Mentuhotep I (2125–2055 BC).

During the 11th dynasty, the local governors increased in strength, and although the country was now ruled by a single king, this king was dependent on these governors. Thus the king needed to appeal to these governors to help him raise an army, with each region producing a number of young men to go on military campaigns, trading expeditions, or border patrols.

However, by the end of the reign of Senwosret III (12th dynasty), the king had regained enough control to raise an army without the help of the local governors.

The Middle Kingdom kings were keen on expanding Egypt's boundaries, slowly pushing further into Nubia. With each successful push, they secured the area by building a fortress. For example:

- Amenemhat I of the 12th dynasty built a row of fortresses in the north-eastern Delta to protect the borders from Asiatic attack.

- Between the reigns of Senwosret I and III, a series of 17 fortresses in Nubia – ten near the second cataract of the Nile past the boundary between Egypt and Nubia – were erected to prevent infiltration by the Nubians as well as to control the trade from the gold mines and stone quarries in the region.

Sometimes these fortresses were over-large, just to prove a point that the Middle Kingdom kings were a military dynasty and to let the Nubians know that the Egyptians were there to stay.

The ten fortresses near the second cataract share a number of architectural elements, including

- **Bastions** (protruding areas from the enclosure walls rather like towers) from within which soldiers could fire on the enemy.

- **Walls** built of mud brick with wide stone bases. The thick walls had a walkway at the top so that soldiers could patrol the perimeter.

- **Ditches** surrounding the enclosure walls making an obstacle for anyone trying to get into the fortress. The ditches were painted white so anyone in the ditch would be spotted from the walls.

- **Walled stairways** to the Nile where supplies would come in and naval attacks could be launched. The stairways were the safest part of the fortress.

Other fortresses had fortified towns and religious temples constructed nearby. The fortress of Buhen included arrow slits high up in the walls, showing that archery was the main method of defence. Written evidence from the expulsion of the Hyksos (see the following section 'Second intermediate period') suggests that the fortified enclosure walls at Avaris also had arrow slits from which soldiers could shoot without being exposed to the enemy.

In addition to standing as symbols of Egyptian power, these fortresses also provide a great deal of information about the life of soldiers, including their pay, weapons, armour, and food (see the section 'Creating an Army: A Key to the New Kingdom', later in this chapter).

Second intermediate period

The Middle Kingdom collapsed around 1782 BC in a similar way to the Old Kingdom, perhaps due to floods and a subsequent famine. Many historians contend that the descriptions of terrible living conditions in the 'Admonitions of Ipuwer' (see the section 'First intermediate period', earlier in this chapter) also apply to the second intermediate period.

For some unspecified reason, at the end of the Middle Kingdom, a large influx of people from the area of Palestine and Syria (referred to by the Egyptians as Asiatics) came to the region. This was not an invasion, but rather a small-scale migration. Some historians believe that the Egyptian government may have invited the Palestinians for their boat-making skills, and these immigrants were then housed in the Delta, which was the site of large ports and trading centres.

This influx is unlikely to have been the cause of the collapse of the Middle Kingdom, but these immigrants and the changes they brought ushered in the Hyksos period.

The Hyksos period

Towards the end of the second intermediate period (1663–1555 BC), Egypt experienced a period of divided rule, with the 15th dynasty ruling in the north from the Delta site of Avaris and the 17th dynasty ruling from Thebes in the south:

- ✔ The 15th-dynasty kings were known as the Hyksos and had risen to power from the Syro-Palestinian community living in the Delta during the Middle Kingdom.

- ✔ The 17th-dynasty kings were of Egyptian origin, but may have been *vassal rulers* of the 15th dynasty, which means that they were only being allowed to rule because they were quiet and didn't cause trouble.

STRANGE BUT TRUE

The unknown soldiers

At Deir el Bahri in Luxor, a mass grave for soldiers was discovered in a site overlooking the temple of Mentuhotep I (11th dynasty), near the mortuary temple of Hatshepsut.

At least 60 bodies were discovered in this tomb, all male, with an average height of 5 feet 6 inches and aged between 30 and 40. Many of the men had a number of old wounds that had healed, indicating that they were war veterans. Most of the wounds were on the left side of the head, which is common for battle wounds, because most soldiers are right handed. The wounds were caused by:

✔ **Arrows:** Ten of the men were killed by puncture wounds from ebony-tipped arrows, and some fragments of these arrows were still embedded in the bodies. One soldier had an arrow embedded, while another was hit in the back from an angle that suggests he was shot from high battlements. (Most arrows were collected after battle and reused by the surviving army, but some were missed or too difficult to retrieve.)

✔ **Blunt objects:** Other soldiers were killed by blunt objects like stones falling from battlements, and many died from being hit with force by a blunt instrument.

This battle was clearly harsh and bloody, but these men died when there was no outside warfare, indicating that they were involved in a civil war, perhaps Mentuhotep I reuniting a divided Egypt.

REMEMBER

The Hyksos rulers are often said to have invaded Egypt from Palestine using chariots, which had not been introduced to Egypt at this time. In fact the Hyksos kings came from the local Asiatic community in the Delta. These communities had been living in the region for more then 100 years before the start of the Hyksos period. (Also, the chariot was introduced during this period, but not *by* the Hyksos. Both the Egyptians and the Hyksos gained access to the chariot at the same time, so neither had an advantage over the other in skill at charioteering.)

Expelling the Hyksos

Near the end of the Hyksos period (around 1640 BC), Hyksos kings had gained control over the whole of Egypt, serving as the undisputed kings of Upper and Lower Egypt.

However, the members of the 17th dynasty at Thebes weren't over keen on the Hyksos kings interfering in local affairs. So Seqenenre Tao II, a 17th dynasty king, led an offensive against the Hyksos King Apophis.

Burying the evidence

The origins of the Hyksos have always been questioned, but the evidence at Avaris, their capital in the Delta, shows a juxtaposition between an Egyptian and a Syro-Palestinian culture. This mix of cultural influences is highlighted in two of the Hyksos's most bizarre practices – servant and donkey burials:

- Three servant burials have been discovered alongside their master's tomb at Avaris. These servants were buried across the tomb entrance and face the door, as if waiting for orders from their deceased master. All the servants were males – an older adult, an adolescent, and a 25 year old. They all seem to have been buried at the same time as their master, indicating that they were sacrificed when their master died. This practice had been used by the Egyptians, but not for more than 1,000 years at the time of the burials, suggesting it was a foreign idea from the homeland of these Asiatic settlers.

- Seventeen donkey burials have also been discovered at Avaris. Donkey burial was a non-Egyptian practice. The donkeys were typically buried in pairs at the front of large tombs, possibly as a sacrifice on the deaths of the tomb owners. These donkeys may have pulled carts or funerary carriages, but no harnesses were found alongside these burials. The inclusion of donkeys was rare and only attached to very elite burials, which indicates wealth and status within the community.

The battle was not as easy as Seqenenre Tao originally thought, and he died in battle. His mummy includes numerous head wounds, indicating that this was a vicious battle. His son Kamose took up the gauntlet and continued the battle. Kamose was a little more successful and managed to reclaim most of Egypt, pushing Apopis back to the Hyksos capital of Avaris. Kamose died young, although historians are unsure how.

Kamose's brother Ahmose I took over the battle and was more successful than his brother, managing to chase the Hyksos out of Egypt entirely. Ahmose continued to pursue the Hyksos as far as Sharuhen in the Negev Desert between Rafah and Gaza, sacking villages along the way – just to show who was boss.

Ahmose then returned to Egypt and reinforced the eastern borders with a strong military presence to ensure that the Hyksos supporters did not try to re-enter the country. This successful king was the first king of the 18th dynasty and ushered in the New Kingdom. (See Chapter 4 for more on this period of Egyptian history.)

Creating an Army: A Key to the New Kingdom

The start of the New Kingdom (1555 BC) saw a number of changes in government control and organisation. But the main change – and the most successful – was the introduction of a permanent army. Prior to the New Kingdom, when the king needed an army, local governors were called on to gather likely lads from within their regions. Ahmose, however, saw the flaw in this method and introduced a full-time standing army.

As with most positions in Egypt, military roles were passed on from father to son (see Chapter 2). However, based on records of military promotions, Egyptian males, including the uneducated, were able to become soldiers and rise through the ranks. Prior to the start of a permanent army, Egyptians could gain political power or reach the throne only through bureaucracy or the priesthood.

Signing up

Training in the army started as young as 5 years old, although professional military service didn't start until the age of 20. Older recruits may have joined as part of a national service with a requirement of serving at least a year before returning to their villages. However, after training they could be called up at any time.

Just like today, new military recruits needed to get haircuts. Images of this process have been discovered in tombs. The haircuts created an element of uniformity among the ranks.

Surviving texts also describe the start of a new recruit's life in the army. New recruits received a 'searing beating' as a means of demoralising them in order to make them more pliable and susceptible to obeying orders.

The training regime was hard and included

- Weight lifting, using bags of sand as weights
- Wrestling
- Boxing
- Throwing knives at wooden targets to improve aim

- ✔ Sword skills, using sticks for practice
- ✔ Chariot riding
- ✔ Target practice in a chariot with a bow and arrow (see Figure 3-1)

These tasks would be hard in anyone's books, but imagine doing all of this outside in more than 100-degree heat. No wonder the Egyptian army was particularly good and greatly feared by many.

Figure 3-1: Target practice using a copper target (Luxor Museum).

Dividing the army

The New Kingdom was a large operation that needed a great deal of organisation to make it work well. The majority of the army was made up of infantry (foot soldiers) who were separated into divisions of 5,000 men.

Each division was named after a god and had a royal son in the position of general of the division. (Some of the princes who held this title were actually infants, indicating that it was an honorary title.) Specialist divisions included groups of charioteers, archers, spearmen, and foreign mercenaries.

For easier control, the army was further divided:

- ✔ A host consisted of 500 men (at least two companies).
- ✔ A company had 250 men (consisting of five platoons).
- ✔ A platoon had 50 men (consisting of five squads).
- ✔ A squad had 10 men.

A soldier's life

Papyrus Anastasi 3, written during the New Kingdom reign of Sety II, was probably copied from an earlier text. It describes in detail the experience of a typical soldier.

What is it that you say they tell, that the soldier's is more pleasant than the scribe's profession? Come let me tell you the condition of the soldier, that much exerted one. He is brought while a child to be confined in the camp. A searing beating is given to his body, a wound inflicted on his eye and a splitting blow to his brow. He is laid down and beaten like papyrus. He is struck with torments.

Come, let me relate to you his journey to Khor [Palestine and Syria] and his marching upon the hills. His rations and water are upon his shoulder like the load of an ass.

His neck has become calloused, like that of an ass. The vertebrae of his back are broken. He drinks foul water and halts to stand guard. When he reaches the enemy he is like a pinioned bird, with no strength in his limbs. If he succeeds in returning to Egypt, he is like a stick which the woodworm has devoured. He is sick, prostration overtakes him. He is brought back upon an ass, his clothes taken away by theft, his henchmen fled . . . turn back from the saying that the soldier's is more pleasant than the scribe's profession.

This text, as I am sure is clear, was written to try to persuade a young boy to bypass the glamour of military life and enter the scribal profession instead. You wouldn't have to tell me twice.

Tagging along

In addition to soldiers, the army included numerous other important elements, such as:

- ✔ **Musicians:** Trumpets and drums were used to help troops march in time, as well to signal tactical changes and manoeuvres during battles.

- ✔ **Standard bearers:** Military standards were an important part of the battle, because seeing where the troops were situated on the field was vital. Standards were also a source of pride for the troops.

- ✔ **Scribes:** All battle events needed to be recorded, and military scribes accompanied the military onto the battlefield. They were responsible for counting amputated body parts after a battle (a method of counting the enemy dead), as well as recording the amount of booty and number of prisoners collected.

- ✔ **Camp followers:** A number of other individuals milled around the military camps and were responsible for cleaning the officers' tents, fetching water, and cooking. These individuals often included children, who perhaps were later trained to become soldiers.

Performing non-combative duties

In addition to fighting in battles, soldiers were assigned to do a number of boring or difficult tasks:

- One of the most tedious assignments was guarding desert trading routes for up to 20 days at a time. The graffiti on some of these desert sites show that soldiers on duty were bored out of their minds, marking off the days until they returned to civilisation.

- Soldiers were also drafted for transportation of large stone blocks for the construction of sarcophagi and obelisks. Hundreds of strong men were needed, and they didn't come much stronger than the military.

- Because of their strength, soldiers helped with the harvest to ensure that it was completed quickly and efficiently. Whether they travelled to their own village to help with the harvest or were allocated to the place most in need is uncertain, but soldiers were definitely used for this important annual event.

On the march

When the soldiers were sent out on a military campaign, they probably dreamed of quiet guard duties. The journeys to get to the battles were often long and hard – sometimes as dangerous as the fights themselves.

For example, a journey from Memphis to Thebes, if travelled in daylight hours by river, took between 12 and 20 days. (Today it takes nine hours by train or about an hour by plane.) The river journey was quite hazardous, with threats from other vessels, sandbanks, and hippos.

To warn passing vessels and people that the military was on board ship, soldiers hung their cowhide shields on the outside of the boats' cabins. This may also have acted as a beacon to passing bad guys wanting to harm the soldiers.

Historians don't know how fast an Egyptian army marched, but records from Alexander the Great's army (around 336–323 BC) show that his troops covered an average of 13 miles a day, receiving a rest period every five to six days for particularly long-distance marches. On shorter campaigns, these troops covered up to 15 miles a day. The marching army also required a rest period between a long march and actually fighting, in order to recuperate their strength.

Policing and tax collecting

When not involved in military combat, soldiers were often employed in tax collecting and general policing.

One text from the reign of Horemheb (18th dynasty) tells of a court case between some soldiers and tax payers: The soldiers had gone to collect taxes and then nicked half the stuff collected and had the cheek to say they had never been paid in the first place. The king decreed that farmers shouldn't be punished for non-payment if their payments had been stolen (which is only fair, really). The soldiers were punished with 100 blows and five open wounds and were forced to return the goods they took.

In the Graeco-Roman period (332–30 BC), the military was still used for tax collection. One record shows a tax collector, Timcyenes, requesting that his boss send some soldiers to help him collect tax from a reluctant villager.

I have collected taxes from all the residents of the village except Johannes . . . he refuses to pay his account . . . please send two soldiers to the village where he is being held, because in that way we may be able to get the money that is owed.

Historians don't know whether the soldiers were successful, but the record does indicate that soldiers had a certain amount of persuasive power – no doubt with the aid of big sticks.

Eating like a soldier: Military fare

Soldiers often had to carry their sustenance with them (thus increasing the weight of their packs). Alexander the Great recorded that his army of 10,000 men and 2,000 horses had a daily consumption of

- 14 tonnes of grain
- 18 tonnes of fodder
- 90,000 litres of water

Soldiers were given fewer than ten loaves of bread a day each, which they carried in bags and baskets. This bread (probably more biscuit than bread) would have grown mould, which although unknown to the Egyptians was a form of natural antibiotic.

Soldiers also carried the ingredients for making bread if they had access to ovens en route or time to fashion mud ovens while at camp.

Other food items were part of the Egyptian military diet because they stored and travelled well, and included onions, beans, figs, dates, fish, and meat. Many kinds of fruit and meat were dried, but the soldiers also caught fish. Enemy livestock was plundered for meat. Beer may have been brewed on campaign because it didn't keep for long. Drinking water was obtained from wells. Soldiers had to carry or steal wine to accompany their meals.

Because the quantity of food required for an army was so immense, the military probably stored food at numerous forts along the campaign route. The armies also made use of food storage in any town or village along the way. In fact, villages may have been legally obligated to help passing armies. Of course, feeding 10,000 men and numerous horses at the drop of a hat may have bankrupted a few of the smaller towns.

Waiting for pay day

The food that the military needed to survive formed the majority of their wages, because no monetary system existed until the time of Alexander the Great. On campaign, these wages were simply eaten, while in the barracks they were exchanged for other goods.

In addition to official wages, soldiers were able to plunder other goodies to give their wealth a boost. Plunder in the form of gold, cattle, and even women was taken from enemy camps after cities had been sacked and regions conquered. The officers obviously got the best of the booty, but ordinary infantry soldiers also returned with full backpacks.

A formal system of awards also recognised the bravest soldiers for their work. These awards consisted of golden flies (as a sign of persistence), gold *shebyu* collars for valour, 'oyster' shells of gold or shell, and even property. Not only were the soldiers made wealthy by these gifts, they also received recognition within the Egyptian community for their services.

Armed for battle

Egyptian soldiers were bedecked in weapons, equipment, armour, and even religious icons as they headed into battle.

Armed to the teeth

The weapons in the Egyptian army were varied and numerous. Soldiers did not always own their weapons, and in records from Medinet Habu, Ramses III supervises the issuing of weapons for the battle against the Sea People (see Chapter 4). The weapons were stacked in piles, swords in one, bows in another, and arrows in a third.

Weapons varied from the simple to the complicated to the downright unpleasant:

- ✔ **Sticks and stones:** Sticks were good for close combat and were used as clubs. Stones were good for long-distance combat because they could be thrown. Both were readily available.

- ✔ **Mace:** This large piece of hard stone (such as granite or diorite) mounted on a handle was used to club people to death. A New Kingdom adaptation of this weapon was to fit a sharpened curved bronze blade (see *Khepesh swords*, below) to a mace and use that not only to club but also to slice at your opponent.

- ✔ **Slingshots:** Originally used for hunting, these were adapted for military use as well. Ammunition was always available, and the slings were easy to transport.

- ✔ **Throwsticks:** These were primarily used for hunting birds, but were also effective weapons in battle. Their main disadvantage was that as soon as the sticks were thrown, the soldiers were unarmed.

- ✔ **Bow and arrow:** The Egyptian army had a large corps of archers used to protect the infantry from a distance, because arrows travelled up to 200 metres. Archers used both the *self bow* (a straight bow made from a single piece of wood) and the *composite bow* (an arched bow made from a number of small pieces of wood glued together to give greater flexibility). Archers could send arrows travelling up to 300 metres.

- ✔ **Spears:** Many of the foot soldiers were armed with spears with a 2-metre-long shaft and a metal blade. Spears were intended to be thrown, but because this disarmed the spearman, they were also used as stabbing weapons.

- ✔ **Axes, daggers, and swords:** These instruments were used in close-combat battles and were made of bronze, copper, or (in the case of axes only) stone.

- ✔ *Khepesh* **swords:** These New Kingdom weapons were normally used by royalty and featured a type of scimitar with a curved blade.

- ✔ **Shields:** These were used for body protection in place of full body armour. They measured 1 by 1.5 metres and were made of wood. Sometimes they were solid wood, which would have made them heavy; more often they consisted of a wooden frame covered in cow hide. A handle was fixed to the back, to which a soldier could attach a strap to sling the shield over the shoulder while on the march. In the absence of proper armour, Egyptian soldiers were still well protected from the showers of arrows, stones, sticks, and swords raining on them.

The transport of choice

A vital item of military kit was the chariot, which was introduced during the Hyksos period (see the section 'The Hyksos period', earlier in this chapter).

The typical Egyptian chariot had a light wooden semi-circular frame with an open back and an axle with two wheels of either four or six spokes. These wheels were made up of numerous smaller pieces tied together with wet leather thongs, which shrank when dry and pulled the wheel together. A long pole was attached to the axle with a yoke for two horses.

Each chariot had a driver and a man armed with a spear, shield, or bow and arrow. The small, agile chariot allowed the army to pursue the enemy quickly as well as rain arrows down on them at the same time. Archaeologists have only discovered 11 chariots, four from the tomb of Tutankhamun, two from the tomb of Yuya and Tuya (the parents of Queen Tiye), and one belonging to Thutmose IV.

Papyrus Anastasi I from the 19th dynasty describes the adventures of an Egyptian charioteer in Canaan, including a visit to a chariot repair shop in Joppa:

> You make your way into the armoury; workshops surround you; smiths and leather-workers are all about you. They do all that you wish. They attend to your chariot, so that it may cease from lying idle. Your pole is newly shaped. They give leather covering to your collar-piece. They supply your yoke. They give a . . . (of metal) to your whip; they fasten [to] it lashes. You go forth quickly to fight on the open field, to accomplish the deeds of the brave!

Sounds like a very ordinary visit in the life of a charioteer.

Throughout the New Kingdom, all royal sons were trained in driving chariots and firing arrows from moving chariots. Battle reliefs generally show the king alone in his chariot, often with four horses instead of the usual two, to demonstrate his great horsemanship and control.

Dressed to kill

In the New Kingdom, the introduction of bronze weapons led to a greater need for body armour. Armour was probably reserved for the elite members of the army rather than the masses of infantry, and included:

- **Scales of bronze or hard leather:** These were fixed and overlapping on a jerkin of linen or leather.

- **Helmets:** These were generally worn only by Sherden mercenaries (a foreign group who formed part of the Sea People – see Chapter 4) and had weird little horns and a round disc on top.

Ordinary soldiers probably only had their hair as a form of head protection. Some Middle Kingdom soldiers had tightly curled, heavily greased hair that created a spongy layer – a style that was difficult for the enemy to grab hold of in battle.

✔ **Battle crown:** The blue crown of New Kingdom kings is thought to be a royal battle helmet, probably made of leather, with silver or electrum discs fixed to it. However, no royal crowns have been discovered, so no one knows if battle crowns were worn.

✔ **Gloves:** Due to the climate, these were not commonly used other than by charioteers of high status. Gloves were made of leather or thick linen and prevented the reins from rubbing the hands.

✔ **Kilts:** Most of the army wore a single triangle of linen folded into a kilt. Some reliefs indicate that the front may have been stiffened to provide a little extra protection. A wooden model, discovered in a tomb, representing a division of Nubian archers shows them wearing red and green loincloths, which may have been made of leather for additional protection.

Soldiers wore a leather skin over the plain linen kilts. These skins were often made from a whole gazelle skin, slashed with a sharp knife to give extra flexibility. A solid leather patch over the rear provided extra padding while sitting.

Although painted reliefs only show these basic clothes, soldiers probably wore more, especially on winter nights. Tomb reliefs generally show the soldiers in their 'dress uniforms' rather than giving a realistic depiction of battle clothes. Also, during fighting, soldiers were likely to have worn as little as possible; the weather was hot, and loose clothing gave the enemy something to grab on to. Any wounds inflicted through long clothing could also get infected with tiny bits of grubby fabric entering the wounds.

Religious protection

In addition to the equipment and weapons that Egyptian soldiers carried with them (spears, shields, daggers, bows, and arrow quivers), battle reliefs and archaeological records show that the military relied not only on armour, but also on religious icons for protection.

The most prominent icon consisted of the protective wings that the king wore. The wings belonged to Horus and wrapped around the king's chest showing that he was protected by the god. A pair of these wings was discovered in the tomb of Tutankhamun. (They are, in fact, made of linen, and therefore offered no form of protection other than religious.)

Jewellery was both functional and decorative, as the king wore jewellery as a form of protection. One piece of jewellery, also found in the tomb of Tutankhamun, consists of a large collar attached to a thick band of gold scales that protected his king's torso. The collar was made of images of the king smiting enemies in the presence of the god. However, how much protection soft gold provided against a spear or arrow at speed is uncertain, and the king probably wore this type of collar in the military parades before or after the battle.

The ordinary soldiers wouldn't have had this large-scale religious protection and would have relied on amulets to protect them (Chapter 9 has more on amulets).

Recording victories

The Egyptians were very keen on their battle records as a means of broadcasting their victories. Military scribes who accompanied the army on its campaigns created these records. The records are in the form of official reports and include poetic narratives and very elaborate images.

Battle records need to be taken with a large pinch of salt because they were produced for propaganda purposes more than anything else. All battle reports claim, quite baldly, that no Egyptians ever died in battle for a number of reasons:

- ✔ They were too good at fighting.
- ✔ Everyone else was scared of them.
- ✔ All the enemy soldiers were cowards who ran away.

Archaeological evidence shows that this clearly isn't the case, with many mummies showing signs of battle wounds. I suppose that the scribes were only keeping morale up by trying to convince the troops of their invincibility.

Perusing the military annals

Many kings produced a set of annals that recorded their military campaigns. However, only two annals have survived – the Palermo Stone and the annals of Thutmose III (also carved in stone). The Palermo Stone is in fragments in the Palermo Archaeological Museum in Sicily, the Egyptian Museum in Cairo, and the Petrie Museum in London. The annals of Thutmosis III are in situ at Karnak Temple.

The Palermo stone records many events of the early kings, including battles, flood levels, and *heb sed* festivals (see Chapter 9).

The annals vary depending on what the king had achieved. For example, the annals of Thutmose III focus on his military achievements because he was a warrior pharaoh and the first empire-builder in Egypt.

Other records that describe military campaigns include

- ✔ Graffiti on campaign routes
- ✔ Autobiographical texts of army personnel in tombs
- ✔ Temple descriptions and images

Every picture tells a story

The artistic representations of battles in temple reliefs didn't change very much in 3,000 years of Egyptian history – which is a clear warning that these images cannot always be taken at face value.

Several themes recur in these surviving scenes:

- ✔ Scenes often show the king holding his enemies by their forelock as he prepares to hit them with a mace. (This was introduced on the Narmer palette in 3100 BC – refer to Chapter 1.) Regardless of whether the pharaoh is in a chariot, strolling through the battlefield, or seated on his throne, the fallen enemies are always shown in a tangled mess beneath his feet, indicating his power over them.

- ✔ The gods are often represented playing a major role in the battles of kings. In the New Kingdom, in particular, the king is counselled regarding the battle by Amun, who is shown handing the sword of victory to the king. After battle, the king is often shown parading the booty and prisoners of war in front of Amun by way of thanks for the help received in battle.

Chapter 4

Building the Empire: The Glories of the New Kingdom

*T*he expulsion of the Hyksos (see Chapter 3) saw the end of the second intermediate period and the start of the New Kingdom. This period (1570–1070 BC) is one of the most famous, with the 18th–19th dynasties and all the popular kings, such as Tutankhamun, Akhenaten, and Ramses II. See the timeline on the Cheat Sheet for a wider chronology.

The start of the 18th dynasty saw the introduction of a permanent military (see Chapter 3) and also a change in international policy. The kingship ideology also included extending the boundaries of Egypt. This meant that each king tried to claim more land than his father, until eventually a large area of the Near East was under Egyptian control, with vassal kings who remained loyal to Egypt set up in foreign towns.

The New Kingdom was a time of renewal and empire building by some of the most powerful kings of Egypt. This chapter focuses on the people and personalities that made this era possible.

Meeting the Egyptian Napoleon: Thutmosis III

The first true empire-builder of the New Kingdom was Thutmosis III (1504–1450 BC) of the 18th dynasty, the husband and step-son of Hatshepsut (see Chapter 5).

Thutmosis III, the son of Thutmosis II and a secondary wife called Isis, was still an infant when he became king on the death of his father. Once king, he was married to Thutmosis II's widow, his stepmother and aunt, Hatshepsut. For more than 20 years, Hatshepsut and Thutmosis III ruled officially as co-regents, although for the majority of this period Hatshepsut ruled Egypt as pharaoh, pushing the young Thutmosis III aside.

Thutmosis III spent his childhood and teenage years training in the army, until the death of Hatshepsut in year 22 of their reign. At this time, he took over the throne as a fully grown adult and military leader and continued to rule Egypt for more than 20 years on his own. Figure 4-1 shows him at his most regal.

Egyptologists often refer to Thutmosis III as the Egyptian Napoleon because he spent his adult life fighting and claiming land in the name of Egypt. He left some very elaborate military records in the Hall of Annals at Karnak temple, telling of the exploits in Syria that earned him his title.

Figure 4-1:
Thutmosis III
(Luxor
Museum).

Fighting at Megiddo

The most famous of Thutmosis III's battles was at Megiddo in Syria, in the first year of his sole rule (around 1476 BC). The King of Kadesh in Syria had slowly been gathering a number of Palestinian cities to join him in an attack against the borders of Egypt, because he wasn't strong enough to do it alone. This attacking army occupied the desirable and fortified Syrian town of Megiddo (in modern-day Israel), which was strategically placed for trade and protection.

Megiddo was the site of many battles in antiquity. The biblical term 'Armageddon' actually means 'mount of Megiddo' in Hebrew and refers to a particular battle here.

Thutmosis III and his Egyptian militia travelled from the Delta, through the Sinai, until they reached Megiddo. They laid siege to various strongholds along the way so that their line of communication (and potential retreat back to Egypt) was clear and under their control.

Three routes led to Megiddo, and Thutmosis needed to decide which one to take. Two of the longer routes were difficult to defend, whereas the shorter and more direct route left the Egyptians in a vulnerable position because they needed to travel in single file and were under constant threat of ambush from the enemy.

Thutmosis was advised to take one of the longer routes, but he decided on the shorter, more interesting route. Luckily for him, the Egyptians travelled the path with no problems and emerged a short distance from the fortified town, where they set up camp waiting for the remainder of the Egyptian army to arrive.

Time to attack

After the Egyptian army started its approach to Megiddo, the enemy forces tried to organise themselves in a very rough-and-ready fashion to guard their town. The following morning, the Egyptians paraded in full battle regalia to psych themselves up and demoralise the enemy.

Thutmosis III led the attack in a gold and electrum chariot, leading one-third of the army. Battle records state that the Egyptians were greatly outnumbered by the Syrian army, which consisted of more than 330 kings and *'Millions of men, and hundreds of thousands of the chiefest of all the lands, standing in their chariots.'*

Despite being outnumbered, Thutmosis III was valiant:

> *The king himself . . . led the way of his army, mighty at its head like a flame of fire, the king who wrought with his sword. He went forth, none like him, slaying the barbarians, smiting the Retenu (the Asiatics), bringing their princes as living captives, their chariots wrought with gold, bound to their horses.*

The Egyptian forces were too much for the skeleton army guarding the mount of Megiddo. The army at Megiddo quickly fled, leaving all its weapons, chariots, and belongings behind. The Egyptians were close on its heels, but the gatekeepers at Megiddo refused to open the doors to let the Syrians in just in case the Egyptians followed. Those inside the fort let down knotted sheets, rather like the story of Rapunzel – albeit less hairy – so that the rich and powerful among their allies could be rescued and brought within the fortress.

Missed opportunity

After the Syrians fled the mount of Megiddo, the Egyptian army had a perfect opportunity to storm the fortification before the Syrians were able to gather themselves and prepare to attack from within the fortress. However, rather than attacking straight away, the Egyptian soldiers were distracted by all the goodies left by the fleeing army and started to rummage through them. They lost their advantage over the Syrians, but filled their bags with all they could carry.

Thutmosis took control of the situation – albeit it a little too late – and organised for a wall and a moat to be built around Megiddo in preparation for a long siege of the town. It was particularly important for the Egyptians to capture the town to show their strength. They also needed to be able to defend their victory against numerous chieftains from surrounding towns who threatened to cause problems for the Egyptians and weaken the control on their empire. The siege lasted seven months before Megiddo finally fell to the Egyptians.

Giddy up

In year 30 of his reign, Thutmosis III was engaged with the Hittites in battle at Kadesh. Kadesh was particularly important because it was located on an essential trade route and gave the Egyptians access to territories in the north.

During the battle at Kadesh, the Hittites used a devious but common technique to destroy the Egyptian army. Stallions pulled the Egyptian chariots, so the Hittites sent a mare, in season, out into the field in order to distract the horses. Cunning, eh?

Luckily for Thutmosis III, his general, Amenemhab, saw and chased the mare with his chariot. When Amenemhab caught the mare, he sliced open her belly and cut off her tail, which he then presented to the king. A bit of a funny pressie really, although it obviously worked as a lucky charm because Thutmosis III won this battle and went on to fight another day.

Getting bootylicious

After the fall of Megiddo and the battle of Kadesh (see the sidebar 'Giddy up'), the Egyptian soldiers had lots of goodies to boost their salaries (see Chapter 3 for wages information). Of course, the king enjoyed the profits of war as well. Thutmosis III's annals at Karnak include booty lists that detail the following:

> *All the goods of those cities which submitted themselves, which were brought to his majesty: 38 lords of theirs, 87 children of that enemy and of the chiefs who were with him, 5 lords of theirs, 1,796 male and female slaves with their children, non-combatants who surrendered because of famine with that enemy, 103 men; total 2,503. Besides flat dishes of costly stone and gold, various vessels, a large two-handled vase of the work of Kharu, vases, flat dishes, dishes, various drinking-vessels, 3 large kettles, 87 knives, amounting to 784 deben. Gold in rings found in the hands of the artificers, and silver in many rings, 966 deben and 1 kidet [both weights of metal]. A silver statue in beaten work, the head of gold, the staff with human faces; 6 chairs of that enemy, of ivory, ebony and carob wood, wrought with gold; 6 footstools belonging to them; 6 large tables of ivory and carob wood, a staff of carob wood, wrought with gold and all costly stones in the fashion of a sceptre, belonging to that enemy, all of it wrought with gold; a statue of that enemy, of ebony wrought with gold, the head of which was inlaid with lapis lazuli; vessels of bronze, much clothing of that enemy.*

Sadly, Egyptologists don't know what happened to this booty and how it was absorbed into the Egyptian economy.

Changing His Religion: Akhenaten

Another 18th-dynasty king who has held worldwide fame for thousands of years is the heretic king, Akhenaten (1350–1333 BC). He was infamous for changing the religion of ancient Egypt from the worship of hundreds of gods to the worship of one god – the *Aten* or sun disc. Figure 4-2 shows the face of Akhenaten.

Akhenaten's bold religious changes were the product of monotheism, as commentators often state. Although the Aten was elevated to the position of supreme god, only Akhenaten and the royal family were able to worship the sun god. Akhenaten raised himself up to the position of fully fledged god, more divine than any other king – and everyone else had to worship Akhenaten! So in Akhenaten's system, there was not just one god but two.

Figure 4-2:
The face of
Akhenaten
(Luxor
Museum).

Meeting the family

Akhenaten was the youngest son of Amenhotep III and Queen Tiye. He was born under the name of Amenhotep and only later changed his name to Akhenaten ('Spirit of the Aten') as his devotion to the god grew.

Akhenaten's mother, Tiye, was of noble, not royal, birth. Some images show her as a somewhat domineering and frightening woman. She is regularly shown alongside her husband in a complementary rather than inferior position and is represented in her own right without the king, which was unheard of in earlier Egyptian history.

Akhenaten had one older brother, Thutmosis, who died before he could come to the throne, and three sisters: Beketaten, Sitamun, and Isis. The latter two were married to their father, Amenhotep III.

Marrying a mystery

Akhenaten married young, before he became king, and he married one of the most famous women in ancient Egypt – the rather serene and enigmatic Nefertiti. No one really knows where Nefertiti came from, who her parents were, and in fact who she was. But most Egyptologists believe that she was the daughter of Ay, the brother of Queen Tiye. Ay's wife held the title 'wet-nurse of Nefertiti', showing that she wasn't mum but step-mum to Nefertiti, because the title of mother would outstrip that of wet-nurse.

Nefertiti and Akhenaten had six daughters, the first born before the end of Akhenaten's first year on the throne. The daughters are often depicted with the king and queen. Their names were

- ✔ Meritaten
- ✔ Meketaten
- ✔ Ankhesenepaten (later Ankhesenamun)
- ✔ Neferneferuaten
- ✔ Neferneferure
- ✔ Setepenre

Although there is no direct evidence, it is possible that Tutankhamun was also the son of Akhenaten and a secondary wife called Kiya. Some scholars also believe that Smenkhkare, the mysterious king who followed Akhenaten on the throne for a brief spell, was the son of Akhenaten; others believe that he was the son of Amenhotep III, and other scholars think Smenkhkare and Nefertiti are the same person. What chance do the rest of us have if the experts are unable to decide?

Praising the sun god

The main focus of Akhenaten's reign was his religious revolution, which took place over a very short period. Akhenaten ruled for only 17 years, and the entire revolution was complete by year 9 of his reign. Despite the short time that this revolution took, this period is the most written about of ancient Egyptian history by modern writers.

Even stranger, for 12 years of his reign, Akhenaten was probably serving as a co-ruler with his father Amenhotep III, with his father ruling from Thebes and Akhenaten ruling from his brand-spanking-new city at Amarna in middle Egypt. Effectively, theirs was a divided rule – one of the few that was seen as acceptable in the entire span of Egyptian history (see Chapter 1).

The *Aten* is the key element in the reign of Akhenaten. The Aten was not a new deity: He was always part of the wider solar cycle and appears as an embodiment of the light that emanates from the sun disc. This light is represented in images by hands radiating from the sun disc, each ending in little hands that give an *ankh* sign (sign of eternal life, shown in Chapter 11) to the royal family. The entire image suggests that the sun provides life. All Akhenaten did was to elevate this element of the sun god to that of being the only sun god.

The favouring of the Aten over other deities started in the reign of Amenhotep III as part of a campaign to limit the power of the Priesthood of Amun at Karnak, which at the time was almost as powerful as the royal family. Akhenaten, however, went further and began to replace all the main gods with the Aten, although he didn't close all the temples until nine years into his reign, when he diverted all revenue to the new temples of the Aten.

In year 12, Akhenaten started a hate campaign against the cult of Amun. This involved carving out the names of Amun wherever they appeared – even in the name of his own father, *Amen*hotep. This had never happened before in Egypt. Kings often eliminated other kings they didn't like from their personal histories (see Chapter 3), but a king had never removed gods before. Akhenaten's actions must have upset a lot of people.

Meeting an unhappy end

Despite his unpopularity, Akhenaten does not seem to have been assassinated, which is surprising. However, the end of his reign is vague and unrecorded, so historians can only guess at the actual events.

A stream of disasters in his personal life precede Akhenaten's death and the collapse of the Amarna period:

- In Year 12 of Akhenaten's reign, his father Amenhotep III died.
- In Year 13, Nefertiti disappears from the inscriptions, so she probably died, although some scholars believe she changed her name and ruled as co-ruler.
- In Year 14, Amenhotep's daughter Meketaten died as the result of childbirth
- In Year 14, Akhenaten's mother, Tiye, died.

This stream of deaths is often attributed to a plague epidemic referred to as 'the Asiatic illness' that swept Amarna; this epidemic may have been a form of bubonic plague. This plague was viewed by the ordinary people as punishment for the abandonment of the traditional gods – which made the masses very keen to start worshipping the traditional gods again.

Akhenaten died in year 17 of his reign, when he was in his 30s. He left no known male heir, except possibly Smenkhkare, a mysterious character, who co-ruled alongside Akhenaten for three years (see the section 'Marrying a mystery', earlier in this chapter). Some believe Smenkhkare is Nefertiti, although the evidence is not conclusive. Smenkhkare then ruled alone for a few months before dying, presumably from the plague as well. (You wouldn't want to be a member of this family would you? They seem jinxed!)

At the death of Smenkhkare, only one more suitable heir existed, the famous Tutankhamun – a wee nipper at only 7 or 8 years old.

Growing Up a King: Tutankhamun

Tutankhamun is a name that conjures up images of gold and wealth, due to the amazing splendours discovered in his tomb. Prior to the tomb's discovery, very little was known about this king – and to be honest, after the tomb was opened, the world was not enlightened a great deal.

There are many gaps in the life of Tutankhamun, and most studies concentrate on the treasure from his tomb. Many of these treasures were created for the tomb and may not have featured at all in the king's life. However, the mystery surrounding this king has intrigued people since the tomb's discovery in 1922. No doubt Tut will continue to interest people for another 100 years.

Keeping it in the family

Historians think that Tutankhamun was born between years 7 and 9 of Akhenaten's reign, possibly at Amarna. Originally called Tutankhaten ('the living image of the Aten'), his name was changed when he became king.

Egyptologists are even unable to agree on who Tutankhamun's parents were. Theories include:

- Akhenaten and Kiya (a secondary wife)
- Akhenaten and Tadukhipa (a Mitannian princess)
- Amenhotep III and Tiye (making Tutankhamun Akhenaten's brother)
- Amenhotep III and Sitamun (Akhenaten's sister)

The first theory is widely accepted by most Egyptologists today.

At the start of his reign, Tutankhamun married Ankhesenepaten, who later changed her name to Ankhesenamun. Depending on who Tutankhamun's parents are, Ankhesenamun is either his half-sister or his niece. They certainly liked to keep it all in the family. Ankhesenamun was a couple of years older than Tutankhamun, and they may have been raised together at the palace at Amarna.

Sadly, despite their youth and a ten-year reign, Tutankhamun and Ankhesenamun had no surviving children. However, buried in Tutankhamun's tomb in a plain white wooden box were two female foetuses, one who was still-born and another who survived for a short while before dying. These foetuses may be Tutankhamun's children, indicating that this young couple had to endure a very trying time attempting to produce an heir to follow Tutankhamun on the throne.

Restoring the religion

The main task of the decade of Tutankhamun's rule was to restore the religion of Egypt – essentially to correct all the changes that Akhenaten had instigated. Tutankhamun started this by abandoning the new capital at Amarna and using Memphis and Thebes as the capital cities of Egypt, as was traditional and expected. Because Tutankhamun was only young, he may have been controlled by his officials: Horemheb (the general and deputy king) and the vizier, Tutankhamun's Uncle Ay.

At Karnak temple, Tutankhamun erected the Restoration Stela, which outlined some of the plans he had for re-establishing the cults and traditions of Egypt:

> *He restored everything that was ruined, to be his monument forever and ever. He has vanquished chaos from the whole land and has restored Maat [order] to her place. He has made lying a crime, the whole land being made as it was at the time of creation.*

> *Now when His Majesty was crowned King the temples and the estates of the gods and goddesses from Elephantine as far as the swamps of Lower Egypt had fallen into ruin. Their shrines had fallen down, turned into piles of rubble and overgrown with weeds . . . Their temples had become footpaths. The world was in chaos and the gods had turned their backs on this land . . . If you asked a god for advice, he would not attend; and if one spoke to a goddess likewise she would not attend. Hearts were faint in bodies because everything that had been, was destroyed.*

Tutankhamun needed to find trustworthy staff to work in the new temples and shrines that he was building. He employed men and women from well-known families who were loyal to the old king, Amenhotep III, ensuring that they would uphold the traditions of his time.

Death

For years, theories surrounding the death of Tutankhamun have dominated publications. He died when he was young – only 18 or 19 years old. Figure 4-3 shows the famous face of Tutankhamun.

For many years, historians thought that Tutankhamum had died from a blow to the head, because a small fragment of bone was found floating around inside his skull. However, in 2005, a CT scan was carried out on his mummy, which showed that these bone fractures happened *after* his death, probably caused by Howard Carter and his team when they were trying to remove the golden mask. The CT evidence also shows various fractures and breaks to Tutankhamum's body that may have happened prior to death and probably led to death. One new theory is that he died in a chariot accident.

Figure 4-3:
The Tutan-
khamun
death mask
(Cairo
Museum).

Lethal letters and royal drama

When Tutankhamun died, his elderly vizier, Ay, took over the throne. Tutankhamun's widow, Ankhesenamun, was still a young woman, perhaps only 21 years old, and clearly did not want to relinquish her position as king's wife and the power that accompanied it. She was not keen to marry Ay, who was the only likely candidate for marriage.

Many scholars believe that Ankhesenamun wrote a letter to the Hittite king Suppiluliumas, requesting that one of his sons be sent to her, so that she could marry him and make him king of Egypt. In a letter attributed to Ankhesenamun, she states that she does not want to 'marry a servant', which may be in reference to her prospective marriage to the elderly Ay.

My husband has died. A son I have not. But to you they say the sons are many. If you would send me one son of yours, he would become my husband. Never shall I pick out a servant of mine and make him my husband ... I am afraid.

The Hittite king was naturally suspicious and sent an emissary to Egypt to report on the political situation. The emissaries returned to the Hittite king and reported that the situation was as the queen had written. The queen, in her eagerness to marry a Hittite prince, sent her messenger to the king with another letter. The records show that the messenger, Hani, spoke on her behalf:

Oh my Lord! This is ... our country's shame! If we have a son of the king at all, would we have come to a foreign country and kept asking for a lord for ourselves? Nibhururiya, who was our lord, died; a son he has not. Our Lord's wife is solitary. We are seeking a son of our lord for the kingship of Egypt, and for the woman, our lady, we seek as her husband! Furthermore, we went to no other country, only here did we come! Now, oh our Lord, give us a son of yours.

Such a request from an Egyptian queen was very unusual, and the Hittite king did not believe that it was a genuine request. However, he was convinced by the messenger's words and eventually sent his son Zennanza to Egypt. Unfortunately, the son was murdered before he reached the Egyptian border – perhaps on the orders of Ay, who married Ankhesenamun shortly after.

Re-establishing Imperial Power: Sety 1

Whatever the cause of Tutankhamun's death, his passing was a real nightmare for Egypt. He left no male heir, so the succession to the throne was unclear.

- Ay (possibly Tutankhamun's great uncle) became king, even though Tutankhamun's army general Horemheb held the title of deputy king. However, Ay was in his 60s when he came to the throne, which was considered old, and he ruled for only four years before he died.

✔ Horemheb succeeded Ay on the throne and ruled for more than 30 years. He continued with Tutankhamun's restoration work.

Horemheb's most important action was to name Pirameses, a general in his army, as his successor. Horemheb could be called the founder of the 19th dynasty because it was he who found and promoted Pirameses (who became Ramses I on taking the throne) among his unruly rabble of military.

Tutankhamun, Ay, and Horemheb started to re-establish Egypt's borders, but the process needed to be continued. Ramses I came to the throne already elderly and ruled for only a short period (1293–1291 BC).

Fighting at Kadesh, Part 1

The reign of Ramses I's son Sety I (1291–1278 BC) saw the introduction of a number of political problems, which were to develop throughout the reigns of Ramses II and Ramses III (see the section 'Fighting the Good Fight: Ramses II', later in this chapter, for more information).

At the beginning of his reign, Sety I launched a series of campaigns to re-establish the boundaries of the crumbling Egyptian empire that had been neglected during the reigns of Akhenaten and Smenkhkare. In his first year in power, Sety embarked on a campaign across Syria, because he was told by his advisors:

> *The Shasu enemy are plotting rebellion! Their tribal leaders are gathered in one place, standing on the foothills of Khor [a general term for Palestine and Syria], they are engaged in turmoil and uproar. Each one of them is killing his fellow. They do not consider the laws of the palace [a euphemism for the king].*

Throughout the journey to Palestine, petty chieftains attacked Sety, but luckily the army had no problems repelling them. These attacks were more irritating than threatening to the king, but they still needed to be dealt with, because the chieftains' actions endangered the trade route that Egypt relied on.

The following year, Sety travelled further north to Kadesh, a fortified town in Syria surrounded by two moats fed from the river Orontes. The Hittites who were in control of the town were at the time stationed on the Syrian coast, leaving the city badly defended. The Egyptians took the city without much effort, and in fact Sety claimed to have made 'a great heap of corpses' of the enemy soldiers.

Despite this victory, Sety didn't have enough military power to put pressure on the Hittites to gain a real stronghold in Syria. The Egyptians held the area for a short while and then it reverted to the Hittites without any further military action. Sety then left, which allowed the Hittites to widen their area of control slowly, moving closer to Egypt.

One down . . . how many more to go?

After the problems at Kadesh, Sety I didn't rest on his laurels. His battle records at Karnak show that he then needed to subdue Libyans who tried to penetrate the Delta borders and squelch Nubian uprisings against Egyptian control.

The term *Libyans* was used by the Egyptians to describe Bedouin tribes of the Western Desert, rather than the inhabitants of modern Libya.

Sety and his army drove the invading Libyans away, and the Karnak relief shows Sety hitting the chief Libyan with a scimitar. That's one way to ensure he doesn't come back. However, the Libyans proved to be a thorn in the side of Ramses III in later years (see the section 'Sailing to Victory: Ramses III', later in this chapter) because they did not give up easily.

The Sety reliefs at Karnak show fortified Syrian towns surrendering to him, with the enemy soldiers fleeing to other towns or to higher ground to get away from the relentless Egyptian army. Sety no doubt led the battles, and, in one scene from Karnak, he has a captive foreign chief under each arm, showing his military prowess in the battlefield.

Fighting the Good Fight: Ramses II

Sety I was succeeded by his son Ramses II (1279–1212 BC). Ramses II has had many names and titles given to him over the centuries, including

- ✔ 'Sese' by his friends and loyal subjects

- ✔ 'Ramses the Great' by explorers of the 18th and 19th centuries AD

- ✔ 'Ozymandias' by Percy Bysshe Shelley when he wrote his poem based on a colossal statue at the mortuary temple of Ramses at Luxor (Ozymandias is a corruption of Ramses's throne name (User-maat-ra-setep-en-ra) by the Greeks)

Maybe you *can* choose your parents

Due to his non-royal origins, Ramses II made a claim of divine birth in order to legitimise his place on the throne (although in reality, because his father was king, he didn't need to).

The divine birth scene at the Ramesseum, Ramses's mortuary temple at Luxor, depicts Amun as Ramses's father. The image shows Ramses's mother, Muttuya, seated on a bed, facing Amun. Amun is holding an *ankh* sign in his right hand and is reaching for Muttuya with his left hand. This (very demurely) represents the divine conception of Ramses.

Further images at Karnak show Ramses's true divine status. In one image, Ramses is born by being moulded on a potter's wheel by the ram-headed god Khnum; in another, Ramses as a child is suckled by a goddess (this scene is repeated in Sety I's mortuary temple at Abydos).

Becoming royal

Ramses II was born in 1304 BC to Sety I and Muttuya, the daughter of the 'Lieutenant of Chariotry' Raia. Ramses II was not royal at the time of his birth because his grandfather, Ramses I, was chosen by Horemheb from within the army to be king because he had a son (Sety I) and a grandson (Ramses II). Ramses had at least two sisters, Tia and Hunetmire, and a brother, although the latter's name has been lost.

In later years, Ramses married at least one of his sisters, Hunetmire, although what she thought of this set-up would be interesting to know. Because Hunetmire and Ramses were non-royal when they were born, suddenly being married just because their family status changed was certainly strange. Luckily for Hunetmire, she bore Ramses no children; theirs may have been a marriage of convenience rather than a marriage in the true sense. (See Chapter 5 for more on Egyptian marriages.)

Marriage and family (and more family)

During the later years of his reign, Sety had named Ramses as co-regent and marked the occasion by giving him his own harem of beautiful women, consisting of 'female royal attendants, who were like the great beauties of the palace', which I imagine was an exciting yet daunting gift for a young boy still in his teens.

Ramses maintained this harem throughout his 67-year reign, and no doubt greatly enjoyed it. But his two favourite wives were Nefertari, whom he married before he came to the throne, and Isetnofret, whom he married in the early years of his reign.

Although Nefertari and Isetnofret were Ramses's favourite wives, his harem is reputed to have contained more than 300 women who bore him more than 150 sons and 70 daughters. A list of Ramses's children is recorded at Karnak in birth order – although these numbers are likely to be greatly exaggerated to show how fertile he was.

In reality, Ramses II had a maximum of 46 sons and 55 daughters. Yes, this figure is lower than his official records show, but is still an awful lot of kids!

Ramses and Nefertari had numerous children, at least ten of which have been recorded, although they sadly all died before Ramses did. Nefertari had at least six sons, whose names and occupations are recorded:

- **Amenhirwenemef** (first son) was in the army and held the title of general in chief.

- **Prehirwenemef** (third son) was a teenage veteran of the second battle of Kadesh (see the section 'Following in dad's footsteps: Kadesh Part II', later in this chapter) and was rewarded with the titles 'first charioteer of his majesty' and 'first brave of the army'.

- **Meriamun** (16th son).

- **Meritamun** (second daughter) was the consort to Ramses by year 24 and acted as deputy for her sick mother.

- **Baketmut** (third daughter) is believed to have died young, although her tomb has not been discovered.

- **Nefertari II** (fourth daughter) is presented on the façade of the main Abu Simbel temple.

- **Nebettawi** (fifth daughter) was the consort successor to Meritamun after the latter died. She is buried in QV60, which was reused in the Christian period as a chapel.

- **Henoutawi** (seventh daughter) is represented on Nefertari's temple at Abu Simbel, indicating that she was one of Nefertari's daughters, although she was dead before the temple was dedicated.

Isetnofret, Ramses's other wife, had at least six children:

- **Ramses** (second son) was a general in the army and crown prince after the death of his half-brother Amenhirkhepshef. In year 30, he was a judge at the trial of a Theban treasury officer and his wife, who were stealing from royal stores.

- **Bintanath** (first daughter) was married to her father.

- **Khaemwaset** (fourth son) was crown prince after his brother Ramses had died. Khaemwaset is the most documented of Ramses II's children. At 5–6 years old he went with his father and half-brother Amenhirwenemef to fight in a Nubian campaign. Khaemwaset then became a high priest of Ptah, a god associated with the funerary cults.

- **Merenptah** (13th son) succeeded Ramses II to the throne. In the last 12 years of Ramses's reign, Merenptah ruled Egypt as a co-ruler and then became king after his father's death.

- **Isetnofret II** married her brother Merenptah.

Ramses's other children are recorded, although their mothers' names have not been identified; it can be assumed they were born of minor wives or concubines.

The throne eventually passed to Merenptah, Ramses's 13th son born of Isetnofret.

Following in dad's footsteps: Kadesh Part II

Ramses II is well known for many things, but in particular he is remembered for his spectacular battle at Kadesh against the Hittites in the fifth year of his reign. Although Sety had won at Kadesh once, Egypt's lack of military power had enabled the Hittites to encroach on the Egyptian borders. Ramses II needed to put a stop to the Hittites before they got any closer. For the first time in Egyptian history, Egypt was the aggressor in a battle.

The Hittite king had, however, anticipated the attack and gathered a huge army in coalition with a number of neighbouring states – 16 different provinces – which included:

- 2,500 chariots, each with 3 men

- Two groups of cavalry totalling 18,000–19,000 men

The Egyptians were greatly outnumbered by the Hittite army with only 20,000 soldiers to the Hittites' 26,000 or so men. At one point, records show that the Egyptians were outnumbered three to one.

Both the Egyptians and the Hittites utilised many of the same weapons, but their styles of attack differed:

- ✔ The Hittites made greater use of hard, iron-bladed weapons than the Egyptians, who mainly used bronze and copper weapons.

- ✔ Egyptian chariots carried two people (a driver and a weapons bloke), while the Hittite chariots carried three men (a driver, a spear thrower or archer, and a shield bearer to protect the other two). While the Egyptian chariots were lighter and had more manoeuvrability, the Hittites were able to move large numbers of men at one time.

- ✔ The Egyptians also employed a group of runners to surround the chariots as they raced into the centre of the enemy amid a shower of Egyptian arrows. The runners then attacked from ground level while the enemy was recovering from the arrow attack.

The battle

Ramses II's army marched to the Levant (modern-day Israel, Jordan, Lebanon, and western Syria) and the site of Kadesh, via the Gaza Strip, in four divisions named after the gods Ptah, Ra, Seth, and Amun (Ramses II led the Amun division).

The Egyptian army forded the Orontes river 20 kilometres upstream from Kadesh, blocking the way north before entering a wooded area nearby. The army was spread over a large area, which resulted in the four divisions becoming separated.

Egyptian scouts then captured two Hittites who offered some information (a little too readily in my opinion):

Then came two Shosu of the tribes of Shosu tribes to say to his Majesty, 'Our brothers who are chiefs of tribes with the foe of Khatti [Hittites] have sent us to His Majesty to say that we will be servants of pharaoh and will abandon the Chief of Khatti.' His majesty said to them, 'Where are they your brothers who sent you to tell this matter to His Majesty?' and they said to His Majesty, 'They are where the vile Chief of Khatti is, for the foe of Khatti is in the Land of Khaleb to the north of Tunip, and he was too fearful of Pharaoh to come southward when he heard that Pharaoh had come northward.' But the two Shosu who said these words to his majesty said them falsely.

Ramses believed that the Hittites were much further north than he anticipated. The Egyptians continued north to the city, with the Amun division full of confidence that the takeover would be easy, reaching the destination first. As the Amun division approached the city, two more scouts were captured and they revealed that in fact the Hittites were just north of Kadesh and were ready to attack.

Ramses sent an emergency warning to the Ra division behind him, but it was still 8 kilometres away. The Hittites sent 2,500 chariots to the south of the Egyptian camp, under cover of trees, and burst on them from behind. But instead of ambushing the Egyptians unawares, the Hittites came face to face with the Ra division, which was slowly approaching the site from the south. Both sides were very surprised, and as the fleeing Hittite chariots had fallen into the river, blocking it, the new Hittites had nowhere to go but towards the Egyptians.

The Hittites burst through the Ra division, which fled (some back into the woods, some to the hills, some towards the Amun division). Both the Ra division and the Hittites charged at the Amun division at the same time. The Amun division wasn't prepared for the attack and was probably somewhat surprised. Like the Ra division, Amun started to scatter and flee as the Hittites broke through the rudimentary defences of their temporary camp.

Ramses seemed to be the only one to keep his head during this whole ordeal. After saying a quick prayer to Amun, he gathered the chariots and troops nearest him and managed to hold his own against the Hittite onslaught. The texts state that Ramses was fighting the entire Hittite army single handed, which does seem somewhat unlikely – but hey, the Egyptian king *is* a god after all.

Better late than never

Luckily for Ramses, the third Egyptian division, which was travelling along the coastal route (either the division of Set or a crack force of Canaanite mercenaries fighting for the Egyptians), arrived just in the nick of time. Although still greatly outnumbered, the Egyptian army managed to repel the Hittites. (However, in reality, the Hittites only used a small proportion of their army and for some reason decided not to deploy the rest. If they had, this battle would have been the end of Ramses the Great.)

When the Hittites realised that the situation had turned against them, they fled into the fortified town of Kadesh. With the Hittites in the walled town and the Egyptians outside, further fighting was unnecessary. The Egyptians gathered their wounded, cut off the hands of the dead Hittites as an account of the battle, and travelled home claiming a great victory! (Seems more like a giant stalemate.)

Making peace

Sixteen years *after* the second battle of Kadesh, the Egyptians and the Hittites finally halted their hostilities. A peace treaty was drawn up, which is the only complete document of this type discovered in Egypt:

> *There shall be no hostilities between them forever. The Great Chief of Kheta [Hittites] shall not pass over into the land of Egypt forever, to take anything from there. Ramses Meriamun [beloved of Amun] the great ruler of Egypt shall not pass over into the land of Kheta to take anything from them forever.*

In addition to the Egyptian version of this peace treaty, a Hittite copy was also discovered at the Hittite capital of Hattushash in modern Turkey.

However, as ground-breaking as this treaty was, it only lasted for as long as the kings who signed it, meaning that all the fighting had to be done over again with the next set of kings.

Rushing the Borders: Merenptah

Ramses was succeeded on the throne by his 13th son, Merenptah (1212–1202 BC). Merenptah's reign saw a repeat of the Libyan problems that manifested themselves during the reign of Sety I. The war with the Libyans is recorded on an inscription at Karnak as well as numerous stelae.

In year 5 of Merenptah's reign, the Libyans joined with numerous different tribes. Numbering 25,000 men, these forces were collectively known as the Sea People. They were strong enough to penetrate the Egyptian fortresses along the western Delta and overwhelm the Egyptians on guard duty. The Sea People were clearly travelling to Egypt with a plan to occupy it, because many were accompanied by their families and all their belongings stacked on ox-drawn carts.

Merenptah marched on the Delta with the remainder of the Egyptian army, made up primarily of archers. The army's composition enabled the Egyptians to get close enough to fire hundreds of arrows from their composite bows, but not close enough for the enemy to engage in hand-to-hand combat, which was the Libyans' strength.

Ultimately, this was a victory for the Egyptians. Their records show that they killed 6,000 Libyans and took 9,000 prisoners, including the Libyan chief's wife and children.

This victory enabled the Egyptian people to live in peace once more. Records state that the Egyptians were now able to 'walk freely upon the road' and 'sit down and chat with no fear on their hearts'. Just what everyone wants, really.

Of course, sadly the peace was not to last, as Merenptah's son Ramses III was soon to discover.

Sailing to Victory: Ramses III

Ramses III's reign (1182–1151 BC) was a difficult one. It was beset by invasions, the most important being a further attack from the Libyans and the Sea People.

More battles with the Sea People

The invasion by the Libyans in year 5 of Ramses III's reign was very similar to the one that Merenptah dealt with (see the section 'Rushing the Borders: Merenptah', earlier in this chapter). A 30,000-strong army of a mixture of Libyans and Sea People faced Ramses III. Records note Ramses III killing 12,535 men and taking 1,000 prisoners – a great victory, according to the records anyway.

However, in reality, the Sea People were the first army who were strong enough to take on the Hittites and win, thus controlling trade in the Near East on both land and sea. On land, the Sea People fought in a similar fashion to the Hittites, with three-man chariots. But their seafaring vessels were smaller than the Egyptian boats, without separate oarsmen. Instead, Sea People soldiers rowed the boats, which meant that the soldiers were unable to fight and move at the same time. This was a major disadvantage against Egyptian boats, which had 24 dedicated oarsmen, protected by high sides, plus a contingent of soldiers.

Ramses III faced the Sea People on both land and sea and was successful in both areas. His naval battle is one of the earliest recorded in history. The Egyptian fleet followed the Sea People's fleet of ships into the 'river-mouths of the Delta', trapping them between the Egyptian boats and the shore, where the Egyptian archers were waiting to shower them with arrows. The Sea People didn't stand much of a chance really.

The Egyptians used fire-arrows against the Sea People's ships and killed the majority of the enemy solders. The Egyptian ships then rammed the enemy ships with their decorative prows before seizing the Sea People's ships with grappling hooks and engaging the enemy in hand-to-hand fighting. These manoeuvres finished off the Sea People once and for all. Egypt was at peace once more.

Those pesky Libyans – again

In year 11 of the reign of Ramses III, the Libyans thought they'd have another go at breaking through the borders of Egypt. Ten out of ten for determination at least!

This time, the records show that Ramses III killed 2,175 enemy soldiers and took more than 2,000 prisoners. He then drove the enemy 11 miles into the Western Desert to ensure that they didn't return straight away. (Chapter 5 describes the eventual return of the Libyans.)

At the end of the reign of Ramses III, the glory of the Egyptian empire ended. Ramses III was the last king to rule in true traditional style. Later periods were beset by invasions, divided land, and economic collapse. The empire that Thutmosis III built and Sety I and Ramses II maintained was slowly disappearing – and the Egyptian civilisation was vanishing along with it.

Chapter 5

Looking at the Power Behind the Throne: Royal Women

I once made the mistake, when being introduced to someone, of asking, 'You're Toby's girlfriend, right?' To which this person responded, 'No! I'm Clare.'

To modern women, being acknowledged by their connection to their husbands, brothers, or fathers is clearly not acceptable. In ancient Egypt though, this is exactly how women – especially royal women – were identified. This chapter uncovers the less-than-glamorous lives of these ancient mothers, wives, and sisters. (Chapter 2 has information about the lives of non-royal women.)

Nothing without Him: Considering the Roles of Royal Women

The role and relevance of royal women was defined solely by their relationship with the king. This relationship is identified by a number of titles which appear in temples, tombs, and documents of the period. Consider the titles of royal women:

- ✔ King's Principal Wife (or Great Royal Wife)
- ✔ King's Wife
- ✔ King's Mother
- ✔ King's Daughter

Without the king, royal woman had no status or role within the palace, and obviously the power associated with each role increased as the relationship with the king became closer. Each title gave different power and opportunities to the woman, although keeping the king happy was essential.

Royal weddings: Brothers and sisters

For many years, Egyptologists believed the royal line ran through the females. Thus the king needed to marry an heiress to the throne to legitimise his kingship. This theory developed as a means of explaining brother–sister marriages (common within the royal family, although a taboo for everyone else). However, because many kings didn't marry royal women, this theory has now been dismissed and it's clear that the throne ran through the male line – passed on from father to son.

Although the crown was not passed on via a woman's family, princesses had to be married. The throne ran through the male line, but this only worked if male heirs were available. If there were no male heirs, and a princess married a non-royal, the non-royal would have enough of a claim to take over the throne. Through incestuous marriages, all princesses were effectively married off as soon as possible to prevent non-royals from taking the throne. Princesses might marry their brothers, father, or even grandfather to prevent a coup. Sometimes they got lucky and their father married them to a favoured, well-trusted official – no doubt only after the king had a male heir himself. This practice set the royal family apart from ordinary people; incestuous marriages were only for royalty and gods, which indicated the royal family was truly divine.

However, with the king's express permission, the King's Sister could marry outside the royal family if the chap was accepted and of suitably noble but non-royal birth (for example, a member of the royal court, including high military and administrative officials). Ramses II, for example, allowed his sister Tia to marry an official, also called Tia, who was vetted and greatly trusted.

To make matters even more confusing, the title King's Sister was often given to a wife. This may or may not have been the king's biological sister. In ancient Egypt, 'sister' was used as a term of endearment to refer to a lover, even if that person was not related. Confusing, eh?

The Great Royal Wife and others

Being the Wife of the King – whether his sister or not – wasn't all it was cracked up to be. Wives held no power, and potentially hundreds of women were allowed to hold this title.

The only powerful queen was the Great Royal Wife, who was the equivalent of the 'first lady' in the land. (Although kings normally had only one Great Royal Wife, Ramses II had two: Nefertari and Isetnofret.)

In the Old Kingdom, the Great Royal Wife was entitled to have her own pyramid, and in the New Kingdom, her name was written in a cartouche like that of a king (see Chapter 11 for more on cartouches).

Even though the Great Royal Wife was important, the title wasn't permanent. The king could promote any wife to this position if she pleased him – normally by producing a son if the current Great Royal Wife hadn't, or at the death of the Great Royal Wife. Additionally, this queen only ever played a complementary role to the king, acting as a female counterpart who accompanied him, but never participated in royal rituals or ceremonies that the king carried out.

The king would have a number of children with his many wives, although knowing whether all his wives bore his children is impossible – especially if it was a diplomatic marriage and the woman was sent to a remote harem. In most cases, we only know the name of the Great Royal Wife, sometimes giving the false impression of monogamy. In theory, the sons of the Great Royal Wife were superior to those of lesser wives, and the eldest son would be the heir to the throne.

Burial of a queen

The tomb of Hetepheres (the mother of king Khufu, who built the Great Pyramid) was discovered in 1925 at Giza and was surprisingly intact. Hetepheres may originally have been buried at Dahshur near her husband, Seneferu. Robbers may have violated her tomb and her body, causing her son to rebury her close to his own burial at Giza. However, no tomb has been discovered at Dahshur to support this theory.

The burial chamber at Giza was certainly full of goodies suitable for a queen. In addition to the alabaster sarcophagus and canopic chest (see Chapter 10 for more on these items), the tomb included loads of furniture. The collection has been reconstructed in the Cairo Museum and includes a large canopy frame (which was originally draped with linen to give the queen privacy as she sat beneath it), a carrying chair for when the queen was out on the razz, a couple of armchairs, and a bed.

Hetepheres was also accompanied in the tomb by a number of vessels made of gold, copper, and alabaster. These were originally filled with wine, beer, and oil. Some of the queen's jewellery has also survived and consists of 20 beautiful silver bracelets, each inlaid with turquoise, lapis lazuli, and carnelian dragonflies.

Although Hetepheres's canopic chest contained remnants of her preserved internal organs, the sarcophagus was disappointingly empty. Whether the sarcophagus was empty because the queen was reburied or her remains were stolen continues to be an archaeological mystery.

Honour your mother: The King's Mother

King's Mother was a particularly important female title. A woman could hold this title alongside other titles she may have held before her son became king. In an ideal world, the King's Mother (mother of the current king) was also the King's Principal Wife (wife of the current king's dead father – showing that her son descended from a king), or God's Wife (see the section 'Marrying Amun', later in this chapter). If she didn't hold these titles before her son came to the throne, the son often bestowed them on her as honorary titles after he became king, in order to revere her and reinforce his own divinity and importance by proving he came from a line of kings.

Like the King's Principal Wife, the King's Mother was a semi-divine title and represented the female aspect of divine kingship. Both the King's Principal Wife and the King's Mother accompanied the king in rituals and the worship of the gods, although neither participated.

According to divine birth scenes depicted on temple walls, the only time the King's Mother interacted directly with the gods was when she was impregnated by the god, normally Amun, with the king. And it is probably best that her husband wasn't there to witness her impregnation by another!

Daddy's girl: The King's Daughter

The title King's Daughter was never given as an honorary title, although it was used by both daughters and granddaughters of the king. The King's Daughter was sometimes also the King's Wife, in reference to real or political marriages between the individuals, their fathers, or even their grandfathers. The King's Daughter did not hold any real power other than that from her close relationship with the king.

Some of these father–daughter and grandfather–granddaughter marriages resulted in children, which shows some arrangements were marriages in every sense of the word.

The Politics of Marriage

For royal Egyptian women, getting married was never simple – and certainly not romantic. The women had little or no say in who they married and when, and were simply pawns in a wider political game. The challenges were numerous, as the following sections discuss.

Marriage as foreign relations policy

Most New Kingdom kings had diplomatic marriages to cement alliances between two nations. Political marriages have nothing to do with love and attraction.

A number of letters have been discovered that describe two types of diplomatic marriages:

- If the foreign king was on equal terms with the Egyptian king, both parties referred to one other as 'brother', and the arrangements were more on equal terms.
- If the foreign country was a vassal state, the Egyptian king was addressed as 'my lord, my god'. These brides were regarded as booty.

Get rich quick

Ramses II had a number of diplomatic marriages. In at least one instance, the negotiation texts have survived. The Marriage Stela of Ramses records a diplomatic marriage in year 35 between Ramses and the daughter of the Hittite king. Ramses seemed quite excited at the prospect of a new wife and rather impatiently sent numerous letters to her parents enquiring as to her estimated time of arrival.

One letter is particularly surprising, as Ramses asks the Hittite queen why her daughter, and more importantly her dowry, was delayed. He even claims the absence of the dowry is taking its toll on the Egyptian economy. Queen Padukhepa, the bride's mother, was not impressed and sent a letter of rebuke back to him:

> that you my brother should wish to enrich yourself from me . . . is neither friendly nor honourable

The princess, her dowry, her entourage, *and* her mother (I bet Ramses was pleased about that) eventually travelled to southern Syria, where they were met by the Egyptian authorities. The bride was described as 'beautiful in the heart of his [Ramses's] majesty and he loved her more than anything' and he celebrated the wedding with a long inscription, which gives the impression that the marriage is in fact nothing more than tribute offered by a lesser king to his master:

> Then he caused his oldest daughter to be brought, the costly tribute before her consisting of gold, silver, ores, countless horses, cattle, sheep, and goats.

At least he mentioned his wife before the goats. Ramses's new wife had at least one child before being sent to live in the Faiyum region (see the section 'Earning their keep: The harem at the Faiyum', later in this chapter). A laundry list belonging to her has been found and shows that the Faiyum was her home.

This queen soon disappeared from the records, perhaps dying young. Ten years after the marriage – perhaps at her death – the Hittite king agreed to send another daughter and a large dowry to Ramses.

After these diplomatic brides entered Egypt with their entourages of some-times more than 300 people, they were no longer allowed to communicate with their families for fear that they would give away state secrets. In fact, one letter from the Hittite king to Ramses II enquires after the Hittite king's daughter, who was sent to Egypt as a diplomatic bride, and indicates that there was no communication from her at all. (The Hittites had a large empire, with the capital in Turkey.)

Although Egyptian kings married foreign princesses, Egyptian princesses did not marry foreign princes. This distinction is made very clear in one of the Amarna diplomatic letters following a request from the Babylonian king to Amenhotep III for an Egyptian bride. The Babylonian king is told in no uncer-tain terms:

> *From old, the daughter of an Egyptian king has not been given in marriage to anyone.*

This statement would have been rather insulting to the Babylonian king, because his sister was already part of the Egyptian harem.

Vanishing wives

The problem of vanishing wives was particularly rife in the New Kingdom – although it wasn't caused by any supernatural phenomenon or evil wrong-doer. Women were frequently sent to the harem in the Faiyum (see the section 'Earning their keep: The harem at the Faiyum', later in this chapter) never to be heard of again by the king or by the wife's foreign family.

Marrying Amun

As well as marrying the king, royal women might also marry the god Amun. Amun was a solar-creator deity worshipped primarily at Thebes at Karnak Temple. From the 18th dynasty on, the title God's Wife of Amun was very important and held only by royal women.

Taking on responsibility

Ahmose I introduced the title of God's Wife of Amun as a means of honouring his mum Ahhotep (ahh, bless). He gave his wife Ahmose-Nefertari the title of Second Prophet of Amun, which was a title normally held by men only.

As Second Prophet of Amum, Ahmose-Nefertari worked as a deputy to Ahhotep, with the understanding that she would inherit the role.

The title God's Wife of Amun was initially passed on from mother to daughter, although by the 23rd dynasty and the reign of Osorkon III, these royal women were forced to be celibate and had to adopt a 'daughter' to take over the role.

God's Wife of Amun was a position of great power, especially within the temple of Karnak. In the 19th and 20th dynasties, this title enabled the royal family to possess equal power within the temple complex to the High Priests – and through bribery of local officials, that power expanded even further.

Although the names of a number of God's Wives of Amun are known, their exact duties are still unclear. From the 21st dynasty (around 1080 BC), historians know the God's Wives of Amun performed a number of tasks closely associated with kingship, reflecting the power of the role. Specifically, they

- ✔ Wrote their names in cartouches (see Chapter 11 for more information about cartouches)

- ✔ Adopted throne names (a second name after they took the title, a privilege normally reserved for kings)

- ✔ Were depicted in their personal chapels being suckled by the goddess Hathor, which shows their divinity

- ✔ Were addressed by subordinates as 'Your Majesty'

From the reign of Osorkon III (23rd dynasty), the God's Wife of Amun was the power behind the throne. Osorkon forced the High Priest of Amun to donate all his wealth to the God's Wife, diminishing the priest's power. Because the God's Wife of Amun was a relative of the king, she was under his control, which essentially gave the king the power that she held – a cunning if somewhat complicated plan.

In the 23rd dynasty, the God's Wife of Amun also held the title 'God's Hand' in relation to the creation story when the god Atum masturbated to create the next generation of gods. Whether this title had a specific role or ritual associated with it is unknown, but the mind boggles.

Enjoying the privileges

When a queen received the title of God's Wife of Amun, she also received an agricultural estate and personnel. Through these resources, she was able to produce a life-long income, which she kept for herself or used to bribe local officials.

The power associated with being God's Wives of Amun continued into the afterlife. These women were buried in their own small chapels at Medinet Habu. Their tombs were beneath the chapels and included an array of funerary goods befitting their station. Their spirits were nourished through the offering of food and drink in the chapels for a number of years after their death.

The God's Wives of Amun also constructed their own monumental chapels at Karnak temple, which is unusual, because women, royal or otherwise, didn't have their own monuments. (Women were normally depicted on tomb walls and in inscriptions of their husbands.) Yet at Karnak temple, the chapels of the God's Wives of Amun show the women standing before the image of the god Amun, as well as carrying out rituals and ceremonies that the king normally carried out.

Living with the King

Many royal women, whether siblings, wives, or children, rarely – or never – saw the king. The king lived most of the year in his palace in the capital city or travelled the country, staying at various palaces along the way. By contrast, royal women didn't always go with the king and lived in one of several harems sprinkled throughout the country (see the following section).

Harems were secure homes for royal and unmarried elite women. Each harem was a self-sufficient institution with land, cattle, and a number of male attendants (not eunuchs). The royal children lived in a part of the harem known as the household of the royal children. Harems were undoubtedly places of luxury, but royal woman had to stay where they were placed, so freedom was limited.

Location, location, location

The further away a royal wife lived from the king, the further down the royal hierarchy she existed.

The importance of each harem was in direct relation to how close it was to the main residence of the king. The location changed from king to king. A number of New Kingdom harems or women's quarters are known today from various towns in Egypt:

- ✔ Memphis in the north of Egypt
- ✔ Gurob in the Faiyum
- ✔ Malkata, the palace of Amenhotep III

- The North Palace at Amarna
- Pi-Ramesses, the capital city of Ramses II in the Delta region
- Medinet Habu (the mortuary temple of Ramses III) on the West Bank of Thebes

Each king needed a place to house his many royal wives, so more harems probably existed, although they are now lost. Ramses II is said to have had more than 300 wives, and Amenhotep III is rumoured to have had more than 1,000 women, so more harems are clearly left to find.

Living it up: The harem at Medinet Habu

The favoured wives lived at harems close to the king – such as Ramses III's harem at Medinet Habu, Thebes, the centre of the religious capital of Egypt. Thebes was a very metropolitan city in the New Kingdom – the place to be. The king spent much of his time here. The wives at Medinet Habu travelled the country with the king and stayed at other comfortable and luxurious harems on the way on a temporary basis.

The gateway of Medinet Habu is hollow and is decorated with intimate scenes of Ramses III caressing his wives. The inscriptions on the gateway don't say what it was used for, and for many years Egyptologists believed the gateway itself was the harem. However, logically speaking, the royal women are not going to live in a gateway, at danger from people outside the enclosure wall, and with the added risk of them running away.

The gateway was more probably their holiday home, because in addition to a number of chambers (none of which is a bedroom), the site included a roof complex with small structures enabling the women to sit outside and look at the scenery. From this retreat, they could see the landscape, witness processions and religious rituals, and generally watch the world go by without being seen.

The Medinet Habu women were permanently housed at the palace, firmly within the enclosure walls, which has a number of suites of rooms consisting of a bedroom, a dressing room, and a sitting room. The audience chamber has raised daises, where the King's Principal Wife sat on her throne. The palace also includes two showers, complete with drains for run-off, and a pleasure garden with a lake.

The king clearly visited this harem, as drawings on the Window of Appearances leading from the palace to the first court of the temple show. The king appeared here in festivals to bestow gold jewellery on his favoured courtiers – and then perhaps bestowed other favours on his royal favourites later.

Earning their keep: The harem in the Faiyum

Egyptologists have extensive records from the New Kingdom Faiyum harem – a harem where 'unwanted' women were sent. In this remote site the women were not a part of the king's life and would easily be forgotten. A wife would be unwanted for various reasons. Perhaps the woman was too old to bear any more children, was a diplomatic wife, or the king was simply bored of her.

Royal women must have found it terribly depressing to be sent to the Faiyum harem, because they knew they would never leave. And the king was unlikely to visit Faiyum often, which lessened these women's chances of gaining the king's favour through producing a son.

However, the women at Faiyum were quite productive and worked in the on-site textile workshop, producing linen for the other royal palaces. This activity was a means for them to earn their keep, as well as to help them pass the time. The senior women were probably involved in embroidery and close, fiddly work, as well as teaching newcomers the skills for the job. Women not involved in cloth production performed household tasks. Lower levels of the harem women were responsible for serving the King's Principal Wife and other senior wives. Probably not the lifestyle imagined by many princesses.

The Faiyum harem also had a cemetery, which means that those who lived and died there were also buried there. These women had no chance to get close enough to the king to be buried in the more prestigious Valley of the Queens (see the section 'Burying the queens', later in this chapter). Additionally, young princes were buried at Faiyum as well, showing that these males were low princes with little or no chance of ever becoming heir to the throne.

Burying the queens

The more favoured wives and children of the New Kingdom kings were given a tomb in the so-called Valley of the Queens in Luxor, very close to the Valley of the Kings. The use of the Valley changed over the years, and it wasn't used solely for queens' burials:

- ✔ From the 18th dynasty, the Valley was used for the burial of the royal sons (more than 60 burial shafts in total).
- ✔ From the beginning of the 19th dynasty, queens were buried here, the most famous Nefertari, the wife of Ramses II, who was given a richly coloured tomb.

> ✔ From the reign of Ramses III (20th dynasty), the royal princes were once again buried here.
>
> ✔ From the third intermediate period, the site was used for non-royal burials and continued to be used as a cemetery until the fourth century AD.

The tombs in the Valley of the Queens were smaller than those in the Valley of the Kings and less complex in design. The queens' tombs were carved in inferior rock, and many tombs were abandoned half way through construction, leaving many unfinished tombs in the valley. Those that were completed were plastered and painted rather than being decorated with carved relief. (See Chapter 13 for more on the evolution and construction of tombs.)

Plotting revenge

With a large number of women living in such confined quarters as a royal harem, trouble was bound to pop up. And trouble is certainly what happened in the reign of Ramses III when a bungled assassination attempt known as the 'Harem Conspiracy' was discovered. The trial of the main defendants is recorded on the Harem Conspiracy Papyrus, written during the reign of Ramses IV.

Fourteen men from many walks of life were called to stand as judges – rather like a modern jury. They were given the power to call for any evidence or witnesses needed to conduct the case fairly and were responsible for dispensing the verdict and punishments.

More than 40 people, all close to the king or the harem, were tried for the conspiracy. There were two plots – one to kill the king and the other to cause a fracas outside the palace at the same time, ensuring the king was not as well guarded as usual.

The chief defendant was Ramses III's minor wife Tiy, who wanted her son Pentewere to be king, even though he was not an heir. Her name is real but her son's was changed as a punishment for this crime, which made repeating his true name impossible and denied him an afterlife (see Chapter 10 for more on this funerary belief).

The papyrus records four separate prosecutions:

✔ Twenty-eight people, including the major ringleaders, were all condemned to death, possibly by public execution.

✔ Six people were condemned to commit suicide immediately in the court in front of the judges.

✔ Four people, including Prince Pentewere, were probably condemned to commit suicide within their cells after the trial.

✔ Three judges and two officers were accused of entertaining some of the female conspirators (tut tut). One judge was innocent, but the others were condemned to be mutilated by having their nose and ears cut off. One committed suicide before the sentence was carried out; clearly mutilation was too much for him to bear.

Whether Ramses III would've given the same verdicts is uncertain; he died before the verdicts were pronounced. Some say his death was a direct result of the assassination attempt – the plot thickens!

Remembering the First Feminists

Over the 3,000 years or so of Egyptian history, not many women have stood out as strong personalities or powerful individuals, because they were all overshadowed by the dominant personalities of kings.

However, a few women did make their mark, including some who worked against the system to rule in their own right, and others who had to take things in hand in order to get the job done, either due to weak kings or political circumstances.

Perhaps the following three women were products of circumstance – or perhaps they really were some of the world's first feminists.

Ahhotep: Warrior queen

Queen Ahhotep of the 17th and 18th dynasties was the first powerful royal woman of the New Kingdom, although this was more by accident than design. She was married to Seqenenre Tao II and had at least two sons – Ahmose, the founder of the 18th dynasty, and Kamose. Both Queen Ahhotep's husband and her son Kamose died in the battles against the Hyksos (see Chapter 3), and she watched her youngest son, Ahmose, follow in their footsteps.

While the men in her life were at war, Queen Ahhotep was effectively ruling Egypt from the capital city at Thebes. After her husband died and while her son Kamose was too young to rule alone, she acted as queen regent on his behalf. After her first son's death, she ruled again for her second son Ahmose. This was a very unusual role for a woman, but she was clearly a take-control kinda gal.

During such a politically unstable time, Ahhotep turned her hand to many tasks, not just the administration of the country. An inscription at Karnak goes someway to describe her role as regent with Ahmose:

> *She is one who has accomplished the rites and cared for Egypt. She has looked after Egypt's troops and she has guarded them. She has also brought back fugitives and collected together the deserters. She has pacified Upper Egypt and expelled her rebels.*

This inscription indicates that Ahhotep learnt military skills, which is feasible because the palace was probably overrun with soldiers and generals. She would have dealt with the military men because Kamose and Ahmose were too young to rule alone.

Her funerary equipment reflects these military concerns, because it included a necklace of the Order of the Fly, a military honour rather like a medal. Her tomb also included weapons, such as a jewelled dagger and a lapis axe detailed with Ahmose's cartouche in the centre of a smiting scene.

Hatshepsut: The female king

The most notorious royal woman is Hatshepsut, a queen from the 18th dynasty who eventually ruled Egypt as a king rather than a queen and upset virtually everyone in the country.

When her father, Thutmosis I, died, Hatshepsut married her half-brother, Thutmosis II, and they had a daughter before Thutmosis II died. On his death, Hatshepsut married her husband's son by another wife, and he became Thutmosis III. He was less than three years old when he came to the throne, so Hatshepsut ruled on his behalf until he was old enough to rule alone.

Hatshepsut's shopping trip to Punt

The most spectacular event of the reign of Hatshepsut was a shopping expedition to the city of Punt. The expedition was very lucrative for Egypt, and Hatshepsut was remembered for her participation – even though it was an act of a king and not a queen.

The excursion is recorded on Hatshepsut's mortuary temple at Deir el Bahri in Luxor. The location of Punt has been questioned over the years. Many places, from the Indian Ocean to Somaliland (modern Ethiopia), have been suggested as the location; the only thing that is known is that it was reached via the Red Sea.

The trading expedition was primarily for incense trees. Incense was used extensively in Egypt by the cult of Amun as well as by ordinary people as a fumigator. Because incense was not a natural resource of Egypt, it had to be imported. Ever industrious, Hatshepsut wanted to plant the trees in Egypt and make incense a natural resource.

She did indeed plant these trees along the causeway leading to her mortuary temple, and some of the pits can still be seen today.

In addition to the trees, the expedition brought back a number of other goods that were valuable to the Egyptian economy, including aromatic wood, tree gum, ebony, ivory, gold, eye paint, baboons, monkeys, hounds, panther skin, and labourers.

While in Punt, Hatshepsut's expedition was welcomed by the King and Queen of Punt, the latter depicted as being extremely obese. Images of obese Egyptians and non-Egyptians are highly unusual, so loads of discussion between scholars has developed trying to figure out whether the Queen of Punt has a disease or whether artists were trying to indicate that she was wealthy. No decision has been arrived at, and it doesn't look as if one is likely to be reached any time soon.

Initially Hatshepsut used traditional queenly titles like King's Chief Wife or God's Wife, although after a couple of years she used titles modelled on those of kings, like Mistress of the Two Lands. After seven years, she completely abandoned her queenly titles and adopted the fivefold titulary of a king. She is represented on monuments wearing the masculine attire of a king. She probably figured if she was ruling Egypt in the absence of a king suitable for the job, she wanted the power that went with it.

Many misconceptions about the images in artwork of Hatshepsut dressed as a king have persisted over the centuries – some even stating she was a transvestite! However, in order to be treated as a king in the artwork, she had to be represented as such. Kings are male, so this is how the artists presented her (see Chapter 11 for more artistic conventions). Whether she wandered around the palace in a kilt and a false beard is highly unlikely – and highly inappropriate for a royal woman.

Hatshepsut ruled as king alone for about 15 years and then completely disappears from the records when Thutmosis III took over his rightful place as king. Her body has never been found, so historians don't know if she died of old age (she was about 36 years old in the latest record) or whether she was assassinated. Either way, she made her mark on the history books – even if the later kings tried to pretend she had never existed by erasing her name from documents, monuments, and historical king lists.

Tiye: One scary lady

One woman who is often presented as a dominant individual is queen Tiye, the mother of Akhenaten. In reality, historians don't know whether she was dominant, but she was definitely prominent.

Tiye was married to Amenhotep III and gave birth to a number of children, including Akhenaten. She held the title of King's Great Wife, making her the most important royal woman in the palace.

Tiye is represented in art more frequently than any previous queen (although her daughter in law Nefertiti is depicted as frequently, if not more so – see Chapter 16 for more about Nefertiti). Prior to her reign, 18th-dynasty queens were retiring; they supported their husbands when required, but remained very much in the background. However, in images depicting scenes throughout Amenhotep III's reign, Tiye is shown alongside him in a complementary position, participating in the king's ceremonies and rituals – an unusual practice for queens. She is depicted as the same size as her husband, which indicated equality with him. She is also sometimes represented without him – also very unusual.

Tiye has a reputation for being a strong, formidable woman. Some Egyptologists believe she ruled Egypt in the later years of Amenhotep III's reign, when he was more interested in his harem than politics. Some also believe she influenced Akhenaten in his religious revolution (see Chapter 4).

The influence Tiye held over her husband and son remains unknown, but evidence does show Tiye was privy to diplomatic issues. A letter from a foreign king is addressed to her, in which the foreign king complains that since Akhenaten came to the throne, he has sent only wooden statues covered in gold rather than solid gold statues like the previous king Amenhotep III sent. The foreign king appeals to Tiye to talk to Akhenaten and persuade him to send good-quality gifts. Whether she had words with Akhenaten is not recorded, but I wouldn't have messed with her.

Both Tiye and Amenhotep III were deified in life and were worshipped at the temple of Sedinga at Nubia. Here Tiye was worshipped as the goddess Hathor-Tefnut Great-of-Fearsomeness, and is shown making offerings to herself. This title must have been chosen for a reason. Perhaps she had a fearsome reputation even then. Tiye is also shown in this temple as a sphinx trampling female prisoners, an assertive depiction that places her as a counterpart to her divine king/husband rather than in a supporting role.

Chapter 6

Following the Decline and Fall of the Egyptian Civilisation

In This Chapter

▶ Invading other nations and surviving invasions

▶ Dividing the rule among leaders, cities, and nations

▶ Meeting famous figures: Alexander the Great, Cleopatra, and others

*U*ntil the end of the New Kingdom (see Chapter 4), Egypt was a strong, economically solvent, and powerful country, with control over a large number of surrounding areas. Egypt was a country to be reckoned with.

However, by the end of the New Kingdom in the 20th dynasty (1185–1070 BC), the traditional Egyptian culture began to decline. This decline started with a division of the throne of Egypt – from one king to two (and sometimes more) ruling from separate cities. A united Egypt under one king was one of the most important aspect of kingship, so this change did not bode well for ancient traditions.

This chapter ambitiously covers more than 1,000 years of Egyptian history – from the glorious period just after the reigns of Ramses II and Ramses III all the way to the dramas of Cleopatra.

Egyptian history at this point takes numerous twists and turns – some of which modern historians are still working to understand. Try keeping your head straight by focusing on the bigger picture here. While the specifics are interesting, pay more attention to the waves of change and phases of control as led by various groups, cultures, and nations.

To give you an overall sense of the end of the ancient Egyptian empire, these 1,000-plus years can be outlined as follows:

- **Third Intermediate Period (1080–525 BC):** Characterised by numerous rulers reigning at the same time from different regions of Egypt.
- **Late Period (525–332 BC):** Characterised by foreign invasion and regularly changing dynasties.
- **Graeco-Roman Period (332–30 BC):** Began with the invasion of Alexander the Great and resulted in drastic cultural changes due to the influx of the Greeks into Egypt.

Dividing the Two Lands: Ramses XI and After

The decline of the Egyptian empire began during the early years of the reign of Ramses XI (1098–1070 BC).

The power of the king was slowly diminishing due primarily to economic problems. The priests of Amun were gaining in power and wealth. (Rather ironically, the king contributed to this increase in power through a number of gifts, offerings, and building works at the temple of Karnak in Luxor.) Eventually the priests held almost as much power as Ramses XI; the king had control of the army – a difference that kept him one step ahead.

Problems occurred when the Viceroy of Nubia, Panehsy, came into conflict with the high priest of Amun, Amenhotep. Panehsy held the upper hand for nine months, preventing the high priest from carrying out his religious duties. Amenhotep eventually turned to Ramses XI for help.

As a very religious king, Ramses fought against Panehsy. Panehsy was eventually exiled to Nubia, and Amenhotep was reinstated as high priest and remained in the position for a number of years before Herihor succeeded him.

Herihor becomes too big for his boots

Ramses XI maintained his good relationship with the priesthood of Amun and bestowed on Herihor the military titles previously held by the exiled Panehsy. This was a huge mistake, because for the first time one man held religious and military titles, making Herihor more powerful than Ramses.

Herihor made the most of the situation and took over the role of king while poor Ramses XI was still alive. It must have been clear to Ramses that Herihor was just waiting for him to die to complete the transaction. No doubt he watched his back, just in case.

Although Herihor died before he could become a true king, he adopted a cartouche (see Chapter 11) and passed on his elevated position to his son-in-law Piankhy, who also ruled alongside Ramses in the same manner. When Ramses XI eventually died, in 1070 BC, four years after Piankhy's reign started, Piankhy continued to rule Thebes as a king in his own right, albeit only for a few months.

Despite this new elevation of the priests of Amun, their power did not extend outside the Theban region – probably because of a lack of interest on the priests' behalf.

Ruling in the north: Tanis kings

While the high priests of Amun were ruling in the south of Egypt, the north was ruled by Smendes (1069–1043 BC), a man of rather obscure origins. He ruled from the site of Tanis in the eastern Delta (refer to the Cheat Sheet map), built from the remains of Ramses II's city at Pi-Rameses. Smendes legitimised his claim to the throne by marrying a daughter of Ramses XI.

Smendes was followed on the throne by Psusennes I (1039–991 BC), who allowed his daughter to marry the high priest of Amun, Menkhepere. This union indicates that a good relationship existed between the northern and southern rulers.

This generally positive relationship between the north and the south continued throughout the rest of the third intermediate and to a certain extent the late period too. The Tanis dynasty, known as the 21st dynasty, lasted for approximately 350 years, prospering during this time, and improved trade and the economy – even if only those in the north of the country experienced the benefit.

The cemetery of the Tanis kings was discovered in 1939 and included the only intact royal burial to be found in Egypt. (Even Tutankhamun's tomb was robbed in antiquity at least twice.) The artefacts in these tombs were impressive but did not get the recognition they deserved, because the media were tied up reporting the Second World War. Interesting discoveries included:

- ✔ **The burial assemblage of Psusennes I.** Psusennes's mummy featured a gold death mask and a solid silver anthropoid (human-shaped) coffin. These items were placed inside a sarcophagus that was originally used by Merenptah, the son of Ramses II, which shows that trade between the north and south of Egypt was active, despite the north and south being ruled by different kings.

- ✔ **The coffin of Sheshonq I.** Sheshonq's coffin is beautiful and unique – a silver, falcon-shaped box. In fact, silver was more valuable than gold because it was not native to Egypt. The use of silver highlights the wealth of the Tanis dynasties and indicates that their trade relations were strong.

Briefly uniting the two lands: Sheshonq 1

The 21st Tanis dynasty was followed by the 22nd dynasty (945–745 BC), the members of which also ruled from Tanis but are believed to be of Libyan origin. The first king of the period is Sheshonq I (945–924 BC), who legitimised his claim to the throne by marrying a daughter of Psusennes II, the last king of the 21st dynasty.

Sheshonq seems to be a Libyan chieftain – specifically a leader of the Meshwesh, a Libyan nomadic tribe. Sheshonq held military titles and adopted the royal titles of Smendes, who had ruled more than 100 years previously. These titles gave his claim to the throne a bit of a kick start.

Although he was Libyan, Sheshonq I reunited the divided Egypt and effectively ruled both Upper and Lower Egypt, which was especially important for him to be accepted as a true king of Egypt. He managed to gain control over the south of Egypt because his son held the title of high priest of Amun, uniting the northern throne and the southern priesthood.

The end of Sheshonq's peace

Despite Shehonq I's best efforts to rule a unified Egypt and maintain the military prowess of the Egyptian nation, the end of the 22nd dynasty caused unrest and national division. Although the priesthood of Amun was now under the control of the northern king through family ties, near the end of the dynasty the high priesthood experienced a gap in succession that resulted in a civil war lasting for more than a decade.

After this civil war was over, the peace was short lived with further uprisings and hostilities that caused not only north–south divisions but even east–central divisions in the Delta between chiefs of Leontopolis (central) and Tanis (east). The harmony of the reign of Sheshonq I was slowly collapsing into chaos.

Too many kings

The problems in the Delta eventually saw a dynastic change while the seventh king of the 22nd dynasty, Sheshonq III, was still ruling from Tanis.

Three more kings ruled over the next 100 years until the end of the 22nd dynasty, but in the meantime many other rulers emerged throughout the

Delta. Notable among these was Pedibast, a local chieftain in Leontopolis, who took over the rule of the central Delta and split the rule of Egypt into three sections. Members of both Pedibast's and Sheshonq's families (east) travelled south to join the priesthood of Amun, ensuring that royal connections existed with this powerful faction.

Towards the end of the 23rd dynasty, the introduction of yet another dynasty of kings brought about further divisions:

- ✔ King Sheshonq III at Tanis (22nd dynasty)
- ✔ King Iupet at Leontopolis (23rd dynasty)
- ✔ King Peftjauabastet at Herakleopolis (23rd dynasty)
- ✔ King Nimlot at Hermopolis (23rd dynasty)
- ✔ King Tefnakht at Sais (24th dynasty)

Each of these kings ruled only a small area, but all took the full title of king and wrote their names in cartouches. Everyone seemed happy with the arrangement and left one another alone.

However, at the end of the period (around 727 BC), a much bigger threat emerged that stopped any further divisions from developing – the power of Nubia. In fact, this new threat encouraged the kings to join together and work in harmony.

Libyan liberator

In 925 BC, Sheshonq I went to war with Palestine and proved that Egypt's military was still a force to be reckoned with. His campaign has even been compared to that of Ramses III against the Sea People (see Chapter 4). When King Solomon died in 930 BC, his son Rehoboam ruled Judah, and Jeroboam I (the first king of the tribe of Ephraim to rule Israel) ruled Israel. These rulers were in the throws of a civil war when Sheshonq decided to prove that Egypt was still great.

The Egyptian army first marched to Judah and camped outside the walls of Jerusalem, which was governed by King Rehoboam. The Bible records that Sheshonq (Shishak) was bribed with a great deal of gold and the much coveted Ark of the Covenant so that he would not enter and sack the city.

Sheshonq continued his march to Israel until he reached Megiddo, the site where Thutmosis III fought his famous battle (see Chapter 4). Sheshonq erected a stela at this site to commemorate his victory against ancient Israel. He further recorded his victories in the quarries of Gebel Silsila and at Karnak temple.

Exerting Pressure from the South: Nubian Influences

Around 727 BC, the power and influence of the Nubians were spreading north from their homeland as far as the Theban region. If Nubians travelled further north, they may interfere with the tranquillity of a divided north. The northern kings of the 22nd (Tanis), 23rd (Leontopolis), and 24th (Sais) dynasties therefore joined forces to enable them to deal with the Nubian group of rulers (25th dynasty) to prevent the latter's power from expanding further.

Growing power

Nubia had never really been a threat to the Egyptians before. Until the reign of Ramses II (see Chapter 4), the area had been firmly under the control of the Egyptians, who exploited the Nubians' quarries and gold mines. After Ramses II's strength faded, Nubia began to distance itself from the Egyptians and managed to form its own capital city in Napata (near the fourth cataract of the Nile).

During the 21st dynasty, the high priests of Amun gained a great deal of influence over Nubia and even built a large temple to Amun at Gebel Barkal, within Nubian territory. The Nubian priests of this temple also expanded their power throughout the surrounding area and eventually usurped the Nubian kingship.

These Nubian kings used titles and cartouches in the manner of traditional Egyptian kings. After the Nubian dynasty had established itself, it started to move northwards to Egypt, where the Egyptian kingship was obviously in a weakened state because of its numerous divisions. The Nubians saw their advance as an opportunity to turn the tables and control Egypt for a change.

Egypt's the limit: Piankhy

The Nubian king Piankhy (sometimes Piye) confronted the four northern kings of the 22nd–24th dynasties in 727 BC and was victorious against them. Although he stripped them of their kingly titles, Piankhy did allow them to have a certain amount of power in their new positions as local governors, which in all honesty may not have been a great deal different from their roles as petty kings of small regions.

In order to reinforce his position as Egyptian king fully, Piankhy took over the priesthood of Amun, which gave him ultimate power over the Theban region. The kings who succeeded him maintained this connection with the cult of Amun, both in Thebes and in Nubia.

Despite this affiliation with the cult of Amun in Thebes, Piankhy chose to rule from the Nubian capital of Napata. He was buried in a pyramid at el-Kurru, north of Gebel Barkal. Later rulers were also buried in pyramids. These pyramids were very different from the Old Kingdom Egyptian pyramids (see Chapter 14) because they were small but tall and narrow. Many of the Nubian pyramids have produced a number of grave goods, including gold jewellery.

The successor of Piankhy, his son Shabaka, increased the area controlled by the Nubian dynasty to include all of Egypt from the south to the north up to the boundary of the Sais region in the Delta.

Conquering the Near East: The Assyrians

At the same time as Nubian influence over Egypt was expanding, the Assyrian empire was also expanding throughout the Near East. Several Assyrian uprisings happened close to the Egyptian borders, but the Nubian kings quashed these.

However, by the reign of Nubian pharaoh Taharqa (690–664 BC), the Assyrians and the Nubians had engaged in numerous confrontations. Both sides had gained the upper hand alternately, showing that they were equally matched. The situation must have been quite unnerving for the new Nubian dynasties that hadn't long gained the coveted prize of rule over Egypt.

In 671 BC, the Assyrian king, Esarhaddon, actually entered Egypt, gaining control of the north as far as Memphis. This meant that King Taharqa had to flee to the south of Egypt. Although they maintained their control over the Delta, the Assyrians left, only to return in 669 BC. However, Esarhaddon died on the way and was succeeded by his son Ashurbanipal, who finally gained control of Egypt.

Ashurbanipal eventually took control over Thebes in 661 BC, making him the king of Upper and Lower Egypt. This caused Taharqa and his successors to flee further south to the Nubian capital, Napata, outside the boundaries of Egypt, never to enter Egypt again.

The Saite Period: Psamtik 1 and Others

After 665 BC, the Assyrians were in control of Egypt – although they chose local people to take the role of the king, under their rule, of course. Egypt was now a vassal state of the Assyrian empire. The capital city was located at Sais in the Delta, and the kings of the Saite period formed the 26th dynasty. (Because the Nubian 25th dynasty was still in control when the Assyrians captured the north, these two dynasties occurred concurrently.)

Psamtik I (664–610 BC) of the Saite 26th dynasty was given the job of consolidating Assyrian control throughout Egypt, including Thebes. Psamtik sent his daughter Nitocris to the temple of Amun at Karnak, where she was given the priestly title of God's wife of Amun, which placed her rather high in the cult hierarchy. This combination of royal and religious power – as well as the cult's wealth – ensured that the north and south were ruled by one individual.

This unified Egypt was not stable, however, and Psamtik was forced to gather an army to deal with numerous petty chieftains who had arisen in the Delta. The chieftains all wanted a slice of Egypt to control, and the Assyrians wanted a single ruler who was easier to control.

Returning to traditions

Throughout the 50 years or so of Psamtik's reign, he brought a number of changes to Egypt. He tried to bring Egypt back to the traditions of the past, to show a continuity of the culture. To do this, he reintroduced a number of religious, artistic, and ritual elements from the Old and Middle Kingdoms.

However, being a truly traditional king in a traditional Egypt meant freedom from foreign influence. The elimination of outside influence was difficult to achieve, but that was what Psamtik I did. In 653 BC, after a number of internal problems had weakened the Assyrians, Psamtik broke free from the Assyrians and gained control of Egypt in his own right. This separation meant that Egypt was once again the driving force of the Near East.

In the navy

Psamtik's successor, Nekau II, continued to improve Egypt's status in the Near East and took control of Syria-Palestine once again. Nekau formed the first official Egyptian naval service, which included a number of Ionian Greeks. Prior to this, Egypt had been primarily a riverine nation with no real need for a navy.

During the 26th dynasty, Egypt enjoyed increased commerce with the Greeks, whose trade network was growing immensely. In order to increase the scope for trade in Egypt, Nekau began the construction of a canal joining the Wadi

Tumilat to the Red Sea – 2,500 years before the Suez Canal was formed for the same purpose. The completed canal was wide enough to navigate a trade fleet through and changed Egypt's trade relations.

Appeasing the masses

Because of increased trade relations during this period, a number of foreign immigrants settled in Egypt, primarily in the Delta region. Initially they were relatively peaceful, but throughout the reign of Ahmose II (known as Amasis; 570–526 BC), numerous civil wars flared up between different foreign groups.

Ahmose tried to limit these conflicts by giving specific trading rights to foreigners living in the Delta town of Naukratis, thus creating a sort of 'free zone' for immigrants to Egypt. Some may view this action as a little unfair to the native Egyptians living there, but at least the fighting stopped, which further encouraged trade relations and foreign immigration to Egypt.

Not even cold yet

Psamtik's separation from the Assyrians (see the section 'Returning to traditions', earlier in this chapter) led to the gradual decline and eventual collapse of the Assyrian empire, and meant that Egypt was once again the most powerful nation in the region. This status did not last long, because everyone wanted to fill the gap left by the Assyrians. The weakened Assyrian kings were under attack from many people, including:

- ✔ Babylonians under king Naboplassar
- ✔ Medes (ancient Iranians)
- ✔ Scythians (Ukrainian and Southern Russians)

The Assyrians even asked Psamtik (who had separated from them) to help with these attacks. Even so, the Assyrians lost, and in 612 BC the Assyrian empire ended with the fall of Nineveh under the attack of the Persian army.

The celebration of the collapse of this once-great empire was short lived for the Egyptians, because the Persians soon marched on Egypt, entered its borders and took over the throne in 525 BC. The inexperienced king, Psamtik III, tried to stop the Persians from gaining control of Egypt. However, Psamtik III was eventually chased to Memphis before being captured and transported to the Persian capital as a prisoner of war, leaving Egypt unguarded and without a king.

Yet again, invasion led to *another* set of kings and yet *another* dynasty (the 26th), starting the late period of Egyptian history.

Settling of the Persians

The Persian 27th dynasty lasted for more than 100 years (525–404 BC) and is recorded by Herodotus. He records three potential reasons for the Persian king Cambyses II invading Egypt in the first place, although Herodotus wasn't sure of the reliability of any of these explanations:

- ✔ Cambyses wanted an Egyptian concubine and was sent a second-rate noblewoman instead of a princess, so he invaded Egypt.
- ✔ Cambyses may have been half-Egyptian, perhaps the illegitimate son born of a daughter of the Saite king Apries.
- ✔ Cambyses made a promise as a child to invade Egypt in revenge for an insult paid to his mother.

If Herodotus wasn't sure why Cambyses invaded Egypt, how on earth can modern historians be? Whatever the specific inspiration, the Persian invasion was a nasty one, aided by the Bedouins who led the way to the Egyptian borders. After the Bedouins and the Persians arrived, they were violent and cruel and even removed the embalmed body of the Saite king Ahmose (Amasis) and set fire to it. Granted, the Egyptians were not so nice either.

In revenge for a mercenary general's betrayal, the Egyptians paraded his two sons in front of him and the Persian army and slit their throats. The blood was collected in a large bowl, mixed with water and wine, and drunk by all the soldiers. However, in the same way that Herodotus had doubts about the stories of Cambyses, perhaps this description was also an exaggerated myth. No other records exist of the Egyptians drinking human blood.

Ruling Egypt from a distance

Although Cambyses and the Persians had taken on the Greeks and the Egyptians and won, they didn't fancy staying in the country of their victory. Cambyses lived and was buried in Persia (modern Iran). During his reign (525–522 BC) he hired a provincial governor to rule in Egypt on his behalf – although he was represented in Egypt as an Egyptian with his names written in a cartouche as a traditional ruler.

However, Cambyses's successor Darius I (521–486 BC) took a lot of interest in Egypt. He built a number of temples and instigated repairs from the Delta to Aswan. Darius also continued and completed the building of the canal between the Wadi Tumilat and the Red Sea that Nekau of the Saite 26th dynasty started.

In 486 BC, despite the positive influence that Darius had on Egypt, the Egyptians revolted. This revolt was not crushed until the next king, Xerxes, came to the throne. His reign (485–465 BC) was not a peaceful one, and later in his reign the Greeks invaded Egypt.

After a short period of respite, Xerxes was assassinated amid another Egyptian revolt. This fighting went on for some time, with the Persian king being defeated by descendants of the 26th dynasty from the Delta along with the aid of Greek mercenaries.

The Egyptians were finally able to gain control during the reigns of the final two kings of the Persian period, Darius II (423–403 BC) and Artaxerxes II (405–359 BC), following a number of problems within the Persian family, which weakened their defences and left them open for attack.

Yet more dynasties

The decline of the Egyptian culture was really on the final stretch by 400 BC, with kings taking control willy-nilly and causing a great deal of confusion. Perhaps the situation was less confusing for the ancient Egyptians!

- ✔ **The 28th dynasty** (404–399 BC) consisted of only one very little-known king called Amyrtaeus, who had succeeded after six years of guerrilla warfare against the Persian kings to bring the throne back to Egyptian control. He briefly gained control of the whole of Egypt, from his capital at Sais in the Delta down to the Aswan border.

- ✔ **The 29th dynasty** (399–380) moved the capital from Sais to Mendes further south, which indicates that the Egyptian's control was still widespread. Mendes was certainly better placed for government. The two kings of this dynasty were also probably buried at this site, although they have not been discovered yet.

- ✔ **The 30th dynasty** (380–343 BC) was a little more substantial, with a total of three kings. These kings spent a great deal of time supervising building according to ancient traditions to show some continuity between their reign and the earlier dynasties.

This dynasty was also involved in a number of battles defending Egypt from Persian invasion (yet again – they don't give up!).

Nectanebo II was given a short respite from Persian attack because of more Persian internal quarrels and conflicts with the Greeks and the Levantines. In 343 BC, Nectanebo II, with the Egyptian army and 20,000 Greek mercenaries, guarded the Delta borders against a major Persian attack led by Artaxerxes III. The borders were soon penetrated, and the Delta and then Memphis fell to the Persian invaders. Nectanebo fled to Nubia, but shortly afterwards disappeared; presumably he died.

The death of Nectanebo II in 343 BC was a major blow to Egypt for a couple of reasons. First, the Egyptians were yet again under the rule of the Persian kings. Second, Nectanebo was the last Egyptian ruler to govern the country until the first president of the Republic of Egypt, General Muhammad Naguib, in AD 1953. That is a long period of foreign rule.

Another round of Persian rule

The end of the reign of Nectanebo II saw the start of the second Persian period (343–332 BC). The Persians were again a little harsh to their adopted country. The Greek records describe how the Persians razed cities to the ground, robbed temples, killed a number of sacred animals, and taxed the population until the people were broke.

Once again, the Persian kings ruled though a governor while residing in Persia. This dynasty (which some historians consider the 31st) only lasted for 10 years, with the first two kings, Artaxerxes III and Arses, being assassinated, and the cowardly Darius III opening the borders of Egypt in 332 BC to allow Alexander the Great to enter Egypt.

Invading Macedonians: Alexander the Great

The assassination of Phillip II of Macedonia in 336 BC saw the start of Alexander's attack on the Persian empire. Alexander was the son of Phillip and felt that he should continue with his father's campaign. Alexander came to Egypt in 332 BC, which instigated a further decline in the ancient Egyptian culture. If the Persians had not occupied Egypt at this time then perhaps Alexander would have left it alone, producing a very different end to the story.

Becoming divine

Alexander wanted to be accepted into the Egyptian culture. One of the first things he did was to travel to Siwa to consult the oracle of Amun (see Chapter 9 for information on oracles) in order to prove that he was the divine son of the god and therefore a legitimate king of Egypt.

Alexander's coronation was carried out in the traditional centre of Memphis, and to a certain extent he ruled in a traditional Egyptian manner. He saw the renovation of Luxor temple with some elaborate images of himself making offerings to Amun-Min.

Alexander, however, left Egypt to continue his campaigns across the Near East. Before his death in 323 BC, Alexander had extended the Macedonian empire, which included Egypt, all the way to the Indus Valley. Being part of the vast empire brought new rich and exotic imports to Egypt.

Making Egypt a home of his own

When Alexander the Great was not invading and conquering nations, he concentrated on the administration of Egypt. Specifically he:

- **Introduced a monetary system to Egypt,** which had previously relied on a bartering system. The coins introduced by Alexander bore a Hellenistic image of himself on one side and an image of an Egyptian god on the other, showing the juxtaposition of the two cultures.

- **Founded the city of Alexandria,** which became the capital of Egypt at this time. The city was built on the site of an ancient Egyptian settlement called Raqote (also spelt Rakhotis), although not much of this ancient town has survived. Alexander left the building works to his architect Deinokrates and an official called Kleomenes.

Alexandria was large – at its height it had a population of more than half a million including a large number of Greek and Jewish immigrants. It was a very cosmopolitan city and included many famous buildings, such as a library and a museum that were sadly burned down in antiquity. The later city included Roman baths, a theatre, and a gymnasium. The larger houses of the Roman settlement were even decorated with mosaics in true Roman style, as Figure 6-1 shows.

The city of Alexandria was not complete until the reign of Ptolemy II (285–246 BC). Ptolemy I (305–282 BC) started building the Pharos lighthouse in Alexandria, which was one of the Seven Wonders of the Ancient World and the world's earliest lighthouse. This structure has long since disappeared – and may be on the bottom of the sea.

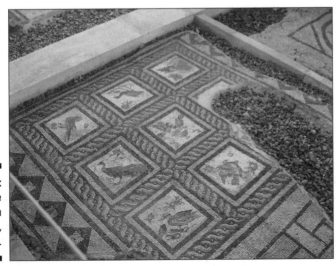

Figure 6-1:
Villa of the Birds, Kom el Dikka, Alexandria.

Alexander the Great died in 323 BC of a fever, leaving no obvious heir to take over his empire. His death led to the gradual collapse of the Macedonian empire, with various generals splitting to their own favoured areas.

Ending the Empire: The Ptolemaic Dynasty

Following the death of Alexander the Great and the collapse of his control over the Persian empire, many petty wars and battles ensued, fought by Alexander's generals. Everyone (especially Alexander's generals) tried to win a slice of the empire.

Ptolemy eventually returned to Egypt as governor under Phillip Arrhidaeus (323–317 BC), the successor to Alexander the Great's son Alexander IV (317–305 BC – born after his father's death). During the reign of Alexander IV, Ptolemy, his childhood friend, was effectively ruling, and on Alexander's death Ptolemy became king in his own right. By 301 BC Ptolemy had gained control of Palestine and Lower Syria, starting a small empire of his own.

However, Egypt could have done with a ruler with more imagination, as Ptolemy started a dynasty of rulers all called Ptolemy (up to Ptolemy XV), and queens called either Cleopatra (seven ruled as queens) or Berenice (four ruled as queens). Can you imagine the chaos when calling your kids in for dinner if they all answered to the same name?

The Ptolemaic dynasty was an example of the juxtaposition between two very different cultures – the ancient Egyptians and the Greeks. The rulers supported the traditional religion of Egypt and contributed to many temples, including building the temples of Dendera, Edfu, Philae, and Kom Ombo. On the walls of all these temples the kings are displayed in traditional Egyptian costume and pose, yet on the coins minted at the time they are presented in traditional Hellenistic fashion.

Sleeping with one eye open

Those in the Ptolemaic family were not a nice group of people. This may sound like a sweeping statement, but this family was obsessed with the power of the throne and did anything to keep this power. They were notorious for marrying their brothers and sisters as a means of legitimising claims to the throne or keeping the throne within the family. (Of course, many ancient Egyptian kings married within their families as well, but not all these marriages ended in children. The Ptolemaic marriages were consummated – regularly.)

Despite these very close family connections, the Ptolemaic family had absolutely no qualms about bumping off their brothers, sisters, husbands, and wives in order to rule alone – or about disposing of unpopular or unsuitable individuals.

As a member of this terrifying family, you really needed to be on your guard. A number of sovereigns and officials were murdered or died in a suspicious manner:

- Phillip Arrhidaeus was assassinated by one of his bodyguards.

- Berenice II was poisoned and scalded to death by her son Ptolemy IV.

- Ptolemy IV's wife, Arsinoe, was poisoned by the brother of Ptolemy's secondary wife, Agathoclea.

- Ptolemy VII was killed by his stepfather and uncle Ptolemy VIII (who was nicknamed Potbelly and was very unpopular).

- Memphites was murdered by his father, Ptolemy VIII, who sent the dismembered body to his sister/wife, Cleopatra II, as a birthday present. (I'm sure she'd have preferred some bath salts!)

- Cleopatra III was possibly murdered by her younger son, Ptolemy X (although, earlier in life, her older son, Ptolemy IX, was accused of plotting to murder her).

- Berenice, the daughter of Ptolemy IX, was murdered within a month of marrying Ptolemy XI. He disliked her and wanted the throne to himself. To be fair, Berenice probably didn't think much of him either.

- Ptolemy XI was lynched by the public after ruling for only 19 days, because Berenice had been very popular.

- Berenice (another one!), the daughter of Ptolemy XII, was murdered by the Romans because of her revolt against her father as she tried to take over the throne. Ptolemy XII asked Julius Caesar, dictator of Rome, for help.

- Ptolemy XIV, the brother and husband of Cleopatra VII (of Mark Antony fame), was probably disposed of by the queen so that she could promote her son Ptolemy XV to the throne, protecting him from the Romans.

The majority of these murders were about power and the throne. However, during many struggles with the Ptolemaic family, Rome was conscripted in to help sort out the arguments. Although Roman involvement ensured that someone won the arguments and had the support and power of Rome behind them, Rome did not forget the debts incurred while aiding the warring Ptolemies. And during the reign of Cleopatra VII, Roman leaders came to collect the debt – eventually leading to the final collapse of the Egyptian civilisation.

Making romantic history: Cleopatra and Mark Antony

The story of Cleopatra and Mark Antony is one of the most famous tragic love stories in the world. This story stars Cleopatra VII, born in approximately 70 BC – the daughter of Ptolemy XII (nicknamed the flute-player) and his sister Cleopatra V. Strange to think, Cleopatra's mother is also her aunt and her father is also her uncle.

Ptolemy XII was not very popular in Egypt because of his sycophantic attitude to Rome. He was also a weak and cruel ruler (which probably made him fit well into the Ptolemaic family). In 60 BC, Ptolemy XII's unpopularity had reached such proportions that he fled Egypt for the safety of Rome, while his eldest daughter, Berenice, took the throne. After a number of years, and with the support of Rome, Ptolemy returned to Egypt and reclaimed his throne. He ruled until his death in 52 BC when Cleopatra VII, aged 19 and married to her 10-year-old half-brother Ptolemy XIII, took over the throne.

Because her husband was so young, Cleopatra ruled Egypt virtually alone and even omitted Ptolemy's face from her coins. Unlike her father, Cleopatra was a popular ruler with the Egyptian people – probably because she was the only Ptolemaic ruler who had bothered to learn to speak Egyptian!

Spinning a web of deceit

Ptolemy XIII's spin doctors used the populace's affection for the queen against her by issuing a decree in her name that all available grain should be sent to Alexandria and none to Middle and Upper Egypt. This angered the Egyptian populace, and they turned against Cleopatra. Cleopatra fled in fear of her life to Ashkelon in Syria.

In 48 BC, Julius Caesar headed towards Egypt to sort out the hostilities between Ptolemy XIII and Cleopatra. At the same time, Cleopatra herself had gathered an army on Egypt's border to charge against her brother.

Caesar arrived in Alexandria determined to put Cleopatra back on the throne, until Ptolemy's courtiers brought him a gift – the head of one of Caesar's friends. This didn't exactly endear the young boy-king to Caesar, and Caesar marched into the city, seized the palace, and generally took charge.

Both Ptolemy and Cleopatra were ordered to dismiss their armies and meet with Caesar, who would settle their dispute (rather like a father and two naughty children). Cleopatra, however, was far from daft and knew that if she entered Alexandria openly, Ptolemy would have her killed. So she sneaked into the palace inside an oriental rug. When the rug was unrolled, Cleopatra fell out and Caesar fell in love.

They became lovers that night and by morning Ptolemy stormed out of the palace because he felt he had been betrayed. He was arrested shortly after, but his army laid siege to the palace. Caesar released Ptolemy, but the siege continued for almost six months and only ended when Ptolemy drowned in the Nile. Alexandria then surrendered to Caesar.

Now a widow, Cleopatra married her brother Ptolemy XIV, who was 11 or 12 years old. Julius Caesar gave them Cyprus as a wedding gift. His own interest in Cleopatra had been awakened.

Enjoying lazy summer days with Julius

The relationship between Cleopatra and Julius Caesar developed, and in 47 BC they went on a romantic Nile cruise. Cleopatra was only 23 years old and pregnant with Caesar's child, nicknamed Caesarion. The baby was born not long after they returned to Alexandria.

In the temple of Hathor at Denderah, a sculpted relief (see Figure 6-2) shows Cleopatra presenting her son Caesarion to the gods and naming him 'Ptolemy Caesar son of Julius Caesar and Cleopatra' to show that he was the heir to the throne.

Figure 6-2:
Cleopatra and Caesarion at Denderah.

More brains than beauty

Despite Hollywood's depiction of Elizabeth Taylor as the Queen of the Nile, Cleopatra does not have a reputation as a great beauty. She was, however, considered witty, charming, intelligent, and bursting with sex appeal.

The Greek historian Plutarch (46–127 AD) records that Cleopatra spoke a total of eight languages, including several African languages, Hebrew, and Aramaic, plus her native Greek. She was also the only Ptolemaic ruler to speak Egyptian, which endeared her to the Egyptian population. Historians have suggested that her father taught her these languages because he was looking further afield than the boundaries of Egypt for eventual rule.

For pleasure, Cleopatra studied fragrant and protective unguents and wrote a beauty book on how to mix these substances to moisturise and protect the skin. While no copies of this book have been discovered, the Romans recorded its existence.

In 46 BC, Cleopatra, Ptolemy XIV, and Caesarion went on a holiday to Rome to visit Julius Caesar. They stayed in Caesar's villa near Rome for almost two years – now that's a holiday and a half. During this time, Julius gave Cleopatra a ton of gifts and titles and even erected a statue of her in the temple of Venus Genetrix. The Romans were horrified at this affair, and it eventually led (in part) to Julius's assassination in 44 BC.

Cleopatra, in fear for her own and her son's life, scurried back to Egypt. Before or on their return to Egypt, Cleopatra's husband Ptolemy XIV mysteriously died at age 15, possibly poisoned, leaving Cleopatra free to marry her son Caesarion and make him her co-regent, Ptolemy XV.

Enter Mark Antony

At the death of Caesar, the Roman empire was divided among three men: Caesar's great-nephew Octavian, Marcus Lepidus, and Marcus Antonius, better known today as Mark Antony.

Cleopatra had met Mark Antony when she was 15, while her father was alive, when Mark Antony had travelled to Egypt in support of Julius Caesar. The next time Cleopatra met Mark Antony, in 42 BC, she was 28 years old and he was over 40. Mark Antony had taken over the eastern section of the Roman empire and was to spend a great deal of time in Egypt over the next 16 years.

Living it up

Mark Antony and Cleopatra's relationship was a jovial one, as recorded by Plutarch:

> She played at dice with him, drank with him, hunted with him; and when he exercised in arms, she was there to see. At night she would go rambling with him to disturb and torment people at their doors and windows, dressed like a servant-woman, for Anthony also went in servant's disguise . . . However, the Alexandrians in general liked it all well enough, and joined good-humouredly and kindly in his frolic and play.

Over the next four years of the relationship, Cleopatra bore twins: Alexander Helios (the sun) and Cleopatra Selene (the moon). Antony acknowledged paternity of both children and actually offered Alexander in marriage to the king of Armenia's daughter in an attempt to appease a quarrel. The king of Armenia refused, and Antony attacked him in 34 BC. That taught him.

In 37 BC, on his way to invade Parthia, Antony enjoyed a rendezvous with Cleopatra, even though Octavian had married Antony to Octavian's sister Octavia as a means of preventing Antony from returning to Egypt. Despite this, from then on Alexandria was Antony's home and Cleopatra was his life. Antony married Cleopatra in 36 BC in Antioch in North Syria, where he dressed as Osiris and she dressed as Isis.

Shortly after this wedding, Cleopatra gave birth to another son, Ptolemy Philadelphus, whom Antony also acknowledged. In 34 BC, Antony made Alexander Helios the king of Armenia, Cleopatra Selene the queen of Cyrenaica and Crete, and Ptolemy Philadelphus the king of Syria.

The beginning of the end

Antony completely abandoned his Roman wife, Octavia, which upset the Romans and Octavian. After three years, Octavian decided to rule alone and turned on Cleopatra and Antony. In 31 BC, Antony's forces fought the Romans in a sea battle off the coast of Actium (northern Greece), aided by Cleopatra and 60 Egyptian ships.

When Cleopatra saw that Antony's cumbersome, badly manned galleys were losing to the Romans' lighter, swifter boats, she fled the scene. Antony abandoned his men to follow her. Although they may have prearranged their retreat, the Romans saw it as proof that Antony was enslaved by his love of Cleopatra, unable to think or act on his own.

Love does not conquer all

In 30 BC, Octavian reached Alexandria, and Mark Antony greeted him with his slowly diminishing soldiers and navy. As soon as the navy saw the Romans, they saluted with their oars and sailed over to join the other side, shortly followed by the desertion of the cavalry and infantry – leaving Antony alone. Cleopatra, now afraid, locked herself in her tomb and sent word to Antony that she was dead! Clearly, things were backfiring.

Antony, feeling somewhat unstable, tried to kill himself, only to mess it up and inflict an eventually fatal wound. While he was bleeding to death, he heard that Cleopatra was in fact alive and demanded that his body be taken to her immediately. When Antony arrived at the tomb, Cleopatra was too afraid to open the door. She and her two serving women let down ropes from a window and pulled Antony up. Distraught, Cleopatra laid Antony on her bed and he died in her arms.

Octavian, meanwhile, had invaded Alexandria and taken control of Cleopatra's palace, with the intention of taking Cleopatra back to Rome and dragging her through the streets in chains. Octavian and his men marched to the tomb, but Cleopatra wouldn't let him in. Instead they negotiated through the closed door, Cleopatra demanding that her kingdom be given to her children.

Meeting Antony for the first time

Julius Caesar, Cleopatra's lover, had just been assassinated, and Mark Antony had taken over control of the eastern part of the Roman empire. Mark Antony sailed to Tarsus (in modern-day Turkey) and summoned Cleopatra to him to interrogate her about her role in assisting his enemies.

The meeting of Antony and Cleopatra is described by Plutarch, writing between AD 46 and 127. It was the stuff of fairytales – and all from the elaborate imagination of the enigmatic Cleopatra. Cleopatra arrived at Tarsus in a boat. To be honest, this was more than a boat: It was a barge with a gilded stern, purple sails, and silver oars. Cleopatra's maids, dressed as sea nymphs, sailed the boat. Cleopatra herself was dressed as Venus, the goddess of love, and she reclined under a golden canopy, fanned by boys dressed in Cupid costumes. Antony, a simple soldier, was impressed by this blatant display of luxury, just as Cleopatra had intended. Cleopatra refused to leave the boat and entertained Antony on the boat that night. This gave her the upper hand by ensuring that they met on Egyptian territory.

The next night, Antony invited Cleopatra to supper, hoping to outdo her in magnificence. He failed, but joked about it in a good-natured way. Like Julius Caesar before him, Antony was enthralled with Cleopatra, becoming the second great love in Cleopatra's life. First impressions clearly count.

As juicy as this story is, it needs to be taken with a pinch of salt. Plutarch, like most authors, wrote with an agenda and may have exaggerated the decadence of the story to highlight the exotic setting and the passions of Antony and Cleopatra. Of course, when Shakespeare incorporates these details into his play, all suddenly becomes fact, of sorts.

While Cleopatra was distracted at the door, Octavian's men set up ladders and climbed through the window. Cleopatra instantly tried to stab herself, but was disarmed and taken prisoner along with her children. Octavian allowed Cleopatra to arrange Antony's funeral, and Cleopatra buried Antony in royal style. After the funeral Cleopatra was so grief stricken, she stayed in bed.

Cleopatra was determined to die to be with her beloved Antony and arranged for an asp (a venomous snake) to be brought to the tomb in a basket of figs, all in secrecy without the knowledge of the Romans. The guards even checked the basket and found nothing suspicious, so they allowed it to be given to the queen. When she reached into the basket the asp bit her and she died. In her final moments, Cleopatra wrote a letter to Octavian asking if she could be buried in Antony's tomb.

Octavian ran to the tomb, but it was too late – Cleopatra was dead. The only person in the way of Octavian's control of Egypt was Caesarion, whom Octavian promptly disposed of. Egypt was now open for Roman rule.

The Romans are coming

Cleopatra's suicide in 30 BC left the path to Egypt open for the Romans to take control. However, Egypt was not made a Roman province, in the true sense of the word, straight away. Octavian (later the Emperor Augustus), used Egypt as a personal estate, governed by an official answerable to him alone. Egypt became the primary provider of grain to the Roman empire and was known in contemporary records as Rome's bread basket.

The emperors who followed Augustus on the throne of Egypt attempted to rule in traditional Egyptian fashion, building temples to traditional Egyptian gods, and even representing themselves as Egyptian kings while performing traditional rituals.

Although the Egyptian culture was unrecognisable because of the Hellenistic invasion by Alexander, many of the Egyptian cults were maintained under the Romans. In AD 394, Philae temple was still in use and in fact this carried the last inscription written in hieroglyphs in Egypt. It was to be another 1,400 years before anyone could read it again (see Chapter 11).

Part III
Living Life to the Full: Culture and Beliefs

The 5th Wave   By Rich Tennant

AT THE EMBALMERS' WORKSHOP

"Wait a minute—if this jar's supposed to hold the body's liver, what's your lunch doing in it?"

In this part . . .

The ancient Egyptians enjoyed parties, feasts, and generally living it up with their mates. Loads of evidence of these parties exist, including menus and lists of the dancers and musicians who attended. For daytime entertainment the Egyptians played board games, listened to stories, went hunting, and participated in sports.

Although relatively hygienic, the Egyptians were beset with disease and illnesses, and the doctors recorded many of the symptoms, diagnoses, and 'cures' – most of which makes our own health service look the biz. From parasitic worms, to teeth abscesses, it's surprising they could concentrate on building pyramids and temples at all!

Ancient Egyptian religion was very imaginative and diverse, with hundreds of gods, different practices, beliefs, and rituals – many dependant on the location. Although the everyday Egyptians weren't allowed to enter the elaborate temples which still dominate the landscape, they worshipped in their homes.

Many of the Egyptians' funerary beliefs were focused on prolonging life for eternity in the underworld, and they preserved bodies and possessions, enabling us to build a compelling image of their life and beliefs.

Chapter 7

Enjoying Food and Entertainment

. . . .

In This Chapter

▶ Storytelling for young and old

▶ Playing games

▶ Training for sport and battle

▶ Hunting and fishing

▶ Planning parties – entertainment, food, and drink

. . . .

*E*veryone likes to have a good time, and the same can be said of the ancient Egyptians. In an age without televisions, radios, or computers, the Egyptians had to find other ways of keeping themselves entertained at the end of a long working day.

And the working week, even for the elite and top craftsmen, was indeed long – ten days on, two days off – with the working day consisting of all daylight hours. Perhaps the poorer classes worked even longer, more difficult schedules, but because they left no records, historians may never know. Chapter 2 offers more details of the day-to-day activities of these ancient Egyptians.

Due to the heat, a midday siesta time was likely, although small details – no matter how important they were to the ancient Egyptians – are unrecorded. With these working conditions, unwinding at the end of the day or the week was extremely important.

Some of the evening and weekend entertainment for the ancient Egyptians was remarkably similar to today's pastimes. Families spent time together, friends met for a gossip and a couple of beers, and people played board games, listened to music, told stories, and enjoyed more active pursuits, such as wrestling and (during the New Kingdom) chariot racing and hunting. The following sections explore some of the most popular ways that ancient Egyptians kicked back and offer some ways in which you can relax like an Egyptian.

Nourishing the Grey Matter

Like any community throughout history, the ancient Egyptians had sporty people and more passive people. Not all Egyptians were physically active, and some chose more studious ways of passing their time, especially if they were literate.

Studious pursuits were not solely the choice of the rich, and physical pastimes were not only for the poor. In fact, the king in most periods was an active hunter. The more studious pastimes were, however, for the literate – who were primarily the elite – but that is not to say a poor illiterate member of the community did not enjoy sketching in the sand, telling stories or playing board games rather than wrestling and stick fighting!

Literacy was very low in ancient Egypt with only 1–5 per cent of the population being able to read and write. (Even today, the estimated literacy rate in modern Egypt is estimated at 25 per cent.) This is a difficult statistic for many to swallow, as the UK today is very highly literate (99.9 per cent). Many of today's pastimes depend on literacy, including reading, crosswords, sudoku, and writing.

One example of an Egyptian crossword has been discovered. Although this crossword didn't have clues, it was discovered with the grid filled in and with all the words interlocking as they do in the modern world. Although sudoku did not exist in ancient Egypt, papyri with a number of mathematical and geometrical riddles, which some Egyptian scribe may have puzzled over for many hours, do exist as well.

Of the numerous Egyptian scribes, one chap is particularly noteworthy: Kenhirkhepshef lived in Deir el Medina during the 19th dynasty (see the Cheat Sheet for a historical timeline) and had a particular interest in the past. He spent his free time, rather like me actually, researching Egyptian history. He wrote an accurate list in chronological order of all the kings of the New Kingdom. (Unfortunately, his list is unusable today because he excluded unpopular kings and those who ruled a divided country.) Researchers believe Kenhirkhepshef may have visited a number of the mortuary temples and gathered information from the priests working there.

Kenhirkhepshef was also a linguist and had a list of official governmental titles that started with 'chief'. Sadly he didn't explain what the titles entailed, and many of them are only known from this list.

Other scribes spent their evenings and weekends writing love poetry. Although some people believe these poems were written by love-sick men and women, they're grammatically correct and cleverly written with rhyming couplets and word play. As such, they're more likely to have been penned by professional scribes. Sadly the authors of this love poetry are anonymous. Some of them were probably well known at the time, and their work was probably oft repeated in the light of the fire.

Telling Tall Tales

Evidence suggests that the ancient Egyptians loved tall stories – although their methods of storytelling and the identities of these storytellers are unknown today. Storytellers did not need to be literate to tell good tales, so they may have hailed from all walks of life.

Stories were most likely told orally. The problem with any kind of oral tradition is that each time a story is told, it changes depending on the story teller's personal agenda, skills and interests – as well as the audience, which included all age groups. Oral traditions do not have rules. As a result, stories can and did take the form of poetry, sing-alongs, or even idle gossip – all of which can provide hours of entertainment.

Some scribes luckily chose to record stories that were part of this oral tradition. The scribes may have felt they were contributing to their heritage by recording these stories. A number of stories have survived, including:

- ✔ The Journey of Sinuhe, in which a man flees Egypt at the death of the king and settles in an Asiatic town, rising in power until he is a chief.

- ✔ The Doomed Prince, in which a young noble's death is foreseen as being caused by one of three fates. Throughout his life he has close shaves with these fates.

- ✔ The Tale of the Eloquent Peasant, in which a simple peasant appeals at the law courts on a daily basis, impressing the king with his eloquence. This long story illustrates that low status does not mean ignorance.

- ✔ The Shipwrecked Sailor (see sidebar), in which a sailor is marooned on an island inhabited by a divine serpent many metres long.

- ✔ The Five Tales of Magic and Wonder, which describe five separate events staged in the Old Kingdom royal court, during which magicians perform various amazing feats of magic for the king's entertainment.

- ✔ The Tale of the Two Brothers, which tells the story of the separation of two brothers because of the treachery of the older brother's wife.

- ✔ The Tale of the (other) Doomed Prince, which tells the story of a man who is foretold the method of his death. The tale recounts his journey and how he nearly comes a cropper on more than one occasion. He also strangely enough meets a princess in a tower who throws her hair down as a means of escape. Does the name Rapunzel mean anything to anyone?

The shipwrecked sailor

A young sailor encountered on the docks a sea captain who had just returned from an unsuccessful expedition. The captain was concerned about explaining himself to the king, so the sailor tried to console the captain by telling his own story of an expedition to the copper mines on a ship with 150 of the best sailors in Egypt.

One day the young sailor and his shipmates encountered a storm that destroyed the ship and killed all the crew, except the sailor who was washed up on an island. He sat alone under a tree suffering from shock for three days. When he came to, he went in search of nourishment and found that the island was abundant in figs, grain, fruit, vegetables, fish, and birds. He loaded up his arms, built a fire, and started to prepare lunch, when he was disturbed by a loud noise.

He initially thought it was a wave from the sea, but the trees shook and the earth moved. The sailor recoiled as he saw a large bearded serpent approaching at speed. Enough to spoil anyone's day!

The snake questioned the sailor as to his presence on the island, but the sailor was too scared to talk, so the snake carried the sailor in his mouth to his lair, where he questioned the sailor again. The sailor recounted what had happened to him and his crew. The snake soothed him and foretold he would remain on the island for four months before a crew he recognised would come to take him back to Egypt.

The snake then told his own story of how he came to be alone on the island. The snake originally lived on the island with 72 other serpents, including his young daughter. One day a star fell from the heavens and burnt the snakes, killing all except the gigantic serpent. He reassured the sailor that although loss hurts at first, the grief disappears with time.

After the four months passed, the sailor spotted a ship on the horizon manned by an Egyptian crew that he recognised. The crew moored, and the snake gave them lots of goodies from the island to take back to Egypt, which the crew promptly loaded onto the ship. The crew then returned to Egypt, and the king summoned the sailor to explain what had happened to his expedition. He was rewarded with land and titles for bringing the goodies from the island. And everyone lived happily ever after!

Playing Board Games

Although a good storyteller can grip a crowd for an hour or so, an evening has many hours to fill. The Egyptians spent many hours playing board games, three of which have survived. These games are known as Senet, Hounds and Jackals, and Mehen – the names surviving down the millennia.

Sadly, the rules for these games have not survived. However, some very bright individuals have come up with rules for them based on the number of squares, the nature of the dice, and the number of pieces.

Have a go at playing the following games – or develop your own alternative rules.

Senet

One of the oldest of the board games is Senet, which means 'game of passing'. Senet is a game of strategy, rather like backgammon. It was played from the Old Kingdom onwards and is often depicted in tombs.

Senet is a two-player game. To play, you need:

- ✔ **Two types of pieces – cones and reels.** Each player chooses which type of piece to use at the start of the game.

- ✔ **A senet board.** Senet boards have a numbered grid of 30 squares arranged in three rows of ten. You can draw and make a Senet board yourself or use the board shown in Figure 7-1.

- ✔ **A set of four 'sticks' or 'knuckle bones'.** The number of squares you move on the Senet board is determined by 'throwing sticks' or 'throwing knuckle bones' – the Egyptian equivalent of casting dice. These four wooden sticks have one plain side and one painted side. The combination of coloured sides visible when you throw the sticks determines the number of squares you move:

  - When only one painted side is visible, move forward one square.

  - When two painted sides are visible, move forward two squares.

  - When three painted sides are visible, move forward three squares.

  - When four painted sides are visible, move forward four squares.

  - When no painted sides are visible, move forward five squares.

You can make your own set of sticks by colouring or painting one side of four ice-lolly or craft sticks.

Figure 7-1:
A sample
Senet board
layout.

1	2	3	4	5	6	7	8	9	10
20	19	18	17	16	15	14	13	12	11
21	22	23	24	25	26	27	28	29	30

Players agree to play with three, five, or seven pieces each. The goal of the game is to be the first to move all your pieces from square 1 to square 30, using the sticks to determine how many spaces you can move on each turn. The following restrictions apply:

- ✔ If Player 1 lands on a square that is occupied by Player 2, the players must swap places: Player 2 must move his or her piece to the square Player 1 started from.
- ✔ All players must land on square 26 before moving off the board.

You and your partner can create other rules and restrictions to make the game more challenging. For example, you may choose to allow players to spilt a roll of 4 between two separate pieces. Or you may decide that players must roll the exact number of spaces to reach square 30 and complete a piece's trek through the board.

Hounds and Jackals

Another popular game from the New Kingdom is Hounds and Jackals – so named because one set of pieces features the heads of jackals and the other hounds. The game is also known as 58 Holes.

Hounds and Jackals is a two-player game. To play, you need:

- ✔ **A game board with two tracks of 30 holes each.** The board can be a flat piece of wood with holes drilled in it – two 'tracks' of 30 holes each. More elaborate 3-D boards are available as well. (The Louvre in Paris has a sculptural board in the shape of a hippo in its collection.)

  Figure 7-2 shows an example layout for a board. You can photocopy this image, stick it onto a ½-inch board and drill holes in each position.
- ✔ **Ten pegs.** Usually five pegs with jackals on the ends and five pegs with hounds on the ends. You can substitute pegs of two different colours.
- ✔ **A set of four sticks.** The number of squares you move on the board is determined by throwing sticks, as the rules for Senet describe.

Each player starts with five pieces (either hounds or jackals). The object of the game is to get all five of your pieces into hole 30, following the track on your half of the board. Each peg needs to go around the track twice to win.

As in Snakes and Ladders, if a player lands in

- ✔ Hole 6, he or she moves directly to hole 20
- ✔ Hole 15 or 25, he or she gets to throw again

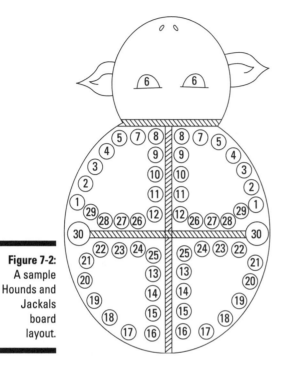

Figure 7-2:
A sample
Hounds and
Jackals
board
layout.

Like Senet, you and your partner can create additional rules and restrictions to make the game more challenging.

Leading a Sporting Life

Some members of the elite preferred more active social lives and participated in a number of sports, including wrestling and weight lifting (with sand bags). While many of these activities were part of military training, it is likely that some individuals chose to train purely to improve their physique and physical strength.

Among a number of children's toys at the town of Kahun in the Faiyum region, archaeologists discovered a few balls made of strips of animal skin stitched together and stuffed with dried grass. Whether the games that children played with these balls were ever played by adults is unknown, but I am sure some people like to think that football was not only 'the beautiful game' but also 'the ancient game'.

The following sections discuss popular forms of recreation for both the Egyptian elite and the masses.

Charioteering

The chariot was not introduced to Egypt until the late Second Intermediate Period. Kings and some noble men of the New Kingdom were trained from young boyhood in charioteering in preparation for the battlefield. See Chapter 4 for more on historical periods.

Chariots in ancient Egypt were small and light. Drawn by two horses, these vehicles carried two people – the driver and a spearman or archer. A king or nobleman was trained in both roles.

Mostly boys were trained in charioteering skills, but at the site of Amarna, the small daughters of Akhenaten (see Chapter 4) are shown on tomb and temple walls driving their own chariots – an image which is unique to this period. A small sketch in the Cairo Museum shows a queen, thought to be Hatshepsut, driving a chariot and firing arrows at the enemy, which indicates perhaps that some royal women picked up charioteering skills. At Amarna, most of the elite members of society owned a chariot, because it was their main mode of transport.

After an Egyptian mastered steering a chariot, evidence suggests that chariot races took place. Nothing of the calibre of *Ben Hur*, but racing nonetheless. Just outside Malkata, the Theban palace of Amenhotep III, is a temporary lodge called the Kom el 'Abd, overlooking a very long, straight road. The road was cleared for the use of high-speed chariot races, in which no doubt Amenhotep III participated. These races were probably semi-private events, only seen by people living at Malkata and nearby.

Target practice

After young princes or military trainees were able to drive chariots, developing archery skills was the next task. Not only was marksmanship essential on the battlefield, but it was useful in the desert while hunting game.

Before being let loose in the desert on potentially dangerous animal targets, marksmen practised in a safe environment. The typical target consisted of a copper sheet set up at shoulder height along a course. The charioteer rode at speed and tried to hit the target with arrows. A stone block in Luxor Museum shows the 18th-dynasty king Amenhotep II using one of these targets. He is particularly skilled and has hit the target with five arrows, each one hitting with such force that it protruded through to the other side.

Hunting

Tomb scenes of the elite often depict the deceased hunting in the desert for gazelles, bulls and lions as well as in the marshes for fish and birds. While these images carry a funerary symbolism of virility and fertility, they also reflect the fact that hunting and fishing were popular activities for ancient Egyptians. Additional imagery in temples depicts hunting scenes as well, indicating that these pastimes probably crossed social boundaries between the elite and royalty.

In the desert

Egypt is surrounded by land on both the east and the west bank of the Nile and supported lions, gazelles, deer, and bulls. Evidence shows that many of these animals may have been caught and housed in large pens to make the hunting safer for the king and the elite. Rather like a safari park – but not with conservation as a goal! The hunter rode along in a chariot, probably with a driver, and sometimes accompanied by pet dogs that retrieved the felled animals.

Images of the king and elite hunting normally show the kings hunting with bow and arrow, although they could possibly have hunted with spears or – if they wanted to catch the animals alive – lassoes.

A wonderful scene is depicted at Medinet Habu – Ramses III's mortuary temple in Thebes – which shows the king in the midst of a wild bull hunt. The king is riding his chariot with the reins of the horses tied around his waist, leaving his hands free to fire arrows at the animals. He has become so excited by the hunt that he has thrown his leg over the front of the chariot to give him more support while bracing himself against the force of the bow. One bull that he has hit is already collapsed in the reeds.

Most hunting was for food, and catches provided tasty meals for the king, noblemen and their families. The skins of lions were often used for luxurious throws in the palace or home. Evidence suggests that Ramses II and III actually had a pet lion, which perhaps they hunted themselves.

In the marshes

Hunting in the marshes was equally popular among the elite, particularly in the favoured holiday marshland spot of the Faiyum. This area became so popular that in the New Kingdom, a royal palace and a harem were built here so that hunters could stay overnight in luxurious surroundings. The Faiyum supported a lively array of wildlife, although visitors to the site were interested only in the fowl and fish.

Many tomb scenes depict marsh hunting scenes in which the tomb owner stands on a small papyrus skiff or boat holding a throw stick in his raised arm. To scare the birds from the marshes, a trained cat or a servant was sent into the bushes to startle the birds. As they flew into the air, the tomb owner threw the stick, felling two or three birds with each stick. The trained cat or servant then went into the marshes and retrieved the birds. (I would love to see how they trained the cat to do anything!)

Birds caught by hunting with a throw stick were prepared for eating (feathers were plucked from the bird and it was hung out to dry in the sun). However, this method of fowling was not employed on a daily basis for food production. To catch birds for food, ancient Egyptians used a large drag-net thrown over the marshland, which was pulled in and gathered birds in its path.

Fishing

The Nile and its canals were abundant with many types of fish, so fishing was a popular pastime. Fishing as a sport was carried out using spears. The fisherman stood on the papyrus skiff, waited for a fish to swim by, and at the most opportune moment thrust the spear into the water. In tomb scenes, the tomb owner is always shown with two fish on the end of his spear, showing that he can not only catch one fish but two with one thrust.

In addition to vegetables, fish was the primary food of most Egyptians. When fishing for food, the Egyptians threw large nets into the river and dragged in vast quantities of fish. Their catch was then prepared for eating by eviscerating the fish, drying them in salt, and leaving them in the sun.

Throwing Big Bashes

The Egyptians were a sociable bunch and had frequent get-togethers to share gossip and to eat and be merry. Not much information on get-togethers for the lower classes exists, but parties for the elite are well recorded.

Many images on New Kingdom non-royal tombs show the elite enjoying themselves at elaborate banquets, entertained by musicians and dancers. Although these images are of particular feasts associated with the funeral and funerary festivals, they no doubt reflect the types of parties that took place in the houses of the rich and influential.

These tomb images provide several intriguing details:

- Guests are seated, normally with the men and women segregated. This may be an oddity of the funerary scenes, but it is still noteworthy.

- Guests are given as much food and alcohol (wine and beer) as they can stomach. In fact, in one tomb there is a delightful image of a woman purging herself into a bucket after over-indulging.

- Teams of servants attend to guests. Everything at these banquets was designed to make the guests feel pampered and special. Servants are shown filling goblets, distributing food, and adorning the guests in floral collars and perfume cones.

Perfume cones were structures made of animal fat impregnated with scented oils. The cones were placed on guests' heads and emitted a pleasant aroma as they melted. A combination of flowers and lard – hmmm, nice! After the cones melted, servants replaced them with fresh ones.

Making music

The hosts of these parties provided entertainment, often in the form of a band – the Egyptian equivalent of the infamous party DJ. Sadly the music they played is lost, but they may have had a couple of groaners in their repertoire, on a par with today's 'Birdie Song' and 'Agadoo'.

The musicians were normally in small groups of either men or women. It was unusual for the groups to be mixed. The group played a mixture of instruments including lutes, flutes, clappers (ivory sticks tied at the end that clattered together when shaken), and harps (both small hand-held versions and full-sized examples). A small hand drum or a group of men or women clapping rhythmically kept the rhythm going.

No evidence exists suggesting that nobles played instruments in public; banquet musicians were hired especially for the occasion. However, it is possible that as a means of passing the time the elite learned to play instruments. In the sixth dynasty mastaba tomb (see Chapter 13) at Saqqara, Mereruka's wife, a princess no less, sits on her bed playing a harp to entertain her husband, who is also seated on a bed.

Dancing

An Egyptian would not have jumped onto the table and danced the night away to tunes from the party band. Music was typically accompanied by a group of dancers, who, like the musicians, were hired for the occasion.

Dancing was a very erotic form of entertainment. The performers were normally naked, except for an elaborate collar and a decorative belt or loincloth. Some dancers are shown in tomb drawings with perfume cones on their heads, indicating they also smelt nice and gave the audience a waft of perfume as they flitted by. Many dancers used their hair as a tool by flicking it from side to side; some tomb images even show weights tied into the hair, ensuring it moved in the correct way.

Perusing the party menu

Food was a major part of elaborate banquets, and fortunately a lot of information still exists.

Images of divine offering tables show what food the Egyptians considered good enough for the gods. Coupled with food left in tombs and described in offering lists, a detailed list of food that may have been on the menu at a posh party emerges.

Although for the rest of the population it was a luxury, meat was a major part of an elite meal. Some of the cuts would be distasteful to diners today; the ancient Egyptians refused to waste any part of the animal. Some of the most popular meat was ox (including the head, tongue, and entrails), goose, pigeon, and fish.

The meat was accompanied by

- Vegetables, including cucumber, onions, and lettuce
- Pulses and nuts, including lentils, chick peas, watermelon seeds, and almonds
- Herbs, including coriander and garlic
- Fruit, including figs, raisins, grape seeds, dom-palm nut (a type of fruit from the dom-palm tree), dates, and pomegranate leaves (and no doubt the rest of the fruit as well).

Baking the Hovis way

Most of the depictions of parties also show hosts serving various breads and cakes to the guests, including honey cakes and a type of fruit loaf. Bread was the staple of the Egyptian diet, and everyone, rich or poor, ate lots of it. Bread is also included on all offering tables and lists, showing that it was a food fit for the gods.

Different types of bread existed, including varieties made from emmer wheat and barley. The tomb of Tutankhamun even held fruit loaves containing berries from the Christ-thorn plant.

Egyptians baked various types of bread in different shapes (triangles and ovals were common) to make identification easier. Sadly, the exact meanings of these shapes are not known today.

To facilitate the grinding of grain into flour, bakers or women in the households may have added ground stone (quartzite or granite) or sand to their grind stones, which acted as an abrasive and produced flour in half the time. Very productive, but these inclusions in the bread caused excessive wear on the teeth of the Egyptians (see Chapter 8 for the gory details).

Brewing beer

No party is complete without a bar, and the ancient Egyptians loved their alcohol. Their parties would have been abundant in wine and beer. Beer was a staple of the Egyptian diet and was even included in the state wages and rations.

Beer was made in a similar way to bread. It was somewhat thicker than the beer or ale you're familiar with today and may have contained a number of impurities. Egyptian beer was made from stale or partially baked barley or emmer bread (a dough high in yeast), which was placed on a screen over a jar. Water was poured over the bread until it dissolved and fell into the jar, where it was left to ferment. Once fermented, the liquid was then decanted into amphora jars for storage or transportation.

The resulting beer was not overly alcoholic if drunk in moderation, but the ancient Egyptians had one too many on occasion.

Where did I get this traffic cone?

Most people at some point have had a couple of drinks too many at a Christmas party or New Year bash and have gaps in their recollection of what happened. Proving nothing is new, one chap from 19th-dynasty Deir el Medina, probably had more than the average recollection problem. Paneb had a reputation of being a womaniser, a criminal, and a drunk. From a series of legal accusations written by one of his enemies, historians can fill in some of the alcohol-related gaps for him.

On one occasion after a few beers with friends, Paneb got into an argument with his elderly adopted father Neferhotep, which ended in Paneb chasing Neferhotep home:

Charge concerning his running after ... Neferhotep, although it was him who *reared him. And he [Neferhotep] closed his doors before him, and he [Paneb] took a stone and broke his doors. And they caused men to watch over Neferhotep because he [Paneb] said 'I will kill him in the night'.*

Reports also indicate that Paneb horrified a number of his co-workers at the construction site of the royal tombs. At the end of a long day, after the empty sarcophagus had just been placed into the tomb, Paneb got drunk and sat on top of the sarcophagus, singing. Although no doubt egged on by his mates, Paneb's actions would have been seen as the worst sacrilege. Now, if only his song were known! Maybe a little ditty about chariot racers?

For the more adventurous beer drinker, flavours were added to the basic mix, including dates, spices, or honey. The sugar in the dates and honey accelerated fermentation. When the Egypt Exploration Society prepared batches using the ancient recipe, the resulting beverage was found to be very sweet but not unpleasant.

Enjoying wine

Although beer was the staple alcoholic beverage in ancient Egypt, in the New Kingdom, wine was very popular, especially among the elite. Wine was a luxurious alternative to beer and was saved for special occasions.

A number of vineyards existed in this region, and many of the local farmers produced wine. Athenaeus wrote in 200 AD that Egyptian wines were 'pale, pleasant, aromatic, and mildly astringent, with an oily quality'.

Just as in the modern world, each amphora of wine was labelled with the date of the wine, the vineyard, and the vintner. Other labels from the palace of Malkata at Thebes, the home of Amenhotep III, also add what type of wine was in the jar, including 'blended', 'wine for offerings', 'wine for taxes', 'wine for a happy return', and 'wine for merry-making'. All of which indicates that the later Egyptians were truly wine connoisseurs.

The process of wine making was very similar to that in some small modern vineyards. The basic steps include

- ✔ Picking the grapes

- ✔ Treading the grapes in vats of clay, wood, or stone

- ✔ Placing the crushed mulch in large sheets of linen, which were twisted to wring out every last drop of juice

- ✔ Allowing the grape juice to ferment in pottery jars

- ✔ Transferring the fermented juice to racked jars that were stoppered with perforated seals, which allowed carbon monoxide to escape

- ✔ Enjoying the wine after a short period of fermentation

A rare variety of wine known as Shedeh was made from grapes, but was heated, like mulled wine. If served this at a party, guests knew their host was both rich and sophisticated.

Chapter 8

Staying Healthy: Diseases and Medicine

In This Chapter

▶ Meeting the doctors

▶ Combining medicine and magic

▶ Diagnosing illnesses and diseases

▶ Curing ailments

Disease is something that plagues every society (pun intended) – ancient and modern.

Medical papyri and mummified remains provide ample evidence of the diseases from which the ancient Egyptians suffered. These remnants also help paint a clear picture of the medical profession in Pharaonic Egypt, including some ill-conceived treatments as well as some surprisingly effective cures. By the end of this chapter, I'm sure you'll never complain about the Health Service again!

In this chapter, you meet the ancient Egyptian physicians, consult their records, and marvel at the ingenuity – and flat-out bizarreness – of many of the cures, some of which form the basis of modern medicine.

Examining Egypt's Overall Health

Numerous surviving medical records, human remains, and even a close study of the settlements can give a detailed view of the general health of the Egyptians.

By modern standards, the ancient Egyptians would be unhealthy, but much of this was due to their living conditions. In many of the settlements, people lived in very close contact, with more than ten people living in a single four-room house.

Evidence in the workmen's village at Amarna indicates the rampant presence of bed bugs, fleas, and rats – all of which aid the spread of disease. Additional evidence suggests that a plague (similar to the bubonic plague) spread throughout the city of Amarna during the 18th dynasty, killing many people including most of the royal family (see Chapter 4).

Other epidemics probably occurred due to the crowded living conditions, but they are difficult to trace in the archaeological record, especially if they weren't as fatal as the bubonic plague.

The average Egyptian had a tough life and probably suffered from one or all the following ailments:

- ✔ Dental abscesses, which resulted in tooth loss and dissolution of the jaw bone
- ✔ Parasitic intestinal worms, the most common being bilharzia
- ✔ Breathing disorders due to the sandy environment
- ✔ Osteoarthritis
- ✔ Blindness, especially among the workmen who constructed the tombs of the kings

Based on the study of the thousands of mummies from Egypt, the average age at death was only 36 years, although a number of exceptions exist. The individuals who did live into their 40s, 50s, and 60s, however, came from all walks of life, so status and wealth were not necessarily factors in life expectancy. Living to a ripe old age was more luck than judgement; the numerous fatal diseases and infections affected *all* Egyptians.

Becoming an Egyptian Physician

Becoming a physician in ancient Egypt involved study and training – in both medical procedures and religious ceremony. The following sections explore the process of becoming a doctor.

Practising magical medicine

Unfortunately, the medical practice that the ancient Egyptian people had to endure was not totally scientific. They were a superstitious population who believed that many ailments had a supernatural cause – the vengeance of a deity, an evil spirit, or the evil eye cast by an enemy.

As a result, patients turned to gods as well as physicians in times of illness. Practical medicine was very closely tied to religion and was often accompanied by religious incantations recited by medically trained priests. Most physicians were in fact priests who used magic and incantations to supplement practical medicine in an effort to appease the spirit or god. Priests were held in high esteem because they conversed with the divine on a daily basis.

The priests of some deities were more inclined than others to turn to medicine. The most important deities associated with medicine were

- **Sekhmet,** the lioness-headed goddess of war, epidemics, and plagues
- **Selqet,** the scorpion goddess, whose priests were approached to treat bites and stings from venomous reptiles, scorpions, and tarantulas
- **Thoth,** the ibis-headed god of knowledge, who was often accredited with writing the healing formulae

Most professions were passed on from father to son (refer to Chapter 2), so some priestly families who turned their hand to medicine held the profession for generations. A well-trained and effective physician was no doubt busy, well paid, and respected within the community. Neighbouring countries held Egyptian doctors in high esteem, and records show that foreign kings requested the treatment of an Egyptian doctor.

Medical training

In order to qualify as an elite physician, a young medical student was trained in the *House of Life*, an unusual institution of learning that provided medical, scribal, and priestly training, as well as housing an extensive library. See Chapter 2 for more insight into the House of Life.

Medical training and priestly training probably went hand in hand. Most House of Life institutions were attached to temples. This was the case at Bubastis, Edfu, Amarna, and Kom Ombo. The most famous House of Life was set up by Imhotep (the builder of the step pyramid at Saqqara) at Memphis; it was in use from the Old Kingdom until the Graeco-Roman period – a period of more than 2,000 years.

Although doctors were formally trained, they did not need to pass exams in order to practice. Like today's medical profession, a strict hierarchy according to ability and experience was in place:

- *Senenu* (**lay physicians**) were the lowest-ranking doctor. They were often scribes who could read medical texts.

- *Kherep senenu* were controllers of doctors and oversaw the work of a number of senenu physicians.

- *Sau* (**magic physicians**) were generally priests of Sekhmet, who were medically qualified, but only treated individuals whom the goddess had punished in some way.

- *Shepherd of the Anus of Pharaoh* was a spectacular title for the physician who gave enemas to the king.

- *Specialists* were doctors who focused on one particular ailment, much like a medical professional today. Ancient Egyptian specialties included eyes, teeth, mouth, stomach pain, and 'uncertain diseases'.

Rather than a student choosing and pursuing a branch of medicine as a career, the position was dictated by the skills held. Some doctors were therefore more qualified than others.

Equipping the physician's office

After physicians were trained, they needed to establish a practice.

Full-time priests with medical training were resident in the temples. They no doubt only had a small number of patients whom they treated in the House of Life. Other physicians who were not priests had to set up independently and treat the people in their villages, perhaps only on a part-time basis. A physician could also be employed by a rich household. Personal physician would have been a more satisfactory position to hold than village doctor.

Doctors also needed to collect a set of instruments with which to practise their art. In a sixth-dynasty tomb at Saqqara, belonging to Qar, the senior physician of the royal palace, a complete set of surgical tools was discovered, including 30 scalpels and tweezers, which seem to be the primary tools for most treatments.

The temple of Kom Ombo features an image of a complete set of medical tools, which corresponds with the items in the tomb of Qar. A corresponding list on the Edwin Smith Papyrus (a medical papyrus) contains the following items:

- A rush (a plant stem with a sharpened end, used with a knife for cutting treatments)
- A fire drill (two wooden sticks to rub together to burn growths)
- A knife/chisel
- A cupping glass to create a vacuum on the skin
- A thorn (to burst blisters)
- Heated broken glass (for eye treatments – ow!)
- Swabs, tampons, and linen material
- Knives, salve spoons, and mortars

Most of these instruments seem sensible enough and are still used today. For example, popping blisters with a sharp instrument (like a thorn) is commonplace, and burning off warts is an effective way of getting rid of them. Indeed, the only item on the list that seems slightly dubious is the hot broken glass used to treat eye conditions. It doesn't bear thinking about; even if swabs and linen pads could mop up whatever comes out, this treatment would make your eyes more than water!

Two top docs

More than 100 ancient Egyptian physicians are known by name, all of them from the elite of society. Two stand out from these known doctors:

Hesy-re is the first known physician in history, dating back to the third dynasty. Hesy-re held the title of Chief of Dentists and Physicians and was clearly a man of high position in the royal court. His tomb is located just north of the Step pyramid of Djoser.

Peseshet was the only female physician known from Egyptian history, living in the fourth dynasty. She was titled Lady Overseer of the Lady Physicians. Although no other female physicians are known until the Ptolemaic period, the fact that Peseshet oversaw lady doctors suggests enough female doctors existed to require an overseer.

To charge or not to charge?

Although loads of information about ancient Egyptian medicine and doctors exists, no surviving information explains how much certain treatments cost or how services were paid for. No evidence exists that the Government hired state physicians to treat the ailments of the populace, as British general practitioners do. The only exception to this appears to be at the workmen's village of Deir el Medina (see Chapter 2 for more on this village). The Government provided the physicians at this location to ensure only that the workmen were fit to build the tombs. The state paid the Deir el Medina doctors a lower wage than all other workers at the site. Perhaps they subsidised their low wages through charging their patients.

Egypt did not have a monetary system until Alexander arrived in 332 BC, so patients receiving treatment probably paid their doctors in grain, livestock, linen, or craft, depending on the patient's profession, wealth, and satisfaction with the cure. If only you could purchase prescriptions today with a goat and a bag of flour, the pharmacy would be a much more colourful place to visit!

Visiting the Doctor

After they were trained and equipped, new physicians could start practising.

More than 1,200 ancient Egyptian medical records have survived, giving detailed insight into what a consultation with a physician was like. These medical papyri include

- A professional medical oath, similar to the Hippocratic oath
- A description of the process of interviewing patients regarding symptoms and conducting physical examinations
- Information about pregnancy and gynaecology (see the section 'Considering Women's Health', later in this chapter, for more details)
- Descriptions of wounds and diseases of the eye, skin, and anus
- Descriptions of bites from humans, pigs, and hippopotami (the life of ancient Egyptian postmen was clearly a lot more dangerous!)
- Details of recommended treatments and prescriptions

Most of the recommended practices are exactly the same as those in use today, but some fascinating differences appear as well, as the following sections discuss.

Examining patients

There were more male than female doctors, so both men and women may have visited male doctors, although the records are silent on this. One of the medical papyri indicates that male doctors dealt with feminine problems.

The Ebers Papyrus (a medical papyrus) describes in detail the procedure for examining a patient. This method of diagnosis is similar to modern practice. The doctor began an examination with an interview, to try to understand the symptoms from which the patient was suffering.

The doctor then monitored the patient's pulse and carried out studies of bodily discharges, such as urine, stools, phlegm, and blood, noting any irregularities. Then the doctor examined the reflexes.

After all examinations were complete, the diagnosis was announced. Because not all illnesses had names, the diagnosis was normally just a statement about whether the doctor would try to treat the patient. The diagnosis came in three forms:

- An ailment that I will treat
- An ailment that I will contend
- An ailment not to be treated

Only 14 of the 48 cases on the Ebers Papyrus were seen to be hopeless and therefore not treatable. Of the other 34 patients, the physicians thought they would just have a go and see what happened.

They then prescribed whatever they felt was most appropriate. The prescriptions were very specific regarding dosage and duration, and all were adjusted according to age, giving a child a smaller dosage than an adult.

Treating patients

Egyptian physicians were more interested in trying to cure ailments than preventing illness.

Of the few surviving records of preventive methods, most seem fairly straightforward, such as bathing regularly. Physicians recommended wearing eye make-up to reflect the sun from the sensitive eye area and to prevent insects from entering the eye. They also advised the burning of incense (see the section 'Alternative methods', later in this chapter, for more on aromatherapy) to help fumigate houses and temples and keep the malaria-carrying mossies away.

Under oath

Most Egyptian physicians were also priests. Because medicine was not these people's main profession, the Egyptian version of the Hippocratic oath is somewhat abbreviated and has a moral element. The tomb of Nenkh-Sekhmet, Chief of Physicians from the fifth dynasty, includes the following declaration:

Never did I do anything evil towards any person.

To modern eyes, many of the cures and treatments used by the ancient Egyptians could be said to break this oath. But in the ancient Egyptians' mind, they were doing their best to cure whatever ailments came their way.

If an ailment was obvious, like a wound or a broken bone, the prescribed cure was purely medicinal. For example, non-infected wounds were sealed by stitching with a needle and thread, and raw meat was placed on wounds on the first day to aid with the healing. (This method is known today as an efficient way to stop bleeding.)

Although the physicians turned to the gods for aid with difficult cases, they did have a remarkable understanding of human anatomy, due to the practice of mummification. The Edwin Smith Papyrus deals with surgical techniques such as amputations, stitching, and removing rogue objects from within the body (such as arrows).

If an ailment was internal with no obvious cause, it was believed to have a supernatural origin, and the gods were addressed for a cure.

Common afflictions – and their cures

Just like today, ancient physicians seemed prepared to treat most things. Whether the prescriptions worked is open to question, but some of the ingredients used, especially for the less serious cases, form the basis of modern medicine and could have been effective. For example, the ancient Egyptians used:

- **Figs for constipation:** High in dietary fibre, figs are still consumed today to aid in digestive regularity.

- **Honey for coughs and cataracts:** In modern medicine, honey is used to treat wounds, burns, and ulcers and is effective against different types of bacteria, acting as an antibiotic.

- **Copper for cleaning wounds:** Today's scientists know that copper prevents bacteria build-up.

- **Poppies to soothe crying children:** The poppy is the basis of narcotics such as opium and morphine and would indeed have made a child drowsy.

✔ **Yeast for digestive disorders:** The Egyptians also applied yeast to boils and ulcers. Today yeast is known to be a good source of vitamin B complex and is effective as an antibiotic.

Digestive disorders

Parasitic worms were one of the most common ailments that ancient Egyptians suffered with. These critters were virtually impossible to treat, and many mummies contain evidence of worms setting up home in internal organs. Parasites included:

✔ Bilharzia, which was caught from water snails in stagnant water. It caused anaemia, loss of appetite, urinary infection, and loss of resistance to other diseases.

✔ Guinea worm, which was caught through drinking contaminated water.

✔ Trichnella and taenia, which were caught by eating undercooked meat.

✔ Tape worm, which was caught via contact with contaminated animals. It resulted in ulcers, within which the tape worm laid eggs.

Enemas seem to have been common, for the elite at least, and this may have eliminated some of the worms, but not many. The Egyptians, sadly, would just have had to live with them and deal with the symptoms.

Other diseases and disorders

For more serious cases, the cures were a little hit and miss and may not have been so successful. Because many of the following diseases are internal conditions, Egyptian doctors were unable to identify the causes and only treated the symptoms, which were pain, coughing, or physical changes. Common diseases and treatments included:

✔ **Tuberculosis:** No cure existed, but doctors eased coughing by having patients inhale mixtures of cream, carob, date kernels, and honey.

✔ **Sand pneumoconiosis:** No cure existed for this condition, caused by breathing in the sand and dust from the surrounding environment. Doctors relied on the same cough-soothing remedies as for tuberculosis.

✔ **Arthritis and osteoarthritis:** Doctors massaged patients with fragrant oils that eased pain.

✔ **Broken bones:** Wooden splints were used for mending long bones. Splints of linen were inserted into the nostril to mend a fractured or broken nose. Plaster casts – made of cow's milk mixed with barley or acacia leaves mixed with gum and water – were used to set breaks or fractures.

✔ **Cataracts:** Doctors applied a mixture of tortoise brain and honey to the eye and recited a religious incantation.

Keep ya jaw on

A treatable bone disorder in ancient Egypt was dislocation of the jaw. The cure for this is described in the Edwin Smith papyrus.

When you examine a man with a lower jaw that is displaced, and you find his mouth open, so that you cannot close his mouth; then you should put your finger on the end of both jaw bones in the inside of his mouth, and put your thumbs under his chin; then you must let them [the displaced joint bone]

fall together in their places . . . bandage them with the imr.w [what this is, is a mystery!] and honey every day until he is better.

None of the records specify why jaw dislocation was so common, but possibly because the biting surfaces of teeth were often very worn (see the section 'Opening Up and Saying "Agh": Dentistry', later in this chapter), many Egyptians ended up moving their mouths in strange ways to be able to chew without excessive pain. Just a theory!

Alternative methods

The Egyptians occasionally used alternative curative methods, which have experienced a recent revival in popularity.

✔ **Aromatherapy.** Incense was very popular in Egypt. It was burnt to sweeten the air and fumigate homes (it also acted as a hallucinogen!). It was also regularly used in temple rituals; records from 1200 BC note that at Karnak temple, 2,189 jars and 304,093 bushels of incense were burnt in a single year!

Incense was used in *temple sanatoria*, dormitories where the ill slept overnight in order to be sent messages from the gods via dreams. The sleep was induced by burning incense that produced hallucinations. The priests then interpreted these dreams and instructed patients as to what tasks they needed to perform in order to be cured. Call me a cynic, but the priests were clearly onto a good thing – the assigned tasks inevitably financed the temple in one way or another.

✔ **Enemas.** One aspect of Egyptian preventive medicine that has made a comeback is the regular use of enemas and colonic irrigation. The Shepherd of the Anus was a specialist who performed enemas, which were practised as a means of maintaining general good health.

Enemas were believed to have been introduced by Thoth, the ibis-headed god of knowledge. The ibis was often observed pushing water into its own rectum with its long beak to evacuate the bowels. The Egyptians followed suit – hopefully with a softer instrument!

✔ **Electroshock.** A more bizarre alternative treatment involved giving the patient electric shocks, using the electric ray *(malapterusus electricus)*, which swam in the Nile from at least the fifth dynasty.

Scribonius Largus (45 AD), physician to Emperor Claudius, records how electric rays were used in early Egyptian medicine for the cure of general pain:

> When they come, one places a living electric ray under the foot of the patient. The patient then stands on a wet beach, covered as long as possible with water, until the foot is asleep up to the level of the knee.

How this technique was supposed to stop pain – other than making you forget about it – I don't know. I can't decide what's worse, the pain or the cure!

✔ **Massage and reflexology.** An image from the fifth-dynasty tomb of Ankhmahor at Saqqara shows patients' hands and feet being massaged by practitioners in order to relieve aches and pains. This is thought to be the earliest image of reflexology in the world.

In a literary papyrus known as Papyrus Westcar, from the Middle Kingdom, the 110-year-old magician Djedi instructed 'his servant at his head to smear him and another to rub his legs', which indicates a form of physiotherapy which perhaps relieved some of the aches and pains of arthritis.

Satisfied customers?

Although the records don't mention the costs of medical examinations and prescriptions, patients most likely paid for a doctor's services. Because money was not used for most of the Pharaonic period, patients would have paid in goods. Whether patients paid before, after, or on the success of a treatment is unknown. However, numerous inscriptions are dedicated to various deities in gratitude for curing diseases. Whether a doctor was thanked with a gift was no doubt left to the discretion of the individual.

Opening Up and Saying 'Agh': Dentistry

The ancient Egyptians suffered greatly from dental problems, and clearly their pain threshold must have been very high considering the horrendous things festering in their mouths.

Not many dentists are known from ancient Egypt, although eight dentists have been identified from the Old Kingdom. Three of these names were discovered in three tombs in August 2006 (although the mummies had long been destroyed by looters). Three of these dentists also held the title of doctor. If dentists didn't always have a separate title, identifying them from doctors is difficult.

Wearing thin

The most common problem for all Egyptians, regardless of status or social position, was wear on the biting surfaces of their teeth. This condition was caused primarily by the quartz, greywacke, amphibole, mica, and sand in the grain, which was then ground into flour. These substances were all present in ancient bread and caused friction against the biting surface of the tooth while chewing. Whether these substances were added by the wind or intentionally is debateable – either way, the wear on their teeth was substantial.

The teeth were worn to such an extent that the enamel completely disappeared, leaving the sensitive inner pulp exposed. This exposed dental pulp then became infected, resulting in abscesses, swelling, and huge amounts of pain. In many instances, the abscesses were in the advanced stages and ate away at the bone of the jaw, resulting in tooth loss.

Little could be done to cure these abscesses other than draining the wound. The doctor or dentist used a flint knife to cut into the infection, and inserted a hollow reed to encourage the flow of pus out of the abscess. The ancient doctors knew that if they left any pus within the abscess it would recur, and they would have to go through the whole process again.

The ancient Egyptians seem to have figured toothache was normal, because the absentee records from Deir el Medina, which record excuses for days off work, show that no one took time off for toothache. (I know for a fact that if I had weeping abscesses, I would take at least a couple of days off!)

On a more positive note, the ancient Egyptians did not suffer from caries (decay) because of the very limited sugar in their diet. The elite sweetened their food with honey, but this was a luxury out of most people's reach. Only a handful of mummies show the start of dental caries, but almost every adult mummy has wear on the biting surface of their teeth.

The quest for fresh breath

With a mouth full of abscesses, the breath of the ancient Egyptians would have been somewhat ripe, to say the least.

The Egyptians did, however, do their best to clean their teeth using the frayed end of a twig. This technique resulted in the highly polished appearance of the teeth of many ancient Egyptian mummies.

The medical records have numerous prescriptions for freshening the breath, including chewing on cinnamon, frankincense, myrrh, and fragrant plants mixed with honey.

Considering Women's Health

Some of the medical papyri focus primarily on the health of women – particularly on fertility, childbirth, and health during pregnancy.

Many of the treatments are based on the idea that a woman is joined from the vagina to the head via a series of tubes. If these tubes are clear, she can become pregnant, and if they are blocked, she can't. Most treatments involve oral medicines or vaginal applications or fumigations.

Specific women's health topics included:

- ✔ **Contraception:** Excrement of crocodile dispersed finely in sour milk or honey and natron was used to avoid pregnancy. Both concoctions were used as a tampon and inserted into the vagina. And I am sure the resulting smell encouraged abstinence – a foolproof form of contraception.

- ✔ **Fertility:** The woman was advised to sit over a mixture of sweet ale and mashed dates. If she vomited, she was sure to give birth in the future; the number of times she vomited equalled the number of children she would have. If she didn't vomit, no children.

- ✔ **Pregnancy test:** The woman was supposed to urinate on barley and emmer wheat. If both of the seeds grew, she would give birth. If the barley grew first, she would give birth to a boy; if the emmer sprouted first, she would give birth to a girl. If neither grew, she was not pregnant. (When this method was recently tested, it didn't determine the sex, but, if a woman is pregnant, the grain does grow within a short period of time. When male urine was used, nothing happened.)

- ✔ **Amenorrhoea:** This is the premature stopping of the menstrual cycle and was 'cured' by giving a women a substance to drink for four days that induced vomiting. If the women vomited blood, her menstrual cycle would start again.

Chapter 9

Worshipping like an Egyptian: Religion

When looking at Egyptian religion, simply knowing where to begin can be difficult. With more than 700 different known gods, the ancient Egyptian population may seem very pious.

However, each god represents a different concept, role, or place where he or she was worshipped. And not every ancient Egyptian worshipped all the gods, all the time. They picked and chose which deity suited specific needs.

This chapter examines the many gods that the king and the priests – as well as everyday Egyptians – worshipped. I explore some of the most notable rituals and practices, including the popular practice of worshipping deceased humans.

Surveying the Pantheon of Egyptian Gods

The Egyptians were a very organised people, in religion as well as in almost everything else. Historians can divide Egyptian religious practice into two forms:

> ✔ **State religion** was closely connected with the king and his divinity. This religious practice was virtually inaccessible to most people. The state gods were worshipped in the large temples that dot Egypt, such as Karnak, Luxor, Abu Simbel, and Abydos. These temples were closed to the public; only the king and the priests were allowed to enter and worship.

✔ **Household religion** developed as a response to the exclusive state religion. Household religion involved a different set of gods. The people (without priests) worshipped these gods in their home (rather than in the temples).

Explaining all those unusual forms

Both state and household religion involved gods of somewhat bizarre form – represented as humans with animal heads, as animals, or as humans with inanimate objects for heads.

The Egyptians did not believe that these odd appearances were how the gods actually looked, however. They believed that deities were formless. The depictions represent the *characteristics* of the deity and his or her role in the pantheon of gods. The nature of the animal or object replacing the god's head gives some information about the god. For example:

✔ **Hathor** was a woman with a cow's head, which represents the mothering, nurturing nature of a cow.

✔ **Sekhmet** was a woman with a lioness's head, which represents the aggressive nature of a lioness.

✔ **Selket** was a woman with a scorpion body and human head, which represents that she is the protector against scorpion and spider bites.

Shifting roles and shapes

Like human beings, the Egyptian deities play numerous roles and take on various characteristics throughout their lives, which means that the same god can be presented in many different ways.

The sun god Ra, for example, is presented in four different ways, depending on the time of day:

✔ **Khepri** is the scarab beetle (or beetle-headed human) that represents the sun at dawn.

✔ **Aten** is the sun disc that represents the light that shines from the sun at noon.

✔ **Re-Horakhti** is a falcon-headed human with a sun-disc headdress that represents the sun on the horizon at dawn and sunset.

✔ **Flesh** is a ram-headed human that represents the sun at sunset.

Basking in the sun's rays

In a country as hot as Egypt, the sun was a particularly powerful force in people's lives. As such, the *solar cult* (worship of deities associated with the solar cycle) was particularly prominent from the Old Kingdom to the Roman period (see Chapters 3, 4, and 6 for more on these various eras).

However, rather than keeping matters simple, the Egyptians named and worshipped many different aspects of the sun god, depending on the time of day and the area where the sun god was worshipped. See the section 'Shifting roles and shapes' for more information.

Additionally, the solar gods were closely connected with the creation of the earth – the sun was the first thing to appear on the mound of creation at the start of time. This means that all solar deities are also creator gods. And as creator deities, they were also closely connected with the funerary cult and the rebirth of the deceased.

Many of the other deities wanted to get in on the solar action in order to increase their wealth and power (although in reality the power was probably coveted by the king or the priests rather than the deities themselves!). Many deities solarised their name by adding Ra to it (for example Amun-Ra). Even the kings wanted to be associated with the sun god and included 'son of Ra' in their kingly titles, showing their divine origins.

Making room for more

To add another dimension to this assortment of gods, the Egyptians were keen to mix and match their gods and make new ones. This goes some way towards explaining why the ancient Egyptians had so many gods.

For example, many gods possessed more than one characteristic and were therefore best represented by two different deities:

- ✔ **Amun-Min** was the combination of a creator god (Amun) and a god of fertility (Min).
- ✔ **Amun-Ra** was the combination of a creator god (Amun) and the solar god (Ra).

Some foreign deities were introduced and combined with an Egyptian god to make them more acceptable to the Egyptian population:

- ✔ **Seth** (the Egyptian god of chaos) combined with **Baal** (Canaanite lightning god).
- ✔ **Hathor** (Egyptian mother goddess) combined with **Anat** (Syrian martial goddess).

✔ **Osiris** (Egyptian god of the dead) combined with **Dionysus** (Greek fertility god).

✔ **Isis** (Egyptian mother goddess) combined with **Aphrodite** (Greek goddess of love).

✔ **Imhotep** (Egyptian god of medicine) combined with **Asklepios** (Greek god of medicine).

Deceit, murder – and forestry

One important Egyptian religious myth is that of Osiris and Seth. It serves as the basis for many of the funerary beliefs of the ancients, as well as explaining the divinity of the king.

Long ago, Osiris ruled Egypt. He was considered an ideal ruler, showing the people how to farm, worship the gods, and obey laws. His brother Seth was jealous and wanted the throne for himself. Seth devised a cunning plan to rid the world of Osiris and snatch the throne. First, he gathered all of Osiris's bodily measurements – height, width, inside leg, hair length, even toenail length. Seth then built a beautiful chest that fitted these measurements exactly.

Seth presented this chest at a banquet to which Osiris was invited and announced that whoever could fit into the chest could keep it. In true Cinderella style, everyone at the banquet tried to squeeze into the chest. Some were too fat, others too tall; some had hair that was too long or too thick. (And I'm sure someone had grotesquely long toenails!) Osiris, of course, fitted perfectly. But before he could gloat about his good fortune, Seth slammed on the lid, nailed it shut, and flung the box into the Nile, drowning the king.

When Osiris's wife Isis heard of Seth's exploits, she went in search of the chest in order to give her husband a decent burial. Her search took her all the way to Byblos (located somewhere in present-day Lebanon), where she learnt that the chest had grown into a tree that had been cut down and carved into a pillar in the palace of the king. After some time she managed to persuade the queen to let her take the pillar back to Egypt. When Isis arrived in Egypt, she lay down for a short nap. While she slept, Seth passed by, recognised the chest, removed the body of Osiris, and chopped it into 14 pieces, which he then scattered around Egypt. (Isis was clearly a very heavy sleeper.)

When Isis awoke, along with her sister Nephthys she initiated a search for Osiris's body parts. The duo were able to locate 13 of the pieces. The final part – Osiris's penis – was never found. Seth had thrown it into the Nile, where a fish promptly ate it.

Isis, however, proved herself a creative lass. After reassembling the collected body parts, she made a new, fully functioning 14th part from clay. She then transformed herself into a kite and flew over the body of Osiris. The breeze from her flapping wings gave him the breath of life, reviving him – just long enough for Isis to become impregnated with Horus. Osiris then died and was banished to the afterlife. Isis was left to raise Horus alone in the Egyptian marshes and to protect him from Seth until he was old enough to take over his father's throne.

Meeting the Egyptian State Gods

While the Egyptians worshipped more than 700 gods over the course of ancient history, several emerged as the most prevalent. This section looks at the notable figures in the state religion – primarily the king. Ordinary people worshipped a completely different set of deities at home (see the later section 'Worshipping at home: Household gods').

Identifying the main characters

Despite the large numbers of gods in the pantheon, a few stand out as the most important. The following gods were worshipped nationally, both as part of the state and household religions.

The three most important gods are

- ✔ **Osiris, the god of the underworld.** When the king died, he turned into Osiris so that he could continue to rule in the afterlife. In art, Osiris is represented as *mummiform* (wrapped like a mummy), holding the crook and flail to show his ongoing role as a king.

- ✔ **Horus (the son of Osiris and Isis), the god of order.** The king was believed to be an incarnation of the god Horus on earth. Horus is represented as a human with a hawk head.

- ✔ **Seth (the brother of Osiris), the god of chaos.** Seth was feared by most Egyptians because of his chaotic nature, although some kings adopted him as their personal god (Sety I and II, Ramses II and III). Seth is represented as a human with a strange head and a curved nose and long, erect, square-topped ears.

The three most important goddesses are

- ✔ **Isis (the sister and wife of Osiris, the mother of Horus), a general mother goddess.** Isis is presented as a beautiful woman, sometimes with wings in place of arms. She is also shown in the form of a kite to represent her role of providing the breath of life to the deceased. (See the sidebar 'Deceit, murder – and forestry' for more details.) She is shown with a throne sign on top of her head.

- ✔ **Nephthys (the sister of Isis and Osiris), a goddess closely associated with rebirth.** Nephthys aided Isis in the resurrection of Osiris and (by association) the deceased king. She is shown as a woman with wings for arms or as a kite to show similar characteristics to Isis. Nephthys is clearly identified by a semi-circle above a rectangle on top of her head, the hieroglyphs for her name.

> ✔ **Hathor (the daughter of the sun god Ra), a mother goddess, and deity of sex, love, beauty, fertility, and death.** Hathor is closely connected with the afterlife and the provision of food for the nourishment of the deceased. She is represented as a woman with a cow's head, a human with cow's ears and a cow-horn head-dress, or simply as a cow.

All these deities are interconnected in the same mythological stories, notably the myth of Isis and Osiris and the contending of Horus and Seth. These myths explain not only the role of the king but also the laws of royal succession.

Upholding truth, justice, and the Egyptian way: Maat

Rather than appearing in her own myths, the goddess Maat was believed to be present in absolutely everything that the ancient Egyptians did. She represented the concept of cosmic balance, justice, and truth. Although not worshipped as such, Maat was a major part of the lives of the rich and poor alike.

Maat is normally shown in human form with an ostrich feather on her head – or she is represented solely as a feather, the hieroglyphic sign for truth.

For the ancient Egyptians, the concept of Maat was present in everything – particularly in the law courts, which were overseen by judges called priests of Maat. Prayers were no doubt recited to Maat before court was in session, and a symbol of the goddess was likely in the courtroom. Judges probably addressed Maat on cases that were particularly tricky.

The most important and well-known role of Maat was in the Hall of Judgement, where deceased individuals (typically non-royals) were judged on their honesty and good deeds. The deceased's heart was weighed against Maat (represented as a feather) on huge cosmic scales. If the heart was heavier than the feather, Ammit (the devourer and a scary creature) ate the heart and denied the deceased individual rebirth and eternal life.

The weighing-of-the-heart ritual was carried out in front of Osiris, who had the final say as to who was reborn and who wasn't. Thoth, the ibis-headed god of scribes, recorded the outcome of the weighing of the heart. Fortunately, in the numerous surviving representations of this ritual, no one is ever unsuccessful.

Sibling rivalry: The contending of Horus and Seth

The contending of Horus and Seth is an ancient Egyptian myth that tells of a tribunal lasting for more than 80 years. During the trial, Seth tried to prove his right to the throne over Horus (see the sidebar 'Deceit, murder – and forestry' for details).

Horus was the son of Osiris, so the throne should rightfully have passed to him, a fact of which Seth was very much aware. The tribunal was overseen by eight divinities, including Isis and Re-Horakhty, who had tried to give the throne to Horus many times. Because Seth had never accepted their decisions, they proposed that Horus and Seth settle the argument once and for all with a series of death-defying challenges. The winner of these would be crowned the king.

Seth first suggested that he and Horus turn into hippos and submerge themselves under water for a period of three months; the one to survive wins the crown. Isis ended this task by throwing a copper harpoon into the water for fear her son Horus would die. She speared Horus and then Seth, resulting in them both emerging somewhat short of the three months. When she released them both from her spear, Horus was furious that she had freed Seth and cut off Isis's head. A somewhat extreme reaction – and certainly no way to treat your mum!

When Re-Horakhty learnt of Horus's action, he demanded that Horus be punished. Seth magnanimously offered to do it. What a hero! Seth found Horus asleep (decapitation is tiring work) under a tree and promptly plucked out both of Horus's eyes and buried them. The eyes turned into two bulbs, which grew into lotus flowers and illuminated the earth. This is mythology – go with me on this.

Seth then returned to Re-Horakhty and told him that he had not been able to locate Horus. Hathor, however, discovered Horus and healed his eyes by milking a gazelle into the sockets. She then reported Horus's injuries to Re-Horakhty, who in turn demanded that Horus and Seth stop their arguing.

After many further incidents, Horus decided to take the upper hand and offered to settle the argument with a race in stone ships; the winner gets the crown. This time, however, Horus planned to cheat. He built a boat of pine and covered it with gypsum to give the appearance of stone. Seeing Horus's boat floating in the water and believing that it was stone, Seth sliced off the top of a mountain to create his own racing ship. After the race began, Seth's boat obviously sank and rendered him the loser. Not happy at losing, he transformed himself into a hippo and attacked Horus's ship. Horus was about to throw a copper barb at Seth, but the tribunal gods stopped him.

Horus, his feathers ruffled, gathered up his harpoons and complained that he had been in the tribunal for 80 years, constantly winning battles against Seth, only to have the tribunal's decision ignored.

Eventually the deities came to the conclusion that the throne of Egypt should be given to Horus. However, although Horus was given the crown of Upper and Lower Egypt, many records attempt to maintain a sense of balance: Horus is often depicted ruling Upper Egypt and Seth ruling Lower Egypt. So everyone's a winner!

Worshipping at home: Household gods

The weighing-of-the-heart ritual (see the section 'Upholding truth, justice – and the Egyptian way: Maat', earlier in this chapter, for more information) was used primarily by non-royal individuals.

In fact, regular Egyptians worshipped a number of state deities in the home, using the same methods as in the temples – daily feeding, washing, and anointing of the statues kept in household shrines.

The following sections explore some of the more common gods and associated rituals for regular, everyday Egyptians.

The sublime cow: Hathor

Hathor was worshipped in the home as a goddess of love, marriage, and childbirth. She held spectacular titles such as 'lady of the vulva' and 'lady of drunkenness'.

She was responsible primarily for fertility, conception, and sexual love. At special shrines near the state temples, ordinary people left many offerings to Hathor in the form of necklaces, beads, and stone, clay, or wooden phalli, asking for fertility or thanking her for providing children.

Hathor was also worshipped as the

- **Goddess of the western mountain.** In this role, represented in tombs as a cow emerging from the marshes, Hathor protected the cemeteries situated on the west bank of the Nile.

- **Lady of the sycamore.** In this funerary role, Hathor provided sustenance for the deceased in the afterlife in the form of sycamore figs. She is represented as a woman emerging from a tree or as a woman with a tree on top of her head.

The craftsman: Ptah

At the village of Deir el Medina, which housed the craftsmen who built the Valley of the Kings, the creator god Ptah was worshipped as the patron deity of craftsmen.

The workmen appealed to Ptah for work-related ailments – the most common one being blindness caused by the dark, cramped, and dusty work conditions. Many inscriptions ask him to lift this affliction, which the workmen believed was caused by some blasphemous act on their behalf, rather than their working environment.

Ptah is depicted in mummiform guise, wearing a close-fitting cap rather like a swimming hat. In his hands he holds three staffs, representing stability, power, and eternal life, all of which he bestowed on his worshippers.

Attached to the external walls of some of the state temples, including Karnak, was an *ear chapel* that had a number of stelae dedicated to Ptah, decorated with a number of ears. The people whispered their prayers into the ears and the prayers went directly to Ptah himself. In some of the temples, a priest hole behind the stela allowed a priest to sit and answer the prayers. The worshippers must have believed that this disembodied voice was that of Ptah.

The happy dwarf: Bes

A number of deities were purely part of the household pantheon. Most of them are not the most attractive deities, but appealed more to the lives of ordinary folk. One of the most commonly worshipped was Bes, the god of love, marriage, fertility, and partying. He was also the protector of children and women through his noisy use of singing, music, and dance, which frightened snakes, scorpions, and all other forces of evil. If only all noisy people were as useful.

Bes is one of the only gods depicted face on, rather than in profile, which makes him really stand out from the crowd. He had a lion's head and tail, combined with the body of a dwarf with bowed legs and his feet turned outwards. His arms are often bent at the elbows, placed on his hips, or holding a musical instrument or knife. A rather odd-looking character.

Bes was often invoked during childbirth to protect the woman and newborn child, as well as to ensure a simple and safe birth. Images of Bes were placed on furniture (beds in particular), headrests, pottery vessels, eye make-up pots, and mirrors – all items that were closely associated with sexuality and fertility.

The grumpy hippo: Taweret

Another deity connected with fertility and childbirth is the pregnant hippo goddess Taweret, who is shown standing upright on her hind legs with pendulous human breasts, an abdomen swollen with pregnancy, and a mane formed from a crocodile's tail. So a real looker!

Taweret was an aggressive protector of women in childbirth and is depicted on similar objects as Bes, including head rests and cosmetic items. She also had a role in the afterlife and is depicted on various copies of the Book of the Dead.

The silent one: Meretseger

Some household deities were worshipped in particular regions, as is the case with Meretseger, who was worshipped primarily at Deir el Medina. She is represented as a cobra or as a woman with a cobra for a head, the hood open and ready to strike. She protected the inhabitants of the village from bites from cobras, scorpions, and spiders.

The Valley of the Kings, where the Deir el Medina inhabitants worked, lay in the shadow of a natural pyramid-shaped hill called Meretseger, which means 'she who loves silence'. The goddess was believed to protect the people in the same way as the mountain overpowers and protects the landscape.

Worshipping the Gods

Worship of each of the hundreds of ancient Egyptian gods – regardless of geography or function – was the same throughout the temples of Egypt. Worship in the home was similar except that rituals were carried out by the family rather than priests. The statue of the god was placed within a sanctuary in the rear of the temple, and the priest entered this sanctuary twice a day (at dawn and at dusk) to carry out the rituals:

- ✔ **At dawn,** the priest removed the statue from the shrine, washed it, anointed it with perfumes and ointments, and dressed it in a fresh linen shawl. The deity was then offered food and drink, which were placed at his or her feet. After the deity had taken spiritual nourishment from the food, it was distributed among the priests within the temple.

- ✔ **At dusk,** the same rituals were repeated and the statue was put to bed. The statue was washed, anointed with perfumes and ointments, offered food and drink, again which was placed at his or her feet. This was removed after the deity had taken spiritual nourishment from it. Then the statue was placed inside the shrine until the morning, when the rituals started again.

Throughout these rituals, the priest recited prayers and incantations, which varied in nature depending on the deity and his or her role.

Appreciating sacred geography

Although the rituals that the priest performed were the same, each cult centre had its own specific practices, including forbidden food, sacred animals, sacred symbols, and prayers.

Most of the state deities also had specific locations that served as their main cult centres (refer to the Cheat Sheet map). These sites were specifically revered:

✔ Ra's main cult centre was at Heliopolis. Excavations indicate that his temple was bigger than the temple at Karnak, but sadly this is currently not open to the public.

✔ Amun's main cult centre was at Karnak, although he was worshipped nationally. This is the largest temple complex in the world and is a must on a trip to Luxor.

✔ Osiris's main cult centre was at Abydos, which you can still visit.

✔ Isis's main cult centre was Philae, a common stop-off for tourists.

✔ Horus had three main cult centres; the first two are still standing and worth a visit:

  • Edfu, where he was worshipped in the image of a winged disc.

  • Kom Ombo, where he was worshipped as the son of Re.

  • Heliopolis, where he was worshipped as Re-Harakhti.

✔ Hathor's main cult centre was at Denderah, and you can still visit it.

✔ Seth's cult centres were based in the Delta region at Avaris and Qantir. These sites are not open to the public.

Participating in festivals

Festivals were an important part of worship for both state and household religion. Historical records show many festivals each month, with the most prominent ones being

✔ **Beautiful Festival of the Valley in Thebes.** Families visited their dead relatives in their tomb chapels to feast with them. The statue of Amun was carried in a long procession from Karnak to all of the mortuary temples on the west bank of the Nile.

✔ **Festival of Sokar-Osiris.** This festival was celebrated at night as a mortuary/lunar festival. People wore onions around their necks and brought offerings to the god and the deceased. The relevance of the onions is anyone's guess, but no doubt the area had a particularly pungent smell for a while afterwards.

✔ **Opet Festival at Thebes.** A statue of Amun was carried in procession along the sphinx avenue from Karnak temple to Luxor temple. The statue stayed at Luxor temple for a number of days before returning to Karnak temple.

✔ **Festival of Drunkenness at Deir el Medina.** This festival was in honour of Hathor and, as the name suggests, involved five days of drinking.

The preceding and loads of other festivals enabled everyone to have time off work to watch the processions through the streets – as well as enjoy extra food rations and lashings and lashings of beer!

Protecting the living

All Egyptians – both royal or non-royal – believed in the power of amulets to protect and strengthen their wearers, whether living or deceased.

An *amulet* is a figure made of any kind of material that can be attached to a necklace, bracelet, or ring. Hundreds of different types of amulets existed. Many featured images of specific deities; each provided specific protection from an individual god or goddess. Amulets were worn on necklaces and bracelets, alone or in conjunction with others, rather like a modern charm bracelet.

Other amulets represented aspects of mythology as well as hieroglyphic signs and included:

- **The ankh:** The sign for eternal life.

- **Scarabs:** Beetle-like creatures associated with the sun god that gave hope of new life and resurrection.

- **Eye of Horus:** A human eye with brow and markings below. The right eye was associated with the sun; the left eye with the moon. For the living, the Eye of Horus provided protection against all malicious spiritual or physical forces. Both eyes are frequently found on mummies because they have the power to resurrect.

- **Hedgehogs:** Worn for fertility and rebirth – due to the animal's reappearance after hibernation.

- **A leg:** A leg forms part of the hieroglyphic writing for 'health' and bestowed health on the wearer.

- **Two fingers:** Typically the index and middle fingers. Only found on mummies. Represents the fingers of the embalmers, ensuring that mummification took place as well as to provide extra protection for the vulnerable parts of the body.

- **Flies:** Worn for fertility and protection from persistent insects. Gold examples were a military honour, awarded by the king.

- **Frogs:** Mostly worn by women to absorb the fecundity of the frog.

- **A carpenter's set-square and plumb-line.** These symbols bestowed the wearer with eternal righteousness and stability.

Amulets worn by the living were also a means of showing wealth – the richer the material, the wealthier the wearer. Most were made of *faience* (a glass-like material), although some were made of semi-precious stones like carnelian, amethyst, and onyx.

Doing the voodoo that you do

The Egyptians may sound like a peaceful lot, but in fact some of their religious practices were flat-out vengeful.

Specifically, they believed in the power of clay or wax figures to bring destruction to their enemies – rather like the well-known practice of using voodoo dolls.

These ancient Egyptian figures came in two types:

- ✔ **Execration figures** were used to destroy the political enemies of Egypt and therefore only used by the king. Each figure represented a bound captive. On the captive's torso were lists of the traditional enemies of Egypt (Nubians, Asiatics, Libyans, Syrians). These figures were ritually broken and buried, representing the destruction of the listed enemies.

- ✔ **Curse figures** were made and used by private individuals as a way to immobilise another individual. Something horrible was typically done to the figure – burning or sticking nails in it. In order to make these figures more effective, a strand of the cursed individual's hair or a nail was moulded into the effigy. Curse figures were made of simple materials such as clay or wax. Presumably people could make their own without the need for a third party.

Although these figures were primarily used to cause harm and destruction, some people were creative and used them for somewhat dubious reasons. One figure in the Louvre in Paris (dated to 200–300 AD) depicts a female, bound with her hands behind her back and iron rods poked into her eyes and pubic region. This figure was buried with a lead tablet inscribed with a love charm that indicates that the figure was created out of love. However, according to the tablet, if the actual woman didn't fall for the charms of the man who made the figure, she would be destroyed. Let's hope she fell for him – I'm sure he had hidden depths.

Consulting oracles

In addition to interacting with the goddess Maat (see the section 'Upholding truth, justice, and the Egyptian way: Maat', earlier in this chapter), the Egyptians sought answers to legal issues and arguments in the form of *oracles*. Poor and rich alike used oracles to settle any number of disagreements, including personal issues.

People either addressed oracles within a temple or when the statue of the god was on procession through the streets. People had two ways of asking for help. They could:

- ✔ **Place a written message at the temple before the divine statue.** This would be handed to a priest who would place it before the god. The god answered the message by the use of yes/no tablets (a number of which have been found). This answer was then interpreted by the priests.

- ✔ **Address the statue through the priests who carried the sacred bark (boat containing the statue) during a procession.** People would shout out their questions, and the statue answered by varying the pressure on the shoulders of the priests who held the bark. The way the priests knelt or bowed meant different things to the people.

The genius of the oracle system was that if you didn't like the answer from one god, you went and asked another. There was no limit on the number of divine convictions.

Dreaming of deities

Although Egyptians appealed directly to the gods via oracles, the gods also appeared to people in dreams that dream priests then interpreted. These priests told individuals what they needed to do to have their prayers answered. Interpretations normally involved some contribution to the temple and were a lucrative business for the priests. (Call me cynical, but some of these divine messages may not have been genuine – and with enough greasing of palms, the interpretation could be anything that was required.)

Worshipping Humans

One of the most prominent forms of worship in the villages was the ancestor cult, in which villagers revered deceased members of the family, going back two or three generations. Living Egyptians appealed to the ancestors for help with everyday problems.

The Egyptians believed that after an individual was reborn into the afterlife, he or she became an *akh ikr en re*, or 'excellent spirit of Re' (go to Chapter 10 for more details). These individuals were thought to have the power to affect the life of the living as well as influence the gods of the afterlife. Through keeping the ancestors happy – by offering food and drink on a daily basis – Egyptians ensured that their deceased relatives supported the living members of the family.

The Egyptians embraced their ancestors and included them in their everyday lives, even incorporating false doors in their sitting rooms that allowed the spirits of ancestors to enter the house and participate in family meals and activities. Not something that would appeal to the average homeowner today.

Pocket-sized ancestors

Revered ancestors were included in religious festivals and processions through the use of *ancestral busts*. These were small (maximum 30 centimetres) portable figures of stone or wood representing a generic figure. The busts included the head and shoulders and sometimes wore large wigs. The busts rarely featured inscriptions, but historians believe that they represented male members of a family.

Egyptians placed these busts in their household shrines (see the 'Worshipping at home: Household gods' section above) and asked the departed for assistance. Small stelae (maximum 25 centimetres) sat alongside the ancestral busts in the household shrines. These stelae were inscribed with images of the ancestors as well as an image of the dedicator of the stela. Many have short prayers carved on them and invoke the aid of the deceased.

During the annual Beautiful Festival of the Valley (see the section 'Participating in festivals', earlier in this chapter), the statue of Amun was carried from Karnak in procession to the necropolis on the west bank of the Nile. Many Deir el Medina residents joined the procession with their ancestor busts. This procession ended at the tomb of the deceased, where a commemorative feast took place in which the deceased was believed to participate.

Deifying humans

The traditional household gods, concerned with fertility, childbirth, and danger from the bites of reptiles, insects, and arachnids, were not enough for the average Egyptian, who also worshipped humans, who were raised to the position of deities. This was not the same as the ancestor cult, because deified humans were often those who were revered and well-known in life. Deified humans were worshipped more widely than revered ancestors in the ancestor cult, which was limited to the immediate family.

Some deified humans were worshipped by the ordinary people and others by the kings. Deified humans were addressed for many reasons, including fertility and moral guidance.

Letters to the dead

Pottery vessels in many Egyptian tombs have a letter written on the inside. These letters to the dead were written by the remaining family and asked for help in various matters.

Families wrote the letters on a bowl, which was then filled with a tasty snack, so when the deceased ate the snack and saw the letter, they had to do what was requested because they had already accepted the bribe. Cunning, eh?

One letter of this type, written on papyrus, is particularly interesting:

> To the able spirit Ankhiry. What evil have I done to you that I should land in this wretched state in which I am? What have I done to you? What you have done is to lay your hands on me, although I have done you no wrong. What have I done to you since I lived with you as your husband, until that day [of your death], that I must hide it? What is there now? What you have attained is that I must bring forward this accusation against you. What have I done to you? I will lodge a complaint against you with the Ennead in the West [the divine law-court in the hereafter], and one shall judge between you and me on account of this letter . . .

> What have I done to you? I made you my wife when I was a young man. I was with you when I held all kinds of offices. I stayed with you, I did not send you away . . . 'She has always been with me' I thought . . . And see, now you do not even comfort me. I will be judged with you, and one shall discern truth from falsehood.

> Look, when I was training the officers of the army of Pharaoh and his chariotry, I let them lie on their bellies before you. I never hid anything from you in all your life. I never let you suffer, but I always behaved to you as a gentleman. You never found that I was rude to you, as when a peasant enters someone else's house. I never behaved so that a man could rebuke me for anything I did to you . . .

> I am sending this letter to let you know what you are doing. When you began to suffer from the disease you had, I let a head physician come and he treated you and did everything you asked him to do. When I followed Pharaoh, travelling to the south and this condition came to you, I spent no less than eight months without eating and drinking as a man should do. And as soon as I reached Memphis, I asked from Pharaoh leave and went to the place that you were, and I cried intensely, together with my people, before the eyes of my entire neighbourhood. I donated fine linen for wrapping you up, I let many clothes be made, and omitted nothing good to be done for you. And see, I passed three years until now living alone, without entering any house, although it is not fair that someone like me should be made to do so. But I did it for you, you who does not discern good from bad. One shall judge between you and me. And then: the sisters in the house, I have not entered any one of them.

The last line seems to have been written as an afterthought because it does not flow with the rest of the letter – but it is in fact the crux of the letter. The author is suffering from grief combined with guilt, which he believes is caused by his wife, whereas it is probably due to his activities with the women in the house! He obviously feels that his first wife does not approve and is punishing him.

Some notable deified humans who were worshipped by significant numbers in different regions of Egypt included

- ✔ **Imhotep,** the architect who built the step pyramid at Saqqara (see Chapter 13), was deified as a god of medicine, even though he was not a physician in life.

- ✔ **Senwosret III** was worshipped at the town of Kahun (see Chapter 2 for more details), because he was responsible for founding the city for the workmen who built his pyramid at el-Lahun.

- ✔ **Amenhotep I** was revered by the people at Deir el Medina as the founder of their village.

- ✔ **Amenhotep,** son of Hapu, was the vizier during the reign of Amenhotep III and was worshipped as a sage. He was the patron god of physicians and healing and was believed to aid with conception.

- ✔ **Horemheb** was revered by Ramses II, who set up a shrine in Horemheb's non-royal tomb at Saqqara. This worship was due to the break that Horemheb gave the family of Ramses II by choosing his grandfather to be king on his death.

People made offerings to the statues of deified humans, as well as reciting prayers and incantations to them.

Chapter 10

Exploring Funerary Beliefs and Mummification

- -

In This Chapter

▶ Contemplating life and afterlife, Egyptian style

▶ Unravelling the process of mummification

▶ Assisting the deceased towards the afterlife

▶ Resurrecting the dead

- -

*M*ost information from ancient Egypt comes from a funerary context, giving the impression that the Egyptians were obsessed with death and spent most of their time and wealth preparing for their earthly ends.

The ancient Egyptians were, in fact, obsessed with *life* and wanted to continue living for eternity. Although each individual no doubt had his or her own beliefs, evidence generally suggests that the ancient Egyptians believed careful preparation enabled them to make their lives after death more prosperous than their lives before. In fact, they believed that the afterlife (for ordinary Egyptians at least) was a perfect replica of Egypt, known as the *Field of Reeds*.

The Field of Reeds relied heavily on the solar cycle, and some believed the dead lay in primordial darkness until the sun god started his nocturnal journey in the afterlife. Although this landscape was abundant in water and vegetation, the provision of funerary goods, food, and elaborate tombs ensured the deceased's continuing happiness after death.

This chapter delves into one of the most frequently discussed (and often misunderstood) aspects of ancient Egyptian life – the preparation and burial of the dead through the physical and spiritual process of mummification.

Understanding the Egyptian Essence of Humanity

The Egyptians believed that a human being was made up of six elements or components. On death, these elements spontaneously separated. For a successful rebirth, all six elements were reunited through the funerary rituals, prayers, and offerings normally carried out by the priests and living family members.

The six elements were

- **The ka,** or the life force, which animated the individual – rather like batteries animate a toy.

- **The ba,** which was depicted as a human-headed bird. The ba represented the personality of the deceased.

- **The akh,** which was the name of the spirit created by combining ba and ka.

- **The deceased's name,** which was supposed to be repeated by the living for eternal life to be possible.

- **The shadow,** which is a little known aspect of the individual. It ties in with the solar cult, because without the sun, no shadow exists.

- **The physical body,** which was considered to be the combination of all these spiritual elements. The physical body was preserved by the process of mummification.

The Opening of the Mouth ceremony

The *ba* and *ka* were united in the afterlife through the *Opening of the Mouth ceremony*. This post-mummification ritual ensured the ka could see, hear, smell, breathe, and eat – all essential activities for life. For unknown reasons, the ba did not seem to need these earthly functions; when the ba was united with the ka for a length of time, it was nourished.

A *sem* priest (funerary priest) held a ceremonial *adze* (an axe-like hand tool) to the mouth of the mummy, which was believed to open the airways. The sem priest then offered prayers and anointed the mummy with oils. The ancient Egyptians considered this ceremony so important that they sometimes included images of the pots and jars used in the ritual on the coffin (examples appear on the interior of some Middle Kingdom coffins at the head end) in case the ritual hadn't been completed correctly and as a means of ensuring the instruments for this important ceremony were close to the body, thus increasing the ritual's effects.

The successful union of the ba and ka created another element of the body, the *akh* or spirit. The deceased was transformed into an eternal being of light. Although the akh was not divine, it had characteristics in common with the deities – the akh was able to intervene with the living and converse with the gods.

Cursing the Egyptologists

Mummies have inspired imaginations for centuries, causing both fear and awe. Over the decades, Hollywood has bombarded us with imaginative movies of mummies coming alive and chasing unsuspecting archaeologists around tombs. The mummies of horror movies are always evil, because of a curse placed on the tomb or the mummy itself.

The most famous curse story began during the excavation of the tomb of Tutankhamun in 1922 by Howard Carter and his team. The locals working with the team were very superstitious and believed entering the tomb would activate an ancient curse. To prevent the locals from entering the tomb at night and disturbing the excavations, the excavation team did not deny the curse, and the story was eventually picked up by an English newspaper.

From that point on, every death of a member of the excavation team was blamed on the curse, even those that happened 20 or so years later – a very slow-working curse, which included natural causes!

The only slightly odd event was an electrical blackout in Cairo at the time of Lord Carnarvon's death from an infected insect bite. (See Chapter 15 for more on Lord Carnarvon's contribution to the Tutankhamun excavation.) Of course, blackouts happened in Cairo regularly at the time – and still do, without any rational explanation. If you look hard enough, you can find significance in anything.

Of the thousands of tombs excavated in Egypt, only two have curses as such, to deter tomb robbers (the first is from the Tomb of Ursa, early New Kingdom; the second from a sixth dynasty tomb of Harkkhuf in Aswan):

> *He who trespassed upon my property or who shall injure my tomb or drag out my mummy, the sun-god shall punish him. He shall not bequeath his goods to his children; his heart shall not have pleasure in life; he shall not receive water (for his ka to drink) in the tomb; and his soul shall be destroyed for ever.*

> *As for anyone who enters this tomb unclean, I shall seize him by the neck like a bird, he will be judged for it by the great god.*

Don't worry, Egyptologists aren't in danger from these curses. They don't enter the tombs to injure, but to reconstruct, conserve, and learn about the owners and their history and culture.

For the ancient Egyptians, the repetition of a name ensured a prolonged afterlife. Through the study of the tombs and publication of the findings, Egyptologists are resurrecting the tombs' owners – which is what they desired all those thousands of years ago. Of course, debate continues as to whether placing mummies in museums (in store or on display) is appropriate.

I am sure the ancient Egyptians wouldn't be overly keen on today's flashy exhibitions. However, if modern Egyptologists didn't excavate the tombs, the ancient Egyptian's history, names and lives would be lost for eternity – the oblivion feared by all ancient Egyptians. A museum may not be the resurrection they wanted, but it is a resurrection and an eternal life of sorts.

Getting All Wrapped Up: Mummies for Dummies

The process of mummification can take two forms:

- ✔ **Natural:** The body is preserved in sand, ice, or peat.
- ✔ **Artificial:** The body is preserved by humans using a variety of hands-on methods.

Ancient Egypt offers examples of both forms of mummies.

In the pre-dynastic period (3500 BC), the Egyptians buried their dead in shallow pits dug into the sand on the desert edge. The pits were unlined, and the unwrapped bodies were placed in a foetal position, directly into the sand. Funerary goods consisted primarily of pots containing food and drink needed for the afterlife, which suggests that the Egyptians held a belief in life after death in this period.

When animals and shifting sands uncovered the bodies, the Egyptians realised that the skin and hair had been naturally preserved by the sand in which the bodies had been buried. The Egyptians began attempting to guarantee the preservation of the dead, rather than leaving it to chance. Over the years, the process of artificially preserving bodies evolved.

Experimenting on the dead

Various experimental mummification methods were introduced between 3500 BC and 2600 BC, including

- ✔ **Pot burials.** Fully grown adults were tightly flexed and placed inside large clay pots. The addition of a lid created a cocoon in which the body was sealed, buried in the ground and finally covered with sand.

✔ **Reed trays.** The body was placed on a shallow reed tray in a tightly flexed position and lain on its side. Rather than a lid, a linen cloth or animal skin was thrown over the body. This tray was then placed into a shallow pit and covered with sand.

✔ **Animal skins.** Prior to 3000 BC, the dead were wrapped in animal skins and placed into the shallow burial pits and covered with sand.

All the preceding methods resulted in the disintegration of the soft tissues, because the bodies were removed from contact with the substance that naturally preserved them – the sand. Skeletal remains are all that exist from these early attempts at preserving bodies.

Improving mummification practices

After the failure of early burial experiments, the Egyptians decided to preserve bodies before burial.

The earliest example of mummification was a royal burial of the first dynasty, belonging to King Djer. It was discovered by Petrie in the late 19th century. All that remained of this body was a mummified arm, adorned with bracelets of semi-precious stones. Unfortunately, the archaeologists were more interested in the jewellery than the arm, and the curator of the Cairo museum, Emile Brugsch, threw the arm part away. Luckily, however, they did take a solitary photograph of this early form of mummification – or rather, of how pretty the bracelets looked on the arm.

Mummification was only for the elite of society, and the multitudes of poor Egyptians were buried in pit burials, similar to the pre-dynastic examples, throughout Egyptian history. The only real difference is that mummified bodies after the pre-dynastic period were extended and not flexed.

Looking to the burial professional: The embalmer

Even though many examples of mummified bodies and tombs exist today, no written record from ancient Egypt is available that describes the process of mummification. The most complete record available is from Herodotus, a Greek historian from the fifth century BC.

Buried alive?

After the pre-dynastic period, animal skins were thought to be unclean and weren't used for wrapping the body. However, one example from the 18th dynasty, found in the Deir el Bahri royal cache, is of a young man stitched into a fleece. His hands and legs are tied with rope and no mummification is indicated on the body.

The man's open-mouthed expression suggests that he was stitched into the skin while still alive, and his presence in the royal cache suggests he was of royal blood. He was probably found guilty of a crime, although his crime is unknown. To deny him mummification and a proper burial condemned him to eternal death.

After an ancient Egyptian died, the body was taken to an embalmers' workshop, which was probably a temporary structure in the local cemetery. Because no evidence of these structures survives, historians are unsure of how many might have existed. The embalmers' workshops probably contained ready-made coffins and amulets, so the relatives could choose the appropriate assemblage according to their budget.

The senior embalmers were priests and were held in high esteem. The most senior embalmer in charge of wrapping the body wore a jackal mask, representing Anubis, the jackal-headed god of embalming.

Despite the high esteem in which embalmers were held, Herodotus records that the bodies of rich and powerful women were typically held back for a few days before being taken to the workshop, to prevent the bodies from being defiled. For example, when the 18th-dynasty mummy of Queen Ahmose-Nefertari was unwrapped, her body showed signs of decomposition of soft tissues before mummification. Although she was in her 70s when she died, her position as a queen may have rendered her desirable even after death – to someone who was that way inclined. (Of course, the sources and truthfulness of Herodotus's information are unknown.)

Stepping through the embalming process

The most expensive and comprehensive method of mummification made the deceased look like Osiris, the god of the underworld. Egyptians believed that the deceased king – and by the Middle Kingdom, deceased nobles – become like Osiris on death.

More inexpensive mummification methods were available (see 'Considering budget burials', later in this chapter, for details), but the following outlines the complete process.

Removing the brain

In the New Kingdom, the embalmers usually removed the brain first. Ancient Egyptians believed that thought processes and emotions occurred in the heart, so the brain was superfluous. (Know any people like that?)

The embalmers broke the ethmoid bone at the top of the nose and removed the brain piecemeal with a hook through the nasal cavity. However, experiments have shown that this method would have inefficiently removed the brain in tiny pieces.

To improve this part of the process, a liquid of juniper oil and a turpentine substance was typically poured up the nose and left for a few minutes to dissolve the remains of the brain, which were then poured out through the nostrils and disposed of. Remnants of dissolved and solidified brain matter have been found at the back of skulls.

Liposuction – Egyptian style

After removing the brain, the embalmers then made a cut in the left side of the lower abdomen with a flint knife and removed the whole contents of the abdomen, except the heart. The embalmer who made this initial slit was then ceremoniously chased out of the workshop, with people throwing stones, sticks, and abuse at him for defiling the body. Whether he returned to the workshop is unknown; I for one would have stayed well away.

After the organs were removed, the abdomen was thoroughly cleaned – first with palm wine and again with an infusion of pounded spices with antibacterial properties to stop the cavity from smelling.

After drying the cavity, the embalmers filled it with a mixture of aromatic substances; linen or sawdust was inserted to give the empty cavity shape. The body was then sewn up and the slit hidden by a bronze or leather leaf-shaped cover.

Preserving the innards

The viscera removed from the bodies were treated as carefully as the bodies themselves. They were dried in *natron*, a natural salt substance that came from the Wadi Natron (the Natron Valley). The dried organs were then wrapped in linen and placed inside *canopic jars*, which in turn were placed inside rectangular canopic chests made of the same material as the coffins and sarcophagi.

The canopic jars had lids in the form of four animal heads, which represent the Four Sons of Horus (the hawk-headed god of order). The Four Sons of Horus each had a specific role to play in the afterlife, because they protected a part of the body and then provided the body with its essential internal organs when the deceased was reborn. The Four Sons of Horus were:

- ✔ *Imsety*, a human head, which protected the liver.

- ✔ *Hapy*, an ape head, which protected the lungs.

- ✔ *Duamutef*, a jackal head, which protected the stomach.

- ✔ *Qebehsenuef*, a falcon head, which protected the intestines.

Drying the body

The stuffed body was then placed on an embalming table for 35–40 days with natron packed around the body, completely covering it. Examples of these long, low embalming tables have been discovered in the embalming caches. The location of these tables during drying and the security measures utilised are sadly unknown.

Optional extras

Ever ingenious, Egyptian embalmers developed additional mummification processes to further prepare the bodies of the deceased. Some interesting extras that have been discovered include:

- ✔ **Post-mortem skin treatment.** An elderly priestess, Nesitetnabtaris from the New Kingdom, was bedridden for a large proportion of her later years because of a fracture in her neck. As a result, her back, buttocks, and shoulders were covered in bed-sores and abscesses. After she died, the embalmers stitched up the worst of the abscesses with flax and covered the stitching with resin so it wasn't visible. They then covered the bed sores with a large gazelle skin stitched to the priestess's back, buttocks, and shoulders. This procedure ensured her body was reborn in the afterlife as complete and perfect – albeit with a go-faster stripe!

- ✔ **Gender reassignment.** Mummy 1770 in the Manchester Museum presented a multitude of problems for the embalmers. She died at the age of 14 in the New Kingdom and was rewrapped 800 years later; the newer wrappings are the ones that have survived. She was obviously rewrapped due to the shocking state of her original wrappings, perhaps after a tomb robbery. Before the rewrapping, embalmers did not know her name, identity, or sex. To hedge their bets, the embalmers provided gold nipple covers – to ensure lactation in the afterlife – as well as a penis made of a roll of linen bandages. The expectation was that in the afterlife she would use what she needed. The embalmers presumably thought their ignorance would never be exposed – but modern sexing techniques uncovered the blunder.

After 35–40 days, the body was removed, washed, and prepared for wrapping, which took up to an additional 30 days, ensuring the entire process took no more than 70 days in total.

Interestingly, the star Sirius, associated with Osiris, disappears for 70 days at a time. Osiris also disappeared for 70 days before his resurrection. Symbolically, the deceased becomes Osiris on death, disappearing for 70 days during the mummification process and then being reborn in the afterlife.

Wrapping the body

Wrapping the body was just as important as its preservation, and a priest wearing an Anubis mask (the god of embalming) was responsible for the job.

The priest needed large amounts of linen to wrap a body – up to 400 square metres have been discovered on some mummies, with more than 40 layers of wrappings.

Deceased royalty had their funerary linen specially made by the temple and harem workshops. Some of the wrappings of Ramses II were even woven from blue and gold thread.

Given the amount of linen required for wrappings, and its expense, non-royal bodies were unlikely to be bound in material made especially for burial, or even in linen provided by one household. Because they found different names on wrappings of the same mummy, researchers think that friends and relatives may have provided the linen required. Perhaps if someone died, the whole village donated linen to the family.

The evolution of wrapping

Wrapping styles changed over the years. The dates of mummies can be iden-tified according to certain characteristics:

- ✔ **Old Kingdom:** Each limb was wrapped individually, including each finger and toe. The wrappings were then coated in resin. Plaster was moulded over the bandages of the face and painted in lifelike colours.

- ✔ **Middle Kingdom:** Mummies were wrapped in the traditional shape with all the limbs wrapped together. The hands were placed flat over the thighs or crossed over the genitalia. Mummy masks replaced the painted plaster, and many of these masks have full beards and moustaches, sometimes painted blue or green. Perhaps the earliest punks?

✔ **New Kingdom:** Additions were made to the mummies before wrapping, including eyes inlaid with onyx and crystal to maintain the shape. (However, Ramses IV was given two small onions as eyes – now that would definitely make your eyes water!) The arms of the royal mummies were crossed over the chest and the hands were often closed into fists.

✔ **Ptolemaic period:** Embalmers used very thin strips of fabric, arranged into intricate geometric patterns and decorated with studs and stars.

✔ **Roman period:** Elaborately painted portraits of the deceased in life were wrapped amid the bandages.

✔ **Roman era:** Elaborate mummy portraits were placed among the wrappings, representing the dead when they were alive.

Inclusions in the wrappings

From the New Kingdom onwards, texts from the *Book of the Dead* (refer to the later section 'The Book of the Dead') were sometimes written on the bandages to aid the deceased in the afterlife. These passages were appropriately placed on the relevant body parts to ensure protection.

While each limb of the mummy was bandaged, the priests recited spells from the funerary texts of the period (see 'Guiding the Dead in the Underworld', later in this chapter) to render each limb divine and ensure the deceased was reborn for eternity. No wonder wrapping took 30 days! Amid all the bandages, the embalmers placed numerous amulets that aided the deceased in the afterlife.

Considering budget burials

Cheaper mummification processes were available from the Middle Kingdom onwards, as evidenced in several surviving mummies from these periods. However, as mentioned in the preceding section, 'Looking to the Burial Professional: The embalmer', the exact process is recorded only in Herodotus' writing from the fifth century BC.

In general, these cheaper techniques did not involve removal of the internal organs. The mixture of juniper oil and turpentine was injected into the body through the anus, which was stopped up to prevent the liquid escaping (the most extreme enema!). After a period, the plug was removed and the liquid was drained, releasing the dissolved organs with it. However, the organs of some mummies did not dissolve evenly, and partially dissolved innards clogged the anus.

The body was then soaked in natron for 40 days, after which it was washed and prepared for wrapping. An even cheaper alternative involved dissolving the organs, drying the body, and returning the mummy to the relatives without wrapping.

STRANGE BUT TRUE

An ancient cover-up

The mummy of a 22nd dynasty priest from the temple of Khonsu at Karnak, Nesperenub, was the subject of a British Museum 3D exhibition in 2004. The mummy was placed in a cartonnage coffin, which was made of plastered layers of fibre or papyrus. The coffin couldn't be removed without destroying it. For many years, X-rays highlighted a strange object attached to the back of Nesperenub's head. This irregularity caused much puzzlement. With the use of CT (computerised tomography) scans and digital imaging, researchers were able to look inside Nesperenub's body in a way that had never been achieved before.

The CT scan identified the object as a roughly moulded clay bowl, complete with the potter's fingerprints. It would seem that while the embalmers were gluing the first layer of bandages to the head with resin, they placed the bowl beneath the head to catch the run-off. However, it was clearly the end of their shift, they forgot the bowl was there, and when they returned to work in the morning the resin had set solid, gluing the bowl to the head. Marks on the back of the head indicate that the embalmers tried to chisel the bowl off. They gave up and decided to include it in the wrappings. Who would ever know?

Returning to sender

After the bodies were wrapped, the embalmers returned them to the families for burial. However, bodies were not always buried straight away because family tombs were opened only every few years to limit robberies. While a mummy awaited final burial, it was stored in a room either at the embalmers' workshop for a rich family or in the home for a poorer family.

Getting dressed up: Clothes to be seen dead in

In addition to wrappings, linen clothes were also placed on or around the bodies, although whether embalmers or family members dressed mummies is unknown.

- ✔ A fifth-dynasty female had nine shirts buried with her inside her wooden coffin. Two of them were clearly designed as grave goods because they were very long (142 centimetres) and very narrow, rendering them unwearable in real life.

- ✔ A mummy dated to 2362 BC from Tarkhan, currently in the Petrie Museum, was buried with clothing that shows creasing under the armpits and on the elbows, indicating it had been worn in life and was probably a much loved outfit.

✔ Other clothing examples discovered in tombs were turned inside out and folded, which was a practice that Egyptian laundries used to indicate that garments had been laundered. These inside-out garments indicate that burial clothing was also worn in life.

Tidying up

After the embalmers completed the mummification process and the body was handed back to the family, all the material from each embalming process was buried in an individual cache. This process suggests that one cache should exist for each burial; sadly this is not the case in the archaeological record.

A number of embalmers' caches have been discovered from Thebes and Saqqara, including that of Tutankhamun. These caches include all the material that was used in the embalming process:

✔ Labelled pots and jars containing coloured powders for colouring the mummy

✔ Resins for filling, deodorising, and sanitising the mummy

✔ Linen for stuffing and wrapping

✔ Natron for desiccating

✔ Wax for covering the body and some of the orifices

✔ Various oils for curing and scenting the body, as well as making it supple

✔ Terebinth resin as deodorant and perfume

✔ Sawdust and chaff for stuffing cavities

✔ Lamps and fragments of the funerary feast held after the funeral in the tomb chapel

✔ A broom to sweep the footprints away of the last person to have been in the tomb

Some of the caches also contain the embalming table, which was a low table because most of the mummification process was performed from the squatting position. These tables are stained with natron, oils, and bodily fluids.

At the time of writing, the most recently discovered tomb in the Valley of the Kings (KV63) is being excavated. All seven coffins opened are full of embalmers' material similar to that used in the burial of Tutankhamun, including floral collars worn at funerals. A number of large storage vessels in the tomb are filled with natron, bandages, and various vessels, indicating that the tomb may have been an embalmers' workshop rather than a burial place. The new tomb may be the embalming cache for an as-yet-undiscovered tomb!

Catching the imagination

Although the practice of mummification declined in the Roman period, mummies and the ancient Egyptians' burial processes have remained intriguing to the world ever since.

From AD 50 to the 19th century, the ideas regarding mummies were increasingly bizarre. Because mummies were between 2,000 and 4,000 years old, many believed they held the secret of eternal life. Mummies were commonly ground down to a powder, referred to as *mumia*, and eaten as an elixir of life. The King of Persia even sent Queen Victoria a small vial of bitumen (associated with production of the late-period mummies) for her health. One wonders if her long life was due to taking a little mummia with her tea!

In the late 19th century, the wealthy also frequently purchased mummies to display in their houses. Public unrollings of mummies were elite social events, at which ladies were known to faint at the ghastly sight as men looked on in scientific interest. Because the demand for genuine ancient mummies for unrolling events soon outstripped supply, the enterprising Egyptians made fake mummies, dried and aged in the sun, to sell to unsuspecting rich western tourists.

Guiding the Dead in the Underworld

Although the embalmers preserved the bodies, further precautions were included in the tombs to ensure that the deceased weren't hindered on their journey to rebirth and the afterlife.

These precautions were in the form of 'guide books' to the afterlife. Instructions were written on coffins, walls, papyri, and bandages, and gave the deceased necessary information for travelling through the afterlife and obtaining eternal life. The following sections discuss the most common guides for the dead.

The Pyramid Texts

The *Pyramid Texts* are the earliest funerary texts, and not surprisingly they are written in the pyramids from the reign of Unas of the fifth dynasty until the reign of Ibi, an obscure king from the eighth dynasty.

The texts were inscribed in the burial chamber and antechamber of the pyramid (see Chapter 14 for more on pyramid architecture) and do not include pictures of any kind. The hieroglyphs are painted green to represent regeneration.

The Pyramid Texts were initially designed for royal burials, but by the end of the Old Kingdom some chapters of the text were being used in non-royal tombs. The spells were initially concerned with the afterlife of the king and present different fates for him – all equal in importance. These fates were:

- ✔ The king can ascend to the sky to become a star amid his ancestors.
- ✔ On death, the king can become Osiris, the god of the underworld.
- ✔ The king can join the sun god in his solar bark (divine boat) and accompany him on his nocturnal journey.

Obviously, contradictions existed in the belief system concerning what actually happened after the king died. Even from this early period, the Egyptians appear to have as many ideas about the afterlife as their modern counterparts.

The Pyramid Texts were made up of three categories, consisting of a number of *spells*, or chapters. Different combinations of spells were chosen to decorate the pyramids. The three categories included:

- ✔ **Incantations,** which were of a protective nature. Incantations were use to ward off snakes and other dangers that the deceased king may come across in the afterlife that could affect his rebirth.
- ✔ **Funerary spells,** which associated the deceased with a manifestation of Osiris. These spells describe the king's journey into the afterlife and were often inscribed in the burial chamber. These words are narrated by the king's son in his role as Horus, the son of Osiris. These texts describe offerings and resurrection rituals, including the words of the Opening of the Mouth ceremony (see the sidebar 'The Opening of the Mouth ceremony', earlier in this chapter, for more).
- ✔ **Personal spells,** which the deceased was to use for his or her journey in the afterlife. These spells were placed in the antechamber and the passage leading out of the pyramid, aiding the *ka* as it left the tomb. These spells refer to the landscape of the underworld and include imagery such as crossing water and ascending a ladder to the sky.

The Coffin Texts

At the beginning of the Middle Kingdom, the Pyramid Texts evolved into the *Coffin Texts* – very imaginatively named, because the Coffin Texts were inscribed primarily on coffins (although inscriptions have been found on tomb walls, mummy masks, and papyri as well).

The Coffin Texts were similar to the Pyramid Texts, although new spells were added. They were available for both royal and non-royal individuals.

The Coffin Texts further developed some ideas introduced in the Pyramid Texts, including:

✔ The heavenly travels of the *ba* alongside the sun god in the solar bark.

✔ The idea that existence in the afterlife is reliant on the nourishment of the *ka*. The preservation of human remains is essential so that *ba* and *ka* can unite to become reborn. Because of this, the *offering frieze* was one of the most important elements of the Coffin Texts and consisted of an elaborately painted scene of all the goodies given to the deceased (food, clothes, weapons, and jewellery).

✔ Personal spells were still present, although they were incorporated into *Guides to the Hereafter*, the most common of which was the Book of the Two Ways. *The Book of the Two Ways* was an introduction to the Netherworld, accompanied by a map that showed how to gain access to it and all notable landmarks. Just what any traveller needs. These maps, dominated by two paths consisting of earth and water, can often be seen on the base of coffins.

The Book of the Dead

The New Kingdom was a renaissance for funerary texts, with many different versions being produced, including *The Book of the Dead* with its more than 200 spells compiled from the Pyramid and the Coffin Texts, plus some new, updated additions.

Text from the Book of the Dead was written on coffins, linen mummy shrouds, papyrus, tomb walls, and bandages, and was often illustrated with colourful vignettes relating to the text. (Earlier funerary texts consisted primarily of text only.)

Some noteworthy additions include:

✔ **Spell 125, which relates to the judgement of the deceased and his worthiness to receive eternal life.**

✔ **Specifications that some chapters need to be written on certain objects to obtain the best results.** For example:

- Chapter 6 should be written on *shabti figures*, servant statues that were placed in the tomb to work on behalf of the deceased. (No one wants to think eternity is filled with mundane chores!)

- Chapter 26, 27, 29b, and 30b, were to be written on *heart scarabs*, which were large scarabs placed over the heart. The scarabs were implored not to give away any naughty secrets when the deceased stood before Osiris in the Hall of Judgement.

• Spell 100 should be written on a clean, unused papyrus using a powder of green pigment mixed with myrrh and water. This sheet should be placed on the breast of the mummy without actually touching the body. If this was done, the deceased was able to board the bark (sacred boat) of Re and thus hang out with the most important of the gods! A very important spell indeed.

✔ **Indications that certain spells or sections of spells were to be read aloud by different people, including the *ka* priests, embalmers, and the deceased themselves.** Spells to be read by the deceased were placed in the tomb as close to the body as possible in the burial chamber, so the *ka* would have immediate access to this information as soon as it left the body.

With so many clear specifications, not all 200 chapters of the Book of the Dead were ever written out in full in any one place.

Guides to the Hereafter

Unlike the Book of the Dead, the *Guides to the Hereafter*, which included the Book of Gates and the Book of the Amduat, were not a constantly changing collection of spells, but the first religious books whose contents were set, followed a theme, and were to be viewed in a specific order. The *Guides to the Hereafter* were only ever used by kings and were generally not even allowed in the tombs of queens. These books are currently visible in the tombs in the Valley of the Kings (see Chapter 13).

The Guides to the Hereafter were more illustrated than the Book of the Dead and followed the 12-hour nocturnal journey of the sun god, accompanied by the deceased.

In the story, the nocturnal journey starts at sunset for the sun and at burial for the deceased. The sun carries its light into the underworld and travels to the east to be reborn. Each hour of the 12-hour journey is separated by gates or portals protected by demons and serpents. The deceased needs to recite the name of the demon and the gate to pass through. Many of the hours include demons willing to harm the sun god and his companions – a real good-versus-evil scenario that would make a great film! At the end of the 12 hours, the sun is reborn into the sky, and the deceased is reborn into the afterlife.

It was not necessary to have all 12 hours inscribed on a tomb wall, coffin, or papyri, and often a representative one or two hours were used depending on the space available.

Tipping the balance

After the deceased negotiated his or her way through all the portals and gateways of the afterlife, there was just one tiny task left to perform before the deceased was left alone for eternity. This is to enter the Hall of Judgement, to stand before Osiris, the god of the underworld, and prove their worth.

The heart of the deceased was weighed against the feather of truth (*Maat*). If the heart was heavier, it was devoured by the monster (*Amut*) waiting nearby, thus preventing the deceased from being reborn and cursing the deceased to reside in eternal limbo.

Rather than leaving the weighing of his or her heart to chance, the deceased recited the *negative confession* from the Book of the Dead, which tells the 42 judges of the underworld all the things that the deceased has *not* done. Cunning really, because if you had done something, don't mention it and no one would ever know! The negative confession included the following lines:

> *I have done no falsehood.*
>
> *I have not robbed.*
>
> *I have not been rapacious.*
>
> *I have not killed men.*

The confession continues along these lines, combining trivial things and terrible crimes almost as if they are the same thing. If anything is missed out from the confession, the heart scarab (see preceding section 'The Book of the Dead') was inscribed with a prayer encouraging the scarab not to betray any wrongdoings still present within the heart.

Although the weighing of the heart sounds terrifying, the numerous examples of this scene show that not one person failed. So obviously reciting the negative confession worked.

Nourishing the ka

After the deceased was reborn into the afterlife, it was essential to maintain a *cult of the ka* to ensure he or she lived eternally. For royalty, this cult was practised within a mortuary temple and involved numerous priests. For laymen, however, if they were wealthy enough to have a tomb with a tomb chapel, family members acted as the *ka* priests and kept the cult active, or paid a priest to perform at the tomb. For poorer individuals, family members maintained the cult within the home.

Knowing was beyond even the Egyptians

Despite all the ancient Egyptians' efforts to preserve their bodies for eternity, not everyone was certain that the afterlife existed.

In some tombs from the New Kingdom, blind harpers are shown entertaining the elite at banquets. Above some of these harpers are the lyrics of the following song:

What has been done with them?

What are their places now?

Their walls have crumbled and their places are not

As if they have never been.

No one has ever come back from the dead

That he might describe their condition,

And relate their needs;

That he might calm our hearts

Until we too pass into that place where they have gone

Let us make holiday and never tire of it!

For behold no man can take his property with him,

No man who has gone can ever return again.

Clearly, the Egyptians were uncertain of the reality of the afterlife. But of course they continued with their mummification and funerary preparations, just to hedge their bets!

One of the most important elements of the cult of the ka was the constant food offerings, which were laid before a *stela* (a statue or false door) for the daily sustenance of the *ka*. These offerings consisted of bread, beer, fowl, oxen, and vegetables. Presumably the families tried to ensure that the offerings included food the deceased liked when he or she was alive. Nothing is worse than having to survive for eternity on fish heads and cabbage if you don't like them!

Accompanying these offerings were prayers and incantations, which primarily ensured that the name of the deceased was kept alive through repetition.

For royalty, these prayers and offerings were made twice daily to the *ka* statue of the king within his mortuary temple. For the rest of the community, the level of devotion was time-consuming and intrusive, so ceremonies were likely to be carried out weekly, monthly or annually, depending on the particular family and their commitments.

Part IV

Interpreting Egyptian Art and Architecture

The 5th Wave   By Rich Tennant

IN ANCIENT EGYPT, ONLY NOBLEMEN DROVE HORSEDRAWN CHARIOTS. FARMERS WERE FORCED TO USE MORE PLENTIFUL ANIMALS.

©RICHTENNANT

In this part . . .

Egyptologists are lucky because so many texts, tombs, and temples survive, giving a rounded view of the whole of ancient Egyptian culture. The major breakthrough in Egyptology as a discipline was deciphering hieroglyphs in the early 19th century. Prior to this, explorers could only look on in wonder with no real insight into the Egyptian's culture and beliefs.

The monuments of the ancient Egyptians are closely tied in with religion, and all architectural elements of a temple have a purpose. However, the development of tombs from holes in the ground to pyramids, and back to holes in the ground again has more to do with security than religion. As the tombs became more secretive they became more elaborately decorated; almost as compensation. This part takes you there.

Chapter 11

Deciphering Egyptian Art and Hieroglyphs

*E*gyptian art – including *hieroglyphs*, which are pictures that represent letters, sounds, ideas, and objects – is distinctive and appears strange to the untrained eye. However, after you begin to understand the codes behind the images, these ancient pictures start to speak and give loads of information about the places, events, and people represented, including their age, rank, occupation, and status.

Egyptian art survives primarily in the embellishments of tomb and temple architecture and in objects both beautiful and practical. See Chapter 12 for more on decorating temples and Chapter 13 for more on decorating tombs.

This chapter shows you how to carefully unravel these image-based codes and reveal the secrets of Egyptian art.

Recognising the Artists

Egyptian artists were very well trained and needed to be schooled in the many conventions of Egyptian art, which enabled the images all over Egypt to be the same.

This extensive training was carried out on the job, and like all Egyptian professions, it was passed on from father to son, starting in infancy (see Chapter 2 for more on occupations). First the apprentice practised his drawing and carving on *ostraca* – broken pieces of pottery and limestone used as scrap paper, rather like the modern sticky note. His tutor corrected these rough sketches in a different-colour ink. Many surviving examples show these errors and corrections.

Team players

Unlike the art of many civilisations, Egyptian art cannot be assigned to a particular artist due to the very strict artistic conventions of the time.

Saying that, the archaeological record *has* provided the names of artists who lived at Deir el Medina and worked on the royal tombs. Sadly, although historians know the artists' names and the tombs they worked on, all the artwork was done in close-knit teams, so specific scenes can't be attributed to an individual. From today's point of view, this anonymity and the culture's strict conventions may have been frustrating for artists because they had no means to express their individuality.

Each team was made up of approximately 30 people, including a number of different craftsmen:

- ✔ **A master craftsman** who designed the original composition and double-checked and corrected all the work of his men
- ✔ **Plasterers** who prepared the walls for painted relief
- ✔ **Stone masons** who prepared the walls for carved relief
- ✔ **Outline scribes** who drew the outline for both carved and painted relief
- ✔ **Sculptors** who carved the outlines for carved relief
- ✔ **Artists** who painted the images for both painted and carved relief

All workmen in a team worked at the same time on a sort of production line.

After the plasterers had prepared one area of wall, the outline scribes sketched the images and the plasterers moved on to another part of the wall. As soon as the outline scribes had finished one bit, the sculptors started their work and the outline scribes worked a little further along.

The entire process was well timed to ensure that the men carried out as much work as possible in the shortest amount of time. This process was used primarily on the large-scale compositions that range from one metre square to tens of metres square. The master craftsman had to prepare the entire composition in advance.

Following the master plan

Although the artists were all skilled in the various characteristics of Egyptian artistic style, a grid system was introduced to ensure the artwork was to scale and in proportion throughout a tomb or temple. This grid system was used for both painted and carved relief.

All compositions were initially sketched on papyrus and were copied and enlarged onto the walls of the tombs and temples. The master plan had a grid drawn over the images so artists could easily scale up the images through copying from the smaller grid to one drawn on the wall.

Artists created the grid on the wall by dipping string into red paint, stretching it across the surface, and then snapping it back into place to get a red line. This was repeated with multiple horizontal and vertical lines, creating a grid. These lines disappeared as the rock was carved or was painted over.

Equipping the Artists

The vibrant remains of Egyptian art in the form of tombs, temples, and carved statues are even more remarkable when you consider the very limited array of tools available at the time.

Paintbrushes were either bundles of plant fibres doubled over and lashed together at the doubled end to make a handle, or pieces of reed chewed at one end to make a frayed brush-type implement.

Paints were hand mixed and some ingredients for certain colours needed to be imported, which made paint an expensive commodity. Surprisingly, many of the colours are still amazingly vibrant, even though they were painted more than 3,000 years ago.

Through chemical analysis, researchers have been able to identify the minerals used to make the paint:

- ✔ **Red** was made from red ochre or iron oxide, which are both resources of Egypt.

- ✔ **Blue** was made from azurite, a carbonate of copper found in the Sinai and the eastern desert. The hue was also made of a combination of silica, copper, and calcium.

- ✔ **Yellow** was made from yellow ochre, iron oxide, or orpiment (a sulphide of arsenic); all are found in Egypt.

- ✔ **Green** was made of malachite from the Sinai. It was sometimes made by blending blue frit and yellow ochre, which were both available in Egypt.

- ✔ **Black** was made from soot, lampblack, charcoal, or plumbago (a blue flowering plant), all readily available in Egypt.

- ✔ **White** was made from gypsum, calcium sulphate, or whiting calcium carbonate, all natural to Egypt.

- ✔ **Brown** was created by painting red over black.

Lamps, which lit the dark tombs throughout the work, were also important. Shallow lamp dishes were filled with oil and included flax (a plant) or linen wicks. Because these light sources produced a great deal of smoke, some unfinished tombs show black soot marks on the ceiling – the most famous soot-covered tomb being that of Tutankhamun.

Figuring Out Egyptian Art

Egyptian art is not a photograph. When considering Egyptian art, modern viewers must remember that the Egyptians rarely recorded 'the truth' – a realistic depiction of an object or person.

Although the images can never be viewed as portraiture or a true rendition, every element of a composition is designed to tell you something about the person, event, or ritual. This notion explains the lack of perspective and three-dimensional qualities in Egyptian art, as well as the somewhat bizarre (to our eyes at least) representations of people, animals, and gods.

Everything in ancient Egyptian art is presented from the most recognisable viewpoint, in an effort to eliminate all ambiguity. However, modern Egyptologists aren't the intended audience for these ancient works, so an understanding of some of the key conventions is necessary even to begin to decipher the images.

The following sections explore several key conventions in Egyptian art.

Toying with views

To really understand an object, you often need to look at it from various angles or *views*, including bird's eye, front, and profile. Led by convention, Egyptian artists consistently used certain views of specific objects in their art and sometimes included more than one view of an object in a single image.

For example:

✔ A container is often shown with its contents on the top, even if the contents are sealed within.

✔ Chairs and stools are shown from a side view with two legs visible, and the seat is shown from a bird's eye view on top. If someone is seated on a chair, the cushion is draped over the seat and the back of the chair.

✔ Sandals and scribal palettes are always shown from a bird's-eye view to give the clearest view of the object.

✔ In garden scenes, a pool is shown from a bird's-eye view, but surrounding trees are shown from a front view, which gives them the appearance of lying flat on the ground. Objects in the pool, like fish, boats, or people, are drawn on top of the water with no indication of depth.

Forming an orderly queue

The ancient Egyptians were a very organised people, and their artwork reflects this.

All Egyptian art is divided into a series of registers and larger scenes or figures:

✔ Each register is separated by a *base line*, which often serves as a ground line for figures within the registers.

✔ Large figures (often the tomb owner or god/king) often occupy the end of a wall composition, covering four or five registers. The figures are, to a certain extent, overseeing the smaller scenes.

Although many tomb and temple scenes have the appearance of a comic strip, scenes next to each other don't necessarily follow in the narrative of the event. Compositions were planned well in advance, but individual scenes were often moved around to fit the space available. So a master craftsman might place a short scene on a short wall to allow the larger walls to be free for the larger scenes, regardless of chronological order. (This lack of linearity can be really confusing in tomb art depicting the 12-hour journey of the sun god, for example, because hour one is not necessarily next to hour two!)

Furthermore, registers do not necessarily join the larger scene or scenes in the composition, and in fact registers and scenes can be totally unconnected in space and time. (The ancients sure didn't make things easy!) Registers and scenes, however, are typically connected by a general theme: offering, hunting, war, and so on.

Other conventions related to registers include

- ✔ **Walking in step.** The feet of all Egyptians are typically on the base line and pointing in the same direction, even when large groups are depicted. Egypt represented its orderly, organised culture through this convention.

- ✔ **Rowdy foreigners.** Any people from outside the Egyptian borders are displayed in a more chaotic fashion, not in tidy rows.

- ✔ **Wild locations.** Any environment not within the confines of Egypt's borders – such as a desert or a foreign country – is represented through the use of undulating base lines.

Representing the human figure

The ancient Egyptian depiction of the human figure is one category of image that modern eyes find most bizarre – and most recognisable.

You have probably seen renditions of the 'Egyptian walk' – figures with one arm in front at head height and the other behind at waist height. Although comical, this image does not exist anywhere in actual ancient Egyptian art; modern artists have simply developed it over the years as an attempt to represent the Egyptians' unusual perspective of the human figure.

Ancient Egyptian artists depicted the human body in the same manner as other objects (see the section 'Toying with views', earlier in this chapter). Human figures are a collection of body parts assembled from their most recognisable viewpoints. For this reason, the human figures shown on tomb walls and decorated items stand in positions that are impossible to replicate with a real human body – without dislocating half your joints! (See Figure 11-1.)

Specifically, the human figure in Egyptian art includes

✔ A head shown in profile – but with a single front view of an eye and eyebrow and a profile mouth.

✔ Shoulders shown in full front view with the nipple or breast (on a woman) in profile, often under the armpit.

✔ The waist, elbows, legs, and feet shown in profile; it was traditional to show both feet from the inside with a single toe, normally the big toe and an arch, although from the New Kingdom some images show all five toes on both feet.

✔ Hands normally shown in full view, either open (from the back showing the nails) or clenched (from the front showing the knuckles).

Although the two-dimensional Egyptian figures can sometimes look a little bizarre to us (with the hands on the wrong arms and the feet on the wrong legs), many images show careful musculature, and statues display the Egyptians' amazing artistic talent.

Hand in hand

Hands caused major problems to ancient Egyptian artists, especially if the hands held objects.

For example, convention often dictated which hands held particular staffs. Old Kingdom officials held long staffs in the left hand and short sceptres in the right hand, close to the body. If the person was looking to the left, this arrangement was no problem, and the staffs are easily depicted in the correct hands. But if the figure faces right, big problems result. The left arm with the long staff becomes the front arm and the right hand becomes the rear arm. The long staff then runs the risk of obscuring the face, which spoils the whole image. This problem was typically solved by placing the long staff in the rear arm and the short sceptre in the near arm – but still in the correct hands. The only problem was that the right hand is on the left arm and the left hand on the right arm.

The hands were also sometimes swapped over to ensure the figure always has two thumbs facing away from the body but visible to the observer. These confusions are often viewed as artistic incompetence, but the fact of the matter is the opposite. In order to place the hands in unusual positions and still maintain the recognisable characteristics and strict artistic conventions, the ancient Egyptians had to work with great anatomical drawing skills.

Depicting eternal youth

Most people in ancient Egyptian imagery are shown at the height of physical fitness – young and fit. Even those individuals who are known to be elderly when they were depicted (such as Ramses II who was more than 90 years old when he died) are shown at about 20 years old.

Ancient Egyptian depictions of people were designed to last for eternity on temple or tomb walls and other decorated objects. Who wants to be shown warts and all? Human beings want to be remembered at their best, and the Egyptians were no different.

A handful of tombs at Deir el Medina (see Chapter 2 for more details on this village) show elderly relatives with salt-and-pepper hair or fully white hair. Granted, their skin and bodies don't show the ravages of time, but their hair colour does give away their advanced years.

The only age that is easy to identify in Egyptian art is for pre-pubescent boys and girls. Egyptians below this age are depicted with totally shaved heads and a side lock down the right side of their heads. (At puberty – between 10 and 15 years old – children had their side locks shaved off as a rite of passage.)

Even among the pre-pubescent children, you can further divide them into infants and children. Infants are shown nude, whereas older children are shown wearing clothes.

Colouring their world

When depicting humans, artist adhered to various colour conventions in order to identify the ethnicity of an individual:

✔ Egyptian men have red-brown skin, while Egyptian women are usually shown with yellow skin.

✔ Nubians – people from Nubia (modern Sudan), which was under the control of the Egyptians – have dark brown or black skin and short, curly black hair.

✔ Near Eastern people (from the area which is now Israel, Lebanon, and Syria), are shown with yellow skin and dark, shoulder-length, mushroom-shaped hair.

✔ Libyans (nomadic tribes from the western desert) are sometimes shown with fair skin, blue eyes, and red hair, or have elaborate side locks down one side of their head.

If a crowd of people of the same race are shown standing together, such as a group of Egyptians or Nubians, artists vary the skin colour between darker and lighter shades so no two skin tones of the same shade are next to each other.

Considering fashion

Egyptians are also only ever shown wearing plain white clothes – either tunics or kilts – with the exception of leopard-skin cloaks for funerary and high priests.

In addition to differences in paint colour, non-Egyptians are easily distinguished from Egyptians in temple art by their style of dress:

✔ Nubians wear gold earrings and loincloths made of cow, giraffe, and leopard skin.

✔ Syrians have shoulder-length hair with a hairband around the forehead. Their long tunics are white with a red trim to indicate that their garments were made of rectangular pieces of fabric, wrapped two or three times around the body.

✔ Libyans have elaborate hairstyles of shoulder-length hair with plaited side locks decorated with feathers. They also wear elaborately decorated woollen cloaks with long fringes.

✔ Asiatics (a general term for the people of the Syro-Palestinian region) wear beards and elaborately decorated tunics and cloaks. Asiatic women also wear little booties, which were not worn in Egypt due to the climate.

Most art shows non-Egyptians being suppressed by the Egyptian king, overcome in battle, acting subserviently to the Egyptians, or bringing tribute to the king or an Egyptian official. However, many non-Egyptians lived in ancient Egypt and adopted the Egyptian way of life, including Egyptian names and the language. These individuals are presented as Egyptian in their tomb art.

Size is everything

Egyptian artists used size as a method of depicting rank and status.

As the saying goes, 'The bigger the better'. In Egyptian art, the larger the individual, the more important he or she was. In tombs, the biggest individual is normally the tomb owner; in temples, the large images represent the king or the gods.

In scenes where people are all presented at the same scale, you can still easily identify who is the more important. Individuals of higher status have their feet at a higher level through sitting or standing on a plinth or dais.

Carving Masterpieces

Egyptian sculptors created their art on two-dimensional surfaces – walls, signs, and plaques – as well as three-dimensional creations. Many of the tools used for carving stone were simply made of a harder stone than the one being cut. Other tools used include

- **Copper hand saws** were used from the Old Kingdom.
- **Metal wedges** were used for splitting stone blocks (made of bronze from the 26th dynasty, and iron from the late period).
- **Wooden wedges** were used for splitting blocks. The blocks were inserted into a gap in the stone and then made wet. As the wood expanded in the water, the stone split.
- **Blunt chisels** were made from all kinds of stone, sometimes with a wooden handle. The chisels were hammered using a stone hammer, sometimes attached to a wooden shaft.
- **Drills** with metal drill bits were used from the Old Kingdom. The bow drill was a wooden shaft with a stone or metal drill bit. The drill bit had to be harder than the stone it was carving. A drill cap at the end of the shaft enabled the sculptor to apply pressure by hand. Instead of a drill cap, weights of stones in sandbags enabled a greater weight to be applied, which was particularly useful for a hard stone.

On the march

From the 18th dynasty, the non-royal tomb of Horemheb at Memphis features many carved scenes in which Egyptian artists have carefully depicted Horemheb's military life.

In one scene, an officer is leaving his tent, which is supported by a decorative tent pole in the centre, in order to speak to his commander, probably Horemheb. His batsman is standing at the door of the tent in a respectful manner, and a young naked boy is on his way to the tent carrying water skins. On the other side of the tent, another man gestures to another water carrier with two large water jars on a yoke over his shoulders. Two additional servants are working in the tent – one is pouring water on the floor to settle the dust, while the other sweeps up with a makeshift broom made from a bundle of tied-together sticks. The tent is filled with the possessions of the officer, including a table piled with food and a folding stool, which was easy to carry from camp to camp.

Another damaged scene shows the military cooks preparing food for the soldiers. The fragmentary state of the scene makes identifying what is being prepared difficult, although a clear portion of the image shows a squatting soldier eating a raw onion like an apple. (With this as a dietary staple, it would take more than 'double-mint' to freshen his breath.) Another cook is preparing meatballs or bread by rolling a ball in his hands, and a soldier is helping himself to a bowl of pre-prepared food.

The scene continues by showing the camp on the march. The terrain has undulating base lines, showing that the soldiers are not in Egypt. The tents have been dismantled and rolled up, and soldiers are carrying one tent on their shoulders. These soldiers are wearing open-work leather loincloths with a square patch at the back to provide added comfort while sitting down. The abundance of movement in these scenes gives an insight into busy military life.

The finished statue was smoothed using sand in the same way we use sandpaper to smooth a surface. The statue was buffed to create a shine if the stone wasn't intended to be painted.

Chiselling reliefs

Both painted and carved relief are common in Egyptian art. Painted relief was obviously easier than carving and was often the chosen method if the stone was of poor quality.

For carved relief projects, sculptors used copper chisels in one of two ways:

- **Raised relief** required the background to be cut away, leaving the figures standing out. This more time-consuming technique was used mostly inside tombs and temples, because the shadows created by dim lighting were very dramatic.

- **Sunk relief** was quicker to carve and involved cutting the figures away from the background. This technique was often used on outside walls and produced very dark shadows, which were good in bright sunlight.

The carved images were then painted in many colours, which to modern, minimalist minds may seem gauche and a tad tacky. For the Egyptians, the inclusion of colour offered another opportunity to display wealth and status.

Mistakes happened – even in the distant past. Carving goofs were easily covered with thin layers of plaster. The outlines were then redrawn and carved. However, 3,000 years or so later, the plaster has come off, often revealing extra carved lines. Just goes to show that no one is perfect.

Carving in 3D

Hundreds of statues have survived from ancient Egypt that represent both royalty and officials. The Egyptians didn't really believe in having statues purely for aesthetic purposes, so all the statues have a function. Statues were placed in both temples and tombs and were all *ka statues*, vessels for the spirits of the individuals depicted. Wherever the statue was placed, Egyptians believed the deceased's spirit could participate in the rituals and offerings being carried out.

Statues were of varying sizes and of many materials, depending on the wealth of the individual. Statues were made of stone, metal, or wood; the cheaper ones with resources from Egypt, and the more expensive using imported materials, including

- ✔ Limestone from quarries at Giza and Tell el Amarna
- ✔ Red granite from Aswan
- ✔ Quartzite sandstone from Gebel Ahmar (near Cairo)
- ✔ Alabaster from Hatnub, south east of Tell el Amarna
- ✔ Cedar from Lebanon
- ✔ Sycamore from Egypt
- ✔ Copper from the Sinai and Cyprus

Statues, such as wall reliefs, followed a number of conventions to indicate rank and position. For example:

- ✔ A figure sitting cross-legged on the floor was a scribe.
- ✔ A bald figure with a leopard-skin cloak was a high priest.
- ✔ A figure in a wig with a leopard-skin cloak was a funerary priest.
- ✔ A bald figure with a long kilt tied at the chest was a vizier.
- ✔ Stylised rolls of fat on the abdomen show affluence and wealth.

Hatshepsut: Miss, Mr . . . What?

Hatshepsut (see Chapter 5 for more on this ruler) started her time on the throne as a consort to her brother/husband Thutmosis II. When he died, she married her young stepson Thutmosis III and ruled as regent until he was old enough to rule alone. However, she wanted the power wielded by her young husband and took over the throne and ruled as king. Her actions caused a number of problems – both in artwork and in accompanying hieroglyphic inscriptions.

In order to be recognised in art as king, Hatshepsut needed to be displayed as such – with kingly attire including a kilt, crown, false beard, and crook and flail. This apparel has led some people to claim she was a transvestite, but this is not the case. Ancient Egyptian art was not a portrait; it displayed Hatshepsut in the _role_ she held as king. In fact, some of her statues show her with a combination of kingly attire and feminine features, making her statues easy to identify because the face is clearly that of a woman. Some of the statues of Hatshepsut as king also show her with breasts, but wearing male attire.

This combination of male and female attributes also confused the scribes. In inscriptions, Hatshepsut is described as both male and female; as both the son and daughter of the god Amun. The guidelines the artists and scribes learnt while training did not work when the king was female. I'm sure they were pleased to see the end of her reign so they could get back to normal.

Reading Hieroglyphs

In order to further identify tomb and temple scenes, it is useful to be able to read some of the *cartouches* – the lozenge-shaped enclosures that contain the king's name and names of the gods.

Cartouches are composed of *hieroglyphs* – pictures used to represent letters, although the situation is not quite that simple. Hieroglyphs form a proper language with case endings, tenses, verbs, nouns, and prepositions. More than 700 hieroglyphic signs existed in the Middle Kingdom and the number grew to more than 1,000 in the Ptolemaic period. (As new foreign words were introduced, the Egyptians needed new signs to be able to spell them!)

Losing the language

The hieroglyphic language first appears in Egypt in approximately 3100 BC and the last-known inscription was at the temple of Philae in AD 394 – a history of nearly 3,500 years.

From AD 394 until 1799, with the discovery of the Rosetta Stone and the beginnings of decipherment, knowledge of this ancient language was lost, although many theories arose:

- In the 16th century, the hieroglyphic language was believed to have developed from Armenian or Chinese.

- In the 1630s, a Jesuit priest and scholar, Athanasius Kircher, tried to decipher hieroglyphs and believed each sign represented an individual philosophical concept.

- In the 1750s, people believed that priests had invented hieroglyphs to conceal sacred knowledge.

Cracking the code

By the end of the 18th century, a number of discoveries had been made:

- The Coptic language developed from ancient Egyptian and was used by the Christians in Egypt. Coptic uses the Greek alphabet for the Egyptian words.

- Hieroglyphs (picture writing), and *hieratic* (shorthand hieroglyphs used for paper documents), and *demotic* (the Egyptian script which developed from hieratic used from 650 BC) languages were connected.

- Cartouches contained royal names.

- The hieroglyph system included phonetic elements.

These breakthroughs were aided in 1799 by the discovery of an engraved stone in the town of el-Rashid (Rosetta). The granite-like *Rosetta Stone* changed Egyptology forever. The stone was written in three scripts:

- Ancient Greek

- Egyptian hieroglyphs

- Demotic (a late cursive form of hieroglyphs)

Most historians could read ancient Greek, so this part of the stone was easily translated. In the race to decipher the hieroglyphic text, two main contenders emerged:

- **Thomas Young,** who published his findings anonymously under the name ABCD in case the unrelated research affected his credentials as a physician. Young deciphered the demotic text and identified the names of Cleopatra and Ptolemy within their cartouches. He also identified that the hieroglyphic signs were phonetic and did not individually represent words or concepts.

✔ **Jean-François Champollion,** who corresponded with Young, but was in competition with him to decipher hieroglyphs. At Young's death in 1829, Champollion continued the work and made the final breakthrough in identifying the phonetic value of many signs, thus enabling the transcription of many inscriptions. He also deciphered some of the linguistic and grammatical elements of the language.

Both Young and Champollion read the Greek inscription and matched the occurrence of recognisable words like 'king' and 'god', and looked for a similar number of occurrences in the Egyptian and demotic inscriptions. Real code breakers!

Identifying the signs

The many signs in the hieroglyphic language are divided into four sign types:

✔ **Single (or uniliteral) signs,** like the alphabet, which only have one letter sound; for example *i*.

✔ **Biliteral signs,** which have a two-letter sound (for example, *mn*)

✔ **Triliteral signs,** which are three-letter signs (for example, *htp*)

✔ **Determinative signs,** which have no sound, but are put at the end of a word to reinforce its meaning. For example, the word for cat is spelt out (*miw*) and would have an image of a cat at the end to show it was a cat.

Rosetta . . . again . . . and again

The text on the Rosetta Stone states that there was a copy of the *stela* (the curved top stone monument with carved inscriptions) in every temple in Egypt. A number of stelas have been found, and most are currently in the Cairo Museum:

✔ One was found in Minuf (Nile Delta), being used as a bench in front of a house. The surviving text is in Greek and demotic, although it is badly damaged.

✔ A basalt stela was found near Tell el Yahudiyeh (Eastern Delta) being reused as an oil press. Only the Greek text survives, although the stela was bilingual originally.

✔ Fragments of a trilingual stela of sandstone were found at Elephantine and are now in the Louvre. The section that is badly damaged on the Rosetta Stone is complete here.

✔ A sandstone stela found at Naukratis has a number of errors and was clearly copied from an original by an inexperienced stone cutter who could not read hieroglyphs.

In general, there are no written vowels in hieroglyphs; well, at least not the same as in English. This is the reason there are so many discrepancies in the spelling of names of gods – Amun, Amon, or Amen (from *imn*) – and of kings – Amenhotpe or Amenhotep (from *imn htp*), for example.

Understanding direction and honorific positioning

You can read hieroglyphs from right to left or left to right, as well as from top to bottom.

Don't panic! An easy method tells you which way the text should be read. Look at the direction the animals and birds are facing and read towards them. So if the animals are facing to the right, read the text from right to left, and if the faces are towards the left, read the text from left to right. Simple. If the text is above an image of a person and the animals are facing the same way as the person, it is clear that the text is describing the person depicted.

In kings' names inside a cartouche, you find a hierarchy of signs, which makes reading them difficult. If a god's name forms part of the king's name (like *Ra*mses), the name Ra is placed at the beginning of the cartouche, even if it is not to be read in that order. This is called *honorific positioning*, with the most important name being written first.

Hieroglyphic signs are positioned to fit within a small invisible rectangle in order to make them aesthetically pleasing, rather than placing each sign next to each other in a long line. This is done by placing horizontal signs together and vertical signs together, while at the same time keeping them in the order they are to be read as much as possible. In addition to looking good, this method of positioning enables more text to be placed in a small space. Also, no spaces or punctuation are between the words, keeping the inscription compact.

Learning the alphabet

Although hieroglyphic writing includes more than 700 signs, a number of uni-lateral signs can be used as an alphabet. Take a look at some of the most common unilateral signs in Figure 11-2. This figure shows you the hieroglyph and its English-language equivalent.

A	(Vulture)	
I	(Flowing reed)	
EE	(Two flowing reeds)	
A	(Arm - gutteral as in cockney 'wa'er')	
OO	(Quail chick)	
B	(Leg)	
P	(Stool)	
F	(Horned viper)	
M	(Owl)	
N	(Water)	
R	(Mouth)	
H	(Hut)	
KH	(Placenta)	
CH	(Cow's stomach - as in 'ich')	
S	(Fold of linen - both signs are used for the same letter)	
SH	(Pool)	
Q	(Hill)	
K	(Basket)	
G	(Jar-stand)	
T	(Loaf of bread)	
CH	(Tethering rope)	
D	(Hand)	
J	(Snake)	
L	(Lion)	

Figure 11-2:
Unilateral hiero-
glyphics.

Figure 11-3 shows signs used to express common Western names.

Hieroglyphic writing does not include many vowels. Also, the sign at the end of each name (the determinative sign) tells you whether the person is male or female.

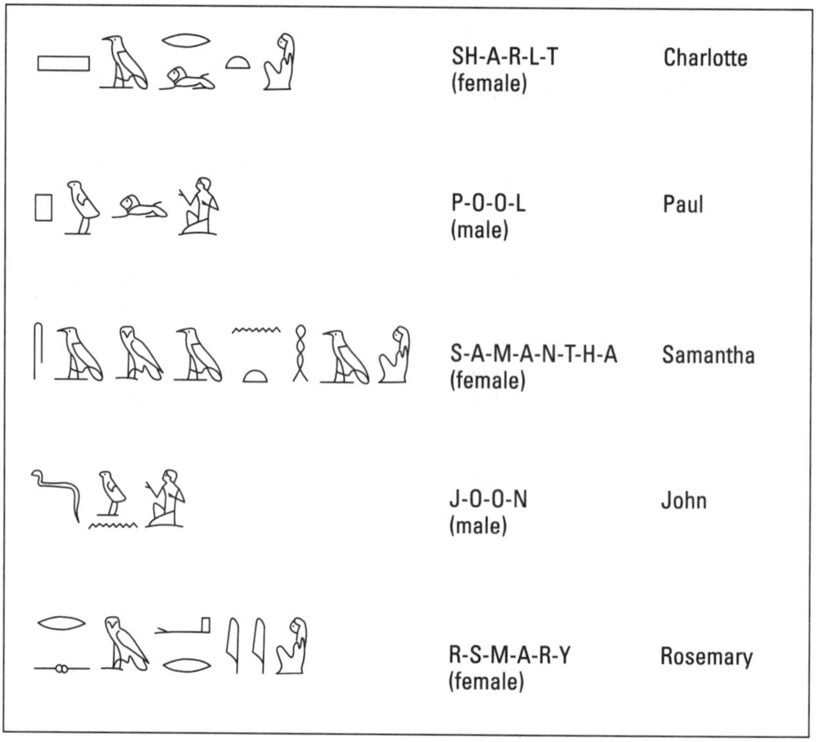

	SH-A-R-L-T (female)	Charlotte
	P-O-O-L (male)	Paul
	S-A-M-A-N-T-H-A (female)	Samantha
	J-O-O-N (male)	John
	R-S-M-A-R-Y (female)	Rosemary

Figure 11-3: Western names expressed in hieroglyphs.

Reading the names of the divine

Most of the royal names and those of the gods are written using bi- and trilit-eral signs (two- or three-letter sounds). However, some of these signs are common in both royal and gods' names. Figure 11-4 shows some of the best-known gods, as well as some common kings' names that incorporate gods' names; all would appear within a cartouche.

These signs aid in identifying the gods and goddesses in artwork and inscrip-tions. These signs appear on the heads of figures and to identify specific gifts given to the king by the gods.

Some of these gods' names appear in the most common kings' names within a cartouche, as shown in Figure 11-5.

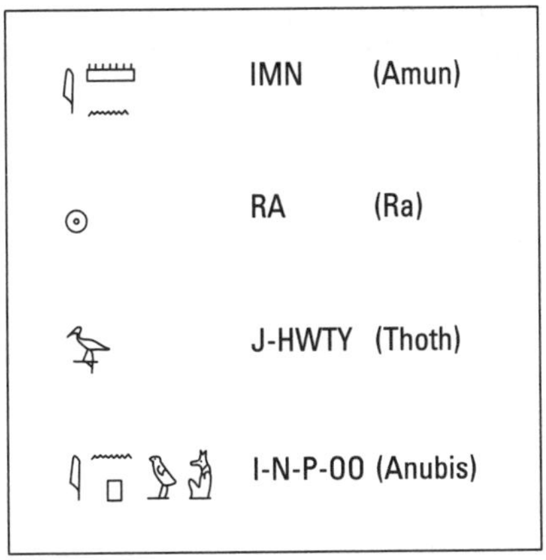

Figure 11-4:
Common
gods'
names.

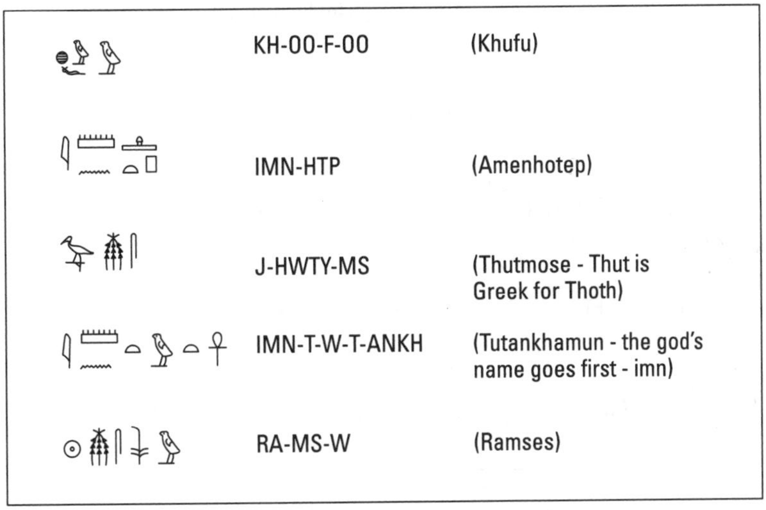

	IMN	(Amun)
	RA	(Ra)
	J-HWTY	(Thoth)
	I-N-P-OO	(Anubis)

Figure 11-5:
Common
gods'
names
appear in
common
kings'
names.

	KH-OO-F-OO	(Khufu)
	IMN-HTP	(Amenhotep)
	J-HWTY-MS	(Thutmose - Thut is Greek for Thoth)
	IMN-T-W-T-ANKH	(Tutankhamun - the god's name goes first - imn)
	RA-MS-W	(Ramses)

Reading Egyptian art

Hieroglyphs also appear in Egyptian art to represent concepts and gods.

Knowing some of the signs featured in Figure 11-6 can make interpreting all Egyptian art a little easier – without needing to read the long inscriptions.

Nothing in Egyptian art is random; everything has a purpose and is carefully placed within the final composition to give a clear description of what is represented.

♀	ANKH	Eternal life
⚐	WSR	Power
𝛶	WAS	Dominion
𝐽	ST	Throne – sign for the name of Isis
🎋	JED	Spinal column – sign for Osiris
🦅	HOOT-HOR	Horus within the palace – sign for Hathor
👤	TYET	The Isis knot represents the goddess
β	MAAT	Sign for truth and justice and the goddess Maat

Figure 11-6: Common Egyptian concepts as hieroglyphics.

Chapter 12

Touring the Temples

Many temples of ancient Egypt are still standing throughout the desert – a beautiful testament to a long-dead religion and a tradition of architecture and design.

The temples dominated the ancient Egyptian landscape. They were awe-inspiring, colourful structures. However, they were closed to the public; only the priests and the royal family had free access. Although the temples were inaccessible to the ordinary people, the activities and function of the temples affected the lives of everyone.

This chapter covers the planning and construction of these buildings, the roles of the priests and royalty, and the opportunities for worship available to both royals and everyday Egyptians.

Building a Temple

The ancient Egyptians built two types of temples:

✔ **Cult temples,** known as houses of the god, were for the worship of a god. These structures were normally situated on the east bank of the Nile. Although the temples were often dedicated to one god in particular (Amun, for example), these gods were often part of a *triad* that included a consort and child. (In the case of Amun, his consort was Mut and his child was Khonsu.) The triad was therefore worshipped at the site too. In a large temple like Karnak, many other gods are also worshipped within the complex – although the main god was Amun.

✔ **Mortuary temples,** known as temples of millions of years, were for the cult of the dead king. These buildings enabled worshippers to keep the king's spirit nourished for the afterlife and were normally situated on the west bank of the Nile. Although they were built in association with the kings' tombs, the temples were often some distance away in order to keep the tombs' locations secret.

The type of worship practised in each temple type was the same, although the statue within each type was different: Cult temples included statues of gods such as Amun or Ra, and mortuary temples housed statues of kings.

The ancient Egyptians believed that architectural design – just like art, religion, and literature – was dictated in the remote past by the gods. For this reason, they believed that they should not change the design of the temples, because improving on perfection was impossible. However, the Egyptian kings still needed to feed their desire to build and therefore constructed larger and larger versions of the same designs.

Going way back: The earliest temples

Very limited evidence of religion and temples prior to 3500 BC has been discovered. The early temples that have been identified bear no resemblance to the New Kingdom monuments still standing in Egypt today. The New Kingdom temples that dominate the modern landscape of Egypt all follow a similar pattern, which took centuries to develop.

Hierakonpolis

The earliest temple in Egypt is at Hierakonpolis just north of Luxor, dating from approximately 3200 BC. Excavations show that the temple consisted of a covered court on a raised mound of sand (probably symbolic of the mound of creation), which looked onto a walled courtyard. Just outside the courtyard, a number of small rectangular buildings probably housed workshops or stores associated with the cult.

The falcon-headed god, Horus (see Chapter 9), was probably worshipped at Hierakonpolis, although no inscriptions or statues have been found at the site. Horus is closely associated with kingship and is the earliest recorded deity.

Medamud

Another early cult temple just north of Thebes at Medamud does not follow New Kingdom conventions. Unfortunately the deities worshipped at this temple are unknown, although in later periods this site was the cult centre for Montu, the god of war.

An enclosure wall surrounded this temple, and an undecorated pylon gateway marked the entrance. This entrance led to a hexagon-shaped courtyard dominated by two mounds, perhaps indicative of the primordial mound of creation. Two corridors led to the top of these mounds.

A mud-brick chamber in the centre was filled with trees. Why these were included is unknown, but the explanation probably has something to do with creation and life sprouting from the mounds of creation. Either that or it's the earliest eco-house.

Evolving design during the Middle Kingdom

By the Middle Kingdom (2040 BC), temples were very symmetrical, although sadly examples from this period are rare, because they were mostly destroyed by the construction of later monuments.

Most of the Middle Kingdom temples were replaced by the New Kingdom (1550 BC) structures, but the Middle Kingdom legacy remains in the design. For example, the Karnak temple features Middle and New Kingdom influences, which makes sense because the structure took 2,000 years to complete and is the largest religious centre in the world.

The Middle Kingdom temples were very simple in design, with an entrance pylon leading to an open courtyard. At the rear of the courtyard, doorways led to three shrines. The central shrine was dedicated to the main god of the temple, and the two others were dedicated to the god's consort and the couple's child (see Chapter 9).

The Middle Kingdom design led to the *traditional temple*. The huge elaborate New Kingdom temples were merely expansions on this design, with each king adding a little to an already complete Middle Kingdom structure.

Adhering to design conventions in the New Kingdom

After the start of the New Kingdom (1550 BC), temple builders began to follow certain rules, and a more stylised and standardised temple design emerged.

Twinkle, twinkle, little star

Rather than being oriented towards the sun or the Nile, a few surviving temples in Egypt are positioned based on a star or stellar constellation.

For example, the temple at Elephantine is oriented towards the star Sothis (the star known today as Sirius). This star's rising announced the start of the annual inundation and was also associated with Osiris, the god of the underworld.

Another stellar temple – the Middle Kingdom temple on Thoth Hill near Luxor – is particularly interesting. This temple is also dedicated to the star Sirius, but archaeological evidence shows two sets of foundations. The temple was clearly re-aligned, because over the centuries the original orientation of the temple no longer aligned with the star's position, which had shifted over time.

Aligning with the elements

One design rule that began in the New Kingdom was the orientation of both cult and mortuary temples. While orientation varies between temples, these buildings were ideally sited on an east–west axis, at a 90-degree angle to the Nile. Of course, sometimes the natural terrain made this orientation impossible, and some temples, like the Luxor and Edfu temples, completely ignore this rule and are positioned north–south to run in line with neighbouring temples.

However, east–west is by far the most common orientation. This position highlights the solar aspect of the majority of temples. The sun rises in the east, so temple entrances often face that way to greet the rising sun.

Minding the rising tides

In addition to choosing a site for a temple according to the location of the Nile, some temples were built in such a way that during the annual inundation, the temple flooded. This flooding reinforced the temple as being like the universe, and a divine place, because the floods represented the primordial waters from which the temple emerged as if created from the waters.

This annual flooding entered all parts of the temple – except the sanctuary (see the section 'Proceeding to the Holy of Holies', later in this chapter, for more information), which was the highest point of the temple. This fact may help to explain why temple decoration rarely extends all the way down to the floor, but stops a metre or so above ground level. Having to repaint the temple once a year would be a major pain in the butt and best avoided at all costs.

Strolling down the processional avenue

Processional avenues or approaches to temples – which were sometimes added years after the main temple was completed, as improvements by later kings – are more commonly known as *sphinx avenues*, because these approaches were lined with multiple sphinx statues.

The most famous of these processional avenues is between Luxor and Karnak temples. A great deal of this avenue is still visible, especially around the two temples. Although Egyptian governmental figures and historians have discussed reconstructing the avenue to allow tourists to walk the full processional way, this plan has not been realised yet.

In addition to Luxor and Karnak, many temples originally had such avenues, including Abu Simbel in Nubia and the Ramesseum on the West Bank at Luxor.

Four types of sphinxes lined the processional avenues, including

- **Ram-headed lions,** which were identified with Amun, who is sometimes shown with a ram's head. Often a small figure of the king was placed under the chin of the sphinx.

- **Falcon-headed lions,** which represented the king in the form of Horus. These are rare and are found primarily in Nubian temples.

- **Sphinxes with the head of a crocodile, jackal, or snake,** which represent the gods Sobek, Duamutef (Anubis) or the cobra goddess Wadjet. These are very rare: Examples have been found only at the mortuary temple of Amenhotep III at Luxor.

- **Human-headed lions,** which bear the face of the ruler who constructed them. These sphinxes normally wear the blue and gold nemes headdress or the crown of Upper and Lower Egypt.

Processional avenues were used during religious festivals (see Chapter 9) when the *sacred bark* (small ceremonial boat) was carried to another temple on the shoulders of the priests. The procession was shielded from the public's prying eyes by a wall behind the two rows of sphinxes with the pathway running through the centre.

Entering the temple

The area by the temple entrance was always wide and open and was the lowest point of the temple. Priests and temple workers progressed through the temple via a system of short staircases or ramps, to reach the sanctuary at the rear (see Figure 12-1).

Take a break

Along the processional route, and therefore not part of the temple proper, a number of way stations offered an opportunity for the priests carrying the statues to stop and rest the sacred bark (boat). The sacred bark often had carrying poles that rested on the priests' shoulders.

The way stations were normally only large enough to accommodate the sacred bark for a short period and did not contain anything other than an altar on which the statue was refreshed with food and drink before continuing its journey.

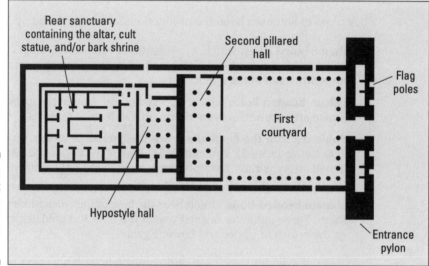

Figure 12-1: The layout of a traditional Egyptian temple.

Because the temples were closed to the public, getting into them was a tricky business. The outside of the temple was not designed to be inviting, and in fact all temples were surrounded by large enclosure walls. These walls were generally built of mud-brick laid over a frame of wooden beams and reed matting. These walls were not for scaling and were sometimes more than 10 metres thick. Not only were these barriers efficient at keeping people out, but they also offered protection for the royal family, priests and anyone else lucky enough to be admitted during times of war or conflict.

The enclosure wall was sometimes designed to represent primeval waters. By alternating the brickwork into convex or concave sections to look like waves, this building element further associated the temple with a representation of a microcosm of the universe.

In the centre of the enclosure wall stood an *entrance pylon*. These structures, generally built of stone, were often hollow and sometimes contained staircases or rooms, or were filled with rubble – anything to create a more stable structure. The shape of the pylon represents the hieroglyph for horizon, with a depression in the centre over the door. Because the pylon was ideally in the east, the sun rose between the sides of the depression over the sacred landscape of the temple. Many pylons exist at Egyptian temples today, including ten at Karnak, three at Medinet Habu and two at the Ramesseum.

A number of flag poles were erected on the wings of the pylon, on either side of the door. The flag poles (sometimes 60 metres tall and possibly made of gold or *electrum*, a mixture of gold and silver) bore flags with the sign of the god. Figure 12-2 shows the entrance at Luxor temple. The photo clearly shows the grooves for the four flag poles, as well as a standing obelisk, which was part of a pair. See the section 'Pointing to the sun: Obelisks', later in this chapter, for more.

Figure 12-2:
The entrance pylon from the Sphinx Avenue at Luxor temple.

Entering via the back door

During processions, the gods (actually their statues carried by the priests) didn't always use the main pylon entrance. Instead, most temples included a river entrance just outside the temple walls that was approached by a landing quay from the Nile or a local canal. In times of procession, the sacred statue began and ended its journey here. The general public may have gathered here for these processions to greet or bid farewell to the god.

Getting a foot in the door: The first courtyard and hypostyle hall

Once through the pylon gateway, the first courtyard loomed ahead. This area was open to the sky and surrounded by a pillared colonnade. The courtyard may have been accessible on special occasions to carefully chosen nobles to receive gifts from the king, to address the oracle of the god, or to receive divine advice (see Chapter 9). This courtyard housed many statues of nobles, priests, and royalty, and was a means for these individuals to be forever present in the temple and in the company of the gods.

At the rear of the first pillared court was the columned *hypostyle hall*. The pillars were believed to hold up the sky and the ceiling was often painted blue with hundreds of stars to represent the night sky. The pillars represented the vegetation that grew in the primordial marshes that surrounded the mound of creation. Entering the hypostyle hall was a symbolic walk in the marshes of creation. The most impressive existing hypostyle hall is at Karnak temple; it was planned by Horemheb, started by Sety I, and completed by Ramses II.

Proceeding to the Holy of Holies

The central axis that ran through both the first pillared courtyard and the hypostyle hall led to the most important part of the temple – the sanctuary. Only the king and the high priest were allowed to enter this part of the temple.

This small chamber was known by many names:

- The inner sanctuary
- The inner sanctum
- The Holy of Holies

The floors ascended as people progressed through the temple towards the sanctuary (see the section 'Entering the temple', earlier in this chapter), and the ceiling descended. Therefore, the sanctuary was the highest point of the temple, but with the lowest roof. This dark raised room represented the mound of creation, from which all life began.

Within the sanctuary, there was an altar with a small shrine. Behind golden or bronze doors, the cult statue stood. The Egyptians believed that this statue was not merely a representation of the god, but in fact housed the spirit of the god. For this reason, access to the statue was extremely limited.

The bark shrine was often within the sanctuary or very nearby. This shrine provided a spot to house the portable bark of the deity when it wasn't needed for processions.

Going for a dip: The sacred lakes

Because the temple represented the universe, and the sanctuary the mound of creation, the complex also needed to include the primordial waters. And indeed every temple had a sacred lake.

Sacred lakes were stone lined with steps that led down into the water. They were filled by the natural water table. Since the Aswan Dam was built in 1960 and the inundation was stopped, most of these lakes have dried up.

The water in these lakes was used in ritual offerings and for the purification of both the temple and the priests. Before the priests entered the temple, they were required to plunge into the lake to be purified by the holy waters.

The sacred lake of Karnak, built by Thutmosis III, had another very creative use. A special tunnel from the lake led to geese pens some distance away. The geese were systematically pushed from the pens through the tunnel, from which they popped up into the water, as if from nowhere. These geese symbolised Amun at creation and proved that the primeval water was still creating new life from nothing.

Supporting the ceiling

Present-day visitors may have difficulty imagining what the temples originally looked like, because the remains indicate very open, bright places. This is in fact the *opposite* of how the temples looked during the New Kingdom. All the temple areas – aside from the sacred lake and first pillared hall – were closed in with heavy stone roofs.

In order to support these roofs, columns were a major aspect of most temples, and indeed of architecture in general. Columns appear in at least two areas of a standard temple – the first pillared hall and the hypostyle hall. In larger temples, pillared courtyards, corridors, and kiosks were also common.

Because pillars were such a dominant architectural element, the Egyptians varied their design. In fact, more than 30 different column designs were used during the pharaonic period.

All pillar types were elaborately decorated with painted and carved images and hieroglyphs. Popular motifs included

- Lotus blossoms, with both open and closed buds
- Papyrus bundles, with both open and closed *umbrels* (flowering heads)
- The face of the cow-headed deity, Hathor

Considering doors and windows

The doors throughout the temples were huge affairs (some more than 20 metres high). Imagine the splendour of these monumental doorways. They were made from wood, ideally cedar wood imported from the Lebanon. These large planks of wood were then inlaid with gold, silver, lapis, and many other semi-precious stones.

As beautiful as they were, the doors served an important function: They were difficult to penetrate, which kept out the public and any invading enemies.

Temples were lit not by windows, but rather by stone grilles high up in the walls or by holes cut into the ceiling blocks, which let in small shafts of light. See Figure 12-3 for an example at Karnak temple. As a result, the temples were very dark and gloomy places, and the light shed by these lighting systems was intermittent and probably very creepy. For extra lighting, the priests and other temple personnel used oil lamps, which no doubt added to the shadow-ridden corners.

Figure 12-3:
A window grill in the hypostyle hall at Karnak Temple.

False doors and ear stelae

In both cult and royal mortuary temples, the sanctuaries included false doors carved into the rear walls. These doors weren't functional but were simply decoration carved onto the wall. (False doors are also found in tombs and tomb chapels; see Chapter 13.)

In a mortuary temple, such doors allowed the spirit of the deceased king to enter freely into the temple from his burial place. The royal burial places were often a distance away from the mortuary temples in an effort to prevent tomb robberies. The tombs were very secret, with no superstructure to act as a beacon to their whereabouts. Because the mortuary temple was the site of the food offerings, the deceased's spirit needed to have access, which the false door provided.

In cult temples, the false doors often backed onto *hearing chapels*. These chapels enabled the ordinary people to speak to the gods from the exterior of the temple (they were unable to enter the temple itself). The chapel wall was decorated with *ear stelae*, stone inscriptions inscribed with images of numerous little ears.

Worshippers spoke into one of the ears – saying a prayer, thanking the god, or asking for something, such as curing of an illness – and their voices went straight to the god's ears. Some of the chapels also had a small priest hole behind the stelae, within which a priest sat and answered the prayers out loud. That would certainly make you jump if you weren't expecting it!

Building the outhouses

In addition to the main temple, a number of outbuildings, essential to the function of the temple, stood around the surrounding grounds.

The most common outbuildings were the stores, or magazines, used to house the foodstuffs that were gathered in payment of taxes and redistributed to the temple and state workers. Some of these structures may also have stored the materials and tools used within the temple.

Other buildings included kitchens, animal and fowl pens, stables, and housing for the priests who resided within the temple enclosure walls. The temple was probably a noisy, busy place – and no doubt very smelly as well. Not the quiet serenity of a modern Christian church.

Several additional outbuildings had a religious function and can therefore be considered part of the temple itself.

The mammissi

From the Ptolemaic period (332 BC), many temples had a building known as a *mammissi*, or birth house. It wasn't a useable building, like a maternity ward, but rather a sacred place that commemorated the birth of the king.

The king had to show that he had a divine birth in order to prove his right to the throne. Prior to the Ptolemaic period, kings from slightly dodgy backgrounds had divine birth scenes added to their temples in order to 'prove' their divine origins and hence their right to rule. Because none of the kings in the Ptolemaic period were Egyptian, they needed to validate their right to rule even more than most. Check out Chapter 6 for more on this era.

In temples dedicated to a male deity rather than being a mortuary temple of the king, the mammissi was symbolic of the birthplace of the deity, and his birth was depicted on the walls. If the deity of the temple was female, the mammissi displayed images of her giving birth to her divine child. A rather splendid mammissi exists at the Ptolemaic temple of Denderah, just north of Luxor.

Sanatorium

Another building common in the Ptolemaic period is the *sanatorium*. Although sanatoria were present at most temples, the only surviving example is at Denderah.

The sanatorium was a dormitory where the sick came in an attempt to be healed. These were open to the general public, although no doubt if you gave the priests a financial gift, your cure was promised to be quicker or better.

After a patient arrived in the dormitory, the priest administered a sleeping draught. When the patient awoke, his or her dreams were interpreted by the priests. Egyptians believed that dreams were messages from the gods (see Chapter 9), so whatever the message of a priest-induced dream was, it would help cure ailments. Risking being called a cynic, I believe that most of these dream interpretations ultimately benefited the temple in one way or another; many of the 'cures' involved making offerings or building shrines at the temple.

Adding Finishing Touches: Obelisks and Decoration

After a temple was completed and the statue of the god had been placed in the shrine, the temple was considered fully functioning. But this didn't mean that kings couldn't keep adding to temples as a means of improving the works of their ancestors, as well as showing their devotion to the gods.

Additions took the form of carved or painted decoration, statues, and obelisks (as well as the processional avenues described in the section 'Strolling down the processional avenue', earlier in this chapter). The following section cover these architectural add-ons.

Pointing to the sun: Obelisks

All temples had at least two *obelisks* – tall, pointing structures that are synonymous with ancient Egypt. Obelisks are characterised by their tapering needle-like shape. At the top of the shaft was a pyramidion, which was gilded in gold or electrum, and takes its shape from the mound of creation. Some of the obelisks were completely covered in gold if the Egyptian economy allowed it.

Obelisks were made from a single block of stone, often red granite from Aswan. The quarry at Aswan has an incomplete obelisk (more than 41 metres long) embedded in the rock, showing that the features (shaft and pyramidion) were carved in situ and removed when complete.

In a standard New Kingdom temple, the obelisks were normally placed in front of a pylon, flanking the doorways, or along the central axis.

Hatshepsut's obelisk adventure

At her mortuary temple at Deir el Bahri and the Red Chapel she built at Karnak, Hatshepsut records her erection of two obelisks at Karnak temple. She even shows their transportation from the quarries at Aswan where they were initially carved.

At Aswan, the obelisks were tied to wooden ledges, which were towed on large sycamore barges, more than 60 metres long, by 27 tow boats to Thebes via the Nile. These boats were rowed by 850 oarsmen – a huge number of rowers, reflecting the weight of their cargo. Each obelisk may have weighed more than 450 tonnes and stood more than 50 metres high. The obelisks were completely covered in gold and were a beautiful sight to behold.

Luckily the currents of the Nile aided the transportation process. The entire journey was accompanied by three ships of priests who chanted incantations and prayers over the boats. I'm sure the rowers appreciated their efforts. After these boats arrived at Thebes, a bull was sacrificed in honour of the event and offered to the gods. Hatshepsut then presented her obelisks to the god Amun.

The whole process from quarry to temple took only seven months and was a phenomenal achievement. Sadly, all that remains of these obelisks are the bases, as the gold and the shafts were removed and reused in antiquity.

A few years later, Hatshepsut erected a further pair of obelisks, standing nearly 30 metres high, one of which is still standing at Karnak temple and is the tallest obelisk in Egypt. Only the tops of this pair were gilded, but still they were an impressive sight.

Journey of a lifetime

The transportation of Cleopatra's Needle to London was not an adventure-free journey. In fact it can be described as disastrous.

Cleopatra's Needle was presented to the United Kingdom in 1819 by Mohammed Ali, the Viceroy of Egypt, in commemoration of victories at the Battle of the Nile and the Battle of Alexandria in 1801. The structure remained in Alexandria until 1877 when the funding for transportation, a total of £10,000, was provided by Sir William James Erasmus Wilson. (Prior to this no one wanted to pay the transportation costs.)

The obelisk was placed in a custom-made, 28 by 4.5 metre iron cylinder, named rather unoriginally *Cleopatra*. This cylinder then floated behind the tow-boat *Olga* – a modern(ish) twist on Hatshepsut's obelisk transportation.

When the boat reached the Bay of Biscay, *Cleopatra* capsized in a storm and floated into the bay. The cylinder was rescued by an English ship and taken to Spain for repairs. It eventually arrived in the United Kingdom in January 1878 and was erected on Victoria Embankment seven months later.

In September 1917, during the First World War, German bombs landed near the obelisk, causing damage to the right-flanking sphinx. This was never repaired, in commemoration of the war, and shrapnel holes are still visible. To be honest, the British are lucky to have the obelisk at all – so what are a few holes?

New Kingdom obelisks were very tall. Due to their height, they were often the first and last point of the temple to catch the rays of the sun, and indeed the shape of the obelisk is believed to represent a sunbeam.

Of the hundreds of obelisks that once existed in ancient Egypt, only 30 are still in existence, and of those only seven are in Egypt. The others have been spread around the world:

- Seven are still in Egypt, two at Heliopolis, one at Gezira Island, one at Cairo, and four at Karnak.

- 13 are in Rome.

- Ten are elsewhere around the world, including Paris, London, New York, Istanbul, Florence, Urbino (a small town in Italy), Catania (in Sicily), Wimborne (United Kingdom), Arles (southern France), and Caesarea (Israel).

Temple décor

One of the easiest ways of making an impact is through decoration, and many kings decorated a wall or chamber of an existing temple and claimed credit for the building work as well. In their logic, if their name was painted or carved on the wall, then they must have built it too.

During particularly weak economic periods, or even just busy times, kings commonly usurped temples in order to reduce time and construction costs. During the New Kingdom, it became the norm for kings to nick the work of their ancestors by simply painting or carving over the cartouches of the original decorator and claiming the work for themselves. Ramses III, however, was determined that he would always be credited for the work he did – he therefore carved his cartouches so deeply into the stone that it was impossible for a later king to usurp his monument without carving half a metre into the wall.

Carvings

Two types of relief were used in temple decoration:

- ✓ **Raised (bas) relief,** in which the background was cut away, leaving the image raised. This was very time-consuming and was kept to a minimum. It was more common on interior walls.

- ✓ **Sunk relief,** in which the subject was cut away from the background. Quick to execute, this type of relief was more common, especially on exterior walls.

Ramses II devised a way of carving which looked like the finer raised relief, but was in fact the quick-and-easy sunk relief. This involved carving a very deep line around the edge of the images, which gives the impression of raised relief. Figure 12-4 shows an example of this carving technique.

After the carved images were completed, they were painted in elaborate colours. Paint also added small details, such as fabric patterns, wings on birds, and plant life.

Figure 12-4:
The image of Hathor and Isis at the Hathor Temple in Deir el Medina is a sunk relief made to look like a raised one.

Interior embellishments

Because the temple represents the universe, the ceilings were always decorated with sky-related images, and the decoration near the floor was always of marshland. Pillars often represented plants, creating a stone universe recognisable to all.

Both cult and mortuary temples featured the same categories of artistic embellishment, including depictions of

- ✔ **Ritual activities,** such as temple rituals, processions, and offerings.
- ✔ **Historical activities,** such as battles, processions (either military or religious), coronation celebrations, sacred birth scenes, and diplomatic treaties.
- ✔ **Environmental scenes,** which were applied to certain elements of the temple architecture and included depictions of the sky, marshes, flora, and fauna.
- ✔ **Making offerings to the gods.**

Although the preceding categories are nicely labelled, many surviving images actually fall into more than one category on occasions. For instance, religious processions or offerings are both ritual activities *and* historical activities because they were real events.

The images were strategically placed throughout the temple, and although artists had a lot of freedom regarding the content of the images, the location was often pre-determined. For example:

✔ The sanctuary had images of offerings being made to a shrine on a sacred bark.

✔ Shrines had images of offerings being made to various gods by the king.

✔ Windowsills were decorated with images of sunrays.

✔ Ceilings were painted with stars or birds to represent the sky.

✔ Food stores were decorated with images of fatted oxen ready for slaughter.

✔ Routes of processions showed the procession in progress.

✔ Pylons and external walls were decorated with violent scenes showing the king smiting enemies in battle or parading bound captives. These images were to act as a deterrent against enemies wishing to cause harm to the temple, Egypt, or the king.

In rooms that did not have a specific function, a variety of images were presented, including historical events such as expeditions, coronations, or public military processions. For example, in the temple of Edfu, the walls were used as archival documents recording the history of temple building and festival calendars.

Who's a pretty pylon?

Luckily for modern visitors and historians, many of the kings described their temple-decoration methods and meanings on temple walls and papyri. These records provide some idea of the splendour that once existed in these vast and now barren places.

For example, the decoration of the third pylon at Karnak is described by Amenhotep III and shows that paint and carving were just the beginning:

The king added a monument for Amun, making for him a very great doorway before the face of Amun-Re, King of the Gods, embellished with gold throughout. [On its door] the sacred ram-headed image, inlaid *with lapis lazuli, is embellished with gold and precious stones: the like will never be done again. A stela of lapis lazuli stands on either side. Its pylons reach to the sky like the four pillars of heaven: The flagpoles thereof, embellished with electrum, gleam brighter that the sky.*

The riches mentioned in this description have long since been stripped and taken away – if they ever existed. The description may be pure propaganda to inflate the piety of the king. For the ancient Egyptians, once something was written in hieroglyphs, it was considered to have been created by the gods and became reality. Now if only those kinds of pens were available in the shops today . . .

Worshipping in the Temple

The temples were busy and vibrant places. Although the temples were closed to the public, the rituals inside were very important.

Attending to the god

All temple activities revolved around the sacred statue in the sanctuary at the rear of the temple. This statue was tiny – perhaps only 30 centimetres high – and was made of gold or gilded wood. Sadly, none of these statues survives, but the shrines within which they were placed survive and give an indication of how small the statues were.

The most important ritual was the first one of the day. Just before dawn, all the temple staff rose, purified themselves, and prepared food for an elaborate breakfast for the statue. Typical duties included baking bread and honey cakes, slaughtering animals, and arranging fruit and vegetables on trays. The meal was then offered to the statue.

A similar meal-preparation ritual was repeated at dusk when the statue was put to bed; for further information see Chapter 9.

Throughout the day, the hour priest offered different hourly prayers to the god. The hour priest kept time by observing the sun and using water clocks, which were essentially bowls with holes that measured the time by the amount of water that had drained away.

Enjoying the festivities

The temple was also the site of many festivals and processions, which enabled ordinary people, typically denied access to the temple, to visit the temple and participate in worship. Records indicate that up to ten processions happened each month, enabling the people to view the sacred bark and perhaps receive blessings and guidance from the priests.

During festivals and processions, temple staff often distributed extra rations so that people could have a feast and celebrate in style, in addition to enjoying the obligatory day off work.

Not only did festivals benefit the villagers, they also benefited the smaller temples. The statues of the deities from the larger temples, like Karnak or Luxor temple, travelled to the smaller ones. To ensure that the god was suitably received, the larger temples supported the smaller temples economically, greatly benefiting the priests working there.

Getting wasted

The Festival of Drunkenness was celebrated annually at Deir el Medina in honour of the cow-headed goddess, Hathor, the lady of drunkenness (see Chapter 9). The aim of the celebration was to drink as much beer and wine as possible over a five-day period. Rather like St Patrick's Day – for the better part of a week!

Texts from Deir el Medina describe the festival in detail:

Come, Hathor, who consumes praise because the food of her desire is dancing, who shines on the festival at the time of illumination, who is content with the dancing at night. Come! The drunken celebrants drum for you during the cool of the night.

Sounds like the party went on well into the wee hours of the morning with lots of dancing – as is normally the case with drunk celebrants.

Egyptians, however, believed that the drunkenness associated with this festival was a means of achieving an altered state that enabled worshippers to see the divine or receive messages from the goddess. If you drink enough, who knows what can happen?

Appreciating the Roles of the King and the High Priests

REMEMBER

The king was officially the high priest of all the cults in every temple in Egypt and was expected to perform all the necessary rituals in order to maintain the cosmic order, or *Maat*. (See Chapter 9 for a further discussion of Maat.)

If the king failed to appease the gods, the land would collapse into a state of chaos resulting in famine, floods, or invasion. If I had this kind of pressure, I would delegate it – and this strategy is exactly what the king followed with his high priests. The high priest of each temple worked in place of the king. Everything the priest did was done in the king's name.

Whenever the king was present at a temple, the high priest was relieved of his role, albeit briefly, enabling the king to perform his duty as high priest.

Laying the foundations

The king's role in the temple started as soon as a location was chosen (and often he chose the location himself). As the section 'Building a Temple' earlier in this chapter explains, most temples were built on older sacred sites, which often required the dismantling of the older temple that originally stood there.

After the site was clear, the king performed the ten foundation rituals:

1. **Fixing the plan of the building by 'stretching the cord'.** This was the most important ritual and was assisted by the goddess of writing, Seshat. During this ritual, the king banged a peg into the earth at the spot where each corner was to be and then stretched cord between this peg until an outline of the temple was established.

2. **Purifying the area by scattering gypsum.**

3. **Digging the first foundation trench.** The trench was dug until the natural water table was reached.

4. **Pouring sand into the first foundation trench.** This represents the mound of creation protruding from the primeval waters at the bottom of the trench.

5. **Moulding the first bricks.**

6. **Leaving *foundation deposits* at the corners of the structure.** These deposits are varied and consist of pottery, model food, model tools, and occasionally jewellery.

7. **Initiating the building work.**

8. **Purifying the finished temple.** This no doubt involved prayers and incantations.

9. **Presenting the temple to its deities.** The king placed the statue of the god in the shrine at the rear of the temple. The statue was the focus of the whole temple. Although a temple could enable worship of numerous deities, each temple had a primary deity. (For example, although Amun, Mut, Khonsu, Montu, Ptah, Opet, and Amum are all worshipped at Karnak, the main deity is Amun. Amun's statue is therefore the most important on the site.)

10. **Making sacrificial offerings to the gods who now resided in the temple.** These sacrifices were probably in the form of geese or oxen.

Because these rituals are only recorded in list form, knowing exactly what each ritual consisted of is difficult, if not impossible.

Feeding the populace: Other temple duties

In addition to being the 'house of the god' where the priests worshipped and revered the statue of the god, the temples were the economic centres of the cities.

Monitoring the river's rise and fall

In order to calculate taxes correctly, temple personnel devised methods for predicting flood levels that helped them determine the type of harvest that was likely to result. If the flood was too high or too low, the harvest failed and resulted in famine. So through prediction, the priest prepared for agricultural abundance or shortfalls.

Each temple had a *nilometer*, which was a deep well that reached the water table. When the Nile started to flood, the priest measured the speed of the rise at the bottom of the nilometer. These measurements were recorded and compared to those made at the same date in previous years. With this information the priests fairly accurately predicted annual flood levels. Clever, eh?

Most temples were supported by their own estates, which the king or wealthy members of the community gave the temples in exchange for the blessings of the god. This agricultural land was rented to farmers, who paid the temple a third of their yields as rent. Much of this income was redistributed in the form of rations (wages) for the army, to the officials (essentially anyone who held a position in government or the priesthood), and for royal construction of temples and tombs. (See Chapter 2 for more details.)

Meeting the priests – civil (not divine) servants

Prior to the New Kingdom, a permanent priesthood did not exist. Priests worked in the temples on a part-time basis and then returned to their jobs in ordinary society. During the New Kingdom, many priests were primarily administrative officials in control of taxes and food distribution – with only a small hint of religion (for the full role of the priest, skip to Chapter 2). Even in the New Kingdom, a large majority of the priests served one month out of four.

A small core of permanent priests lived within the temple precincts, with the high priest in the most senior position. Obviously the number of personnel in a temple varied according to the size of the temple. Karnak, for example, had more than 2,000 employees, whereas most other temples had between 10 and 80 personnel.

Acting as an ancient records office

Because the temples were so involved in the Egyptian economy and the associated administration, they kept extensive records of the local regions, rather like a town hall records office. These records were stored in the House of Life (for further details go to Chapter 2) and included details of

- Locations of holy places
- Pilgrimages, which anyone could participate in
- *Cult centres* (centres of worship of particular deities) and names of personnel
- Local crops
- Local standards and deities
- Dates of principal festivals
- Taboos regarding activities or food
- Portion of the Nile present in the region
- Cultivated fields and marshy lands
- Outgoings, such as support for campaigns to foreign areas, building works, and rations
- Foreign countries and their resources

Recording the days

The priests were also responsible for devising the calendar systems. Three were in use, all for different purposes:

- **Agricultural calendar:** For day-to-day use by the majority of the population. The year was divided into three seasons of four months each – inundation (flood), time of growing, and harvest.
- **Astronomical calendar:** For ritual use and based on the movement of the stars.
- **Moon calendar:** For ritual use for *lunar cults* (cults devoted to gods associated with the moon). Careful records of the lunar phases were kept and these were tied in with religious days and rituals.

All the calendars had certain aspects in common. Each month consisted of 30 days, totalling 360 days in a year. Five religious festival days were then added to the end of the year for the birthdays of Osiris, Horus, Seth, Isis, and Nephthys (see Chapter 9). Of course, this 365-day calendar slowly veered away from the true year. Every four years, the agricultural calendar advanced one day, which meant that eventually the seasons no longer coincided with the calendar. To deal with this discrepancy, the rising of the star Sirius always coincided with the beginning of the inundation, which was seen as the New Year.

Chapter 13

Excavating the Tombs: Houses of Eternity

· ·

In This Chapter

▶ Tracking the development of the tombs

▶ Identifying tomb variations

▶ Protecting bodies and treasure from robbers

▶ Adorning tombs with painting and decoration

▶ Exploring the Valley of the Kings

· ·

*E*gypt is well known for its burial sites, whether pyramids or the elaborately decorated tombs in the Valley of the Kings. This chapter focuses
on the history of tombs, while Chapter 14 delves into the secrets of the
pyramids.

The Valley tombs are the result of years of evolution brought on by changing
religious priorities and increasing security risks.

However, regardless of the tombs' design, the same fundamental belief in the
afterlife is present. The Egyptians saw the afterlife as a place where the
deceased was reborn and lived for eternity (see Chapter 10 for more details),
the ancient equivalent of paradise. In fact, a belief in the afterlife is suggested
in the earliest burials (prior to 3100 BC), before the construction of elaborate
tombs, from the simple inclusion of funerary goods.

As religious beliefs became more complex, the tombs grew more elaborate
and developed into status symbols – like today's Porsche!

But above all, these resting places were intended to last for eternity, as a
home for the deceased in the afterlife. They were therefore referred to as
Houses of Eternity. (It does exactly what it says on the tin!)

Burying the Earliest Egyptians

All civilisations need to dispose of the dead, and in a country as hot as Egypt, decomposition can start immediately. Therefore, in the pre-dynastic period (prior to 3100 BC), burials were simple affairs:

- The deceased was buried individually in a shallow pit dug into the desert edge, a short distance away from the settlements.
- The body was placed into the pit in a foetal position with no coffin or covering of any kind.
- The pit was filled with sand, which fell directly onto the body, preserving it naturally.

Burials were accompanied by a number of grave goods, including pottery vessels and dishes, jewellery, and cosmetic palettes. These objects were clearly connected to a belief in the afterlife and the belief that the deceased would need them again.

Enclosing the dead

Occasionally, animals disturbed the pit burials, uncovering the buried bodies and revealing the natural preservation that had taken place. The bodies sometimes even retained skin and hair, whereas at other times the preservation was not so consistent.

Natural preservation sparked a belief that in order to survive in the afterlife, bodies needed to be preserved. With that, the process of artificial preservation, or *mummification* (see Chapter 10), began. Artificial preservation also led to the development of tombs as a further effort to preserve bodies for eternity.

The earliest attempts to preserve the body artificially took two forms:

- Enclosing the body in something, such as a clay pot, reed tray, animal skin or linen shroud
- Lining the burial pits in bricks or wood

A number of early cemeteries have been discovered (Hierakonpolis; Minshat Abu Omar, 150 kilometres from Cairo; and Adaima, 25 kilometres north of Hierakonpolis) that include simple pits lined with mud brick. The walls were left undecorated, and the bottom of the burial pit was lined with reed matting tied to wooden strips, which created trays to lay the bodies on. A ledge runs around the top of the inside wall, which supported wooden roofing beams. These pits were then covered with desert rubble in order to disguise the burial locations in the desert plateau.

Tomb 100

Tomb 100 from the pre-dynastic cemetery at Hierakonpolis (around 3685 BC) was the first tomb (and the only one known from the pre-dynastic period) to contain decorated walls. Rather than a simple pit, Tomb 100 features a number of subterranean rooms separated by partition walls. In the burial chamber, these walls are plastered and painted. Depictions of men, animals, and riverboats appear in red, white, green, and black paint on a yellow background.

At least three images in Tomb 100 relate to more traditional Egyptian art, including imagery often used to represent the role of kingship. For example, one image in Tomb 100 shows a man smiting three bound captives with a mace; another shows a figure holding two wild animals in his bare hands; and another has a boat holding a figure, probably a chieftain, seated underneath a canopy with a group of men in loincloths worshipping him with their hands outstretched.

Although no texts survived in Tomb 100, these prominent figures suggest that a king, or chieftain, was probably the tomb owner. Sadly, since its discovery in the early 20th century, the location of Tomb 100 has become lost, so further examination of the original paintings is impossible. Photographs and copies of the paintings are in the Ashmolean Museum, Oxford, and the Egyptian Museum in Cairo.

Upgrading the pits

As time went by, the simple brick-lined pits weren't enough. Egyptians wanted something more impressive as their House of Eternity.

Initially the pits were modified to include partition walls, which created a number of chambers to store lots of grave goods. The largest discovered pit tomb is tomb Uj from Abydos from dynasty 0 (around 3100 BC; see the Cheat Sheet for chronology). The tomb is 9.10 by 7.30 metres and is divided into 12 rooms, nine of which contained hundreds of pottery vessels and ivory labels. This elaborate tomb most probably belonged to a local chieftain or mayor.

The Egyptians were still not satisfied, however, and wanted to extend their House of Eternity upwards. The sky's the limit, as they say.

Turning Pits into Palaces: Mastabas

By the start of the Old Kingdom, officials began building superstructures over the pits. The mounds of desert rubble piled over the pits' wooden roofs were extended upwards, making the tombs distinguishable from the surrounding landscape.

Adding superstructures

The size and design of the materials placed on top of the tombs reflected the status and wealth of the individual and no doubt led to a trend of keeping up with the Joneses – or rather, keeping up with the Amenhoteps.

Smaller, less impressive burials consisted of small uneven mounds of rubble covering the burial pit, whereas more elaborate tombs had rectangular brick superstructures built up to heights of 1 metre above ground level.

These superstructures were bench-like in shape, hence they were named *mastaba*, from the Arabic word for bench. The outside of the superstructure was painted white, while offering niches along the west wall were painted a dull red. A brick pavement led to the niches and provided a space where mourners could leave food offerings of bread, beer, and vegetables for the spirit of the deceased.

Because these superstructures were built *after* the burial had taken place, entrances were unnecessary. The lack of entrances meant mastabas were safe from most robbers, but it also meant the tombs couldn't be re-entered. This was soon to change, as family burials became the height of fashion.

Bigger, better mastabas

By the end of the Old Kingdom (2333 BC), family tombs were common, with elaborate hollow mastaba superstructures being constructed.

These superstructures contained numerous decorated chambers, including areas that functioned as funerary chapels and enabled family to leave offerings inside rather than outside. The deceased were still buried in pits beneath the ground and could be reached via a shaft in the floor of the mastaba.

As the mastabas became more impressive, the kings needed to reassert their status and wealth, which led to the design and construction of step pyramids and eventually smooth pyramids (see Chapter 14).

Stepping up: King Djoser

The first step pyramid was built for King Djoser of the third dynasty (2686 BC). The structure started with a traditional mastaba tomb at Saqqara. The burial chamber was 28 metres below ground at the bottom of a shaft and was lined with granite. This remains under the step pyramid that is on the site today.

Room for 11 more?

Just to the east of the original completed mastaba of Djoser, 11 burial shafts were sunk 38 metres into the ground. These 11 shafts each ended in a large galleried chamber and were the intended burial places of the royal family.

Although the chambers were sadly robbed in antiquity, two calcite sarcophagi have survived, one with a gilded coffin containing the remains of an 8-year-old girl.

Leading from the burial chamber are four corridors, which lead to a suite of chambers and storerooms. Some of these rooms included blue faience (a type of ceramic made from sand) tiles decorated with djed pillars, representative of the god Osiris, which is the only decoration in this burial site. The only human remains found in this step pyramid was a mummified foot, which suggests that a burial took place here.

The mastaba superstructure was constructed of desert rubble and clay, encased in limestone blocks 3 metres thick. The initial superstructure was 63 metres long and 8 metres high, which was in itself no mean feat.

At some point in the mastaba's construction, Djoser decided he wanted something more impressive and made a number of alterations:

- ✔ The mastaba was extended lengthways.
- ✔ Three more structures were placed on top of each other, creating a four-step pyramid.
- ✔ The base was extended, and two more steps were added, resulting in a six-step pyramid rising 60 metres from the ground.

This was the first building in the world to be built entirely of stone. This tomb structure was thought to be a staircase that the king would ascend to be with his ancestors, who became stars after death.

After the construction of step pyramids, the next evolution in pyramid development was to fill in the steps to form a true, smooth-sided pyramid. See Chapter 14 for more on these structures. A number of pyramids at Saqqara and Abusir started as step pyramids and were turned into true pyramids by filling in the steps.

More complex than tomb

All the tombs and pyramids built during the Old and Middle Kingdoms were not isolated monuments, but rather part of larger complexes, consisting of temples and a cemetery for nobles and officials.

The step pyramid complex of Djoser, however, is unique. Rather than building a simple temple, Djoser built an entire full-sized kingdom over which he could rule for eternity. This complex covers 146 square metres, and most of the buildings were 'dummies' with no real function.

The complex includes

✔ The king's tomb – the main, step pyramid.

✔ Family and dignitary burial tombs, buried in mastaba fields with hundreds of tombs. The closer the tomb was to the pyramid, the more important the individual.

✔ A pillared hall.

✔ An open courtyard with altars dedicated to the sun god.

✔ A festival courtyard where Djoser performed his rejuvenation ceremony, or *heb sed*, every 30 years. The ceremony involved the king running around markers representing the length and breadth of Egypt to show his strength and vitality.

✔ Two mansions for the spirit of the king to reside in. The mansions also represented his rule over Upper and Lower Egypt.

✔ A mortuary temple, which was the focus of the funerary cult of Djoser.

✔ A *serdab*, which housed a life-size statue of the king. The statue was able to observe rituals through a hole in the wall.

✔ Storage rooms to house objects used in the rituals.

The only structures in the complex with real function were the mortuary temple and the burial tombs of Djoser's family and officials. In the afterlife when the king was reborn, the dummy buildings became real and provided Djoser with the luxuries and necessities of a king – including a kingdom to rule.

Hewing in Rock

During the Middle Kingdom, the mastaba was abandoned and non-royal burials were carried out in rock-cut tombs. These were tombs cut directly into a cliff face and supplemented with a monumental façade, a sloping courtyard, and a colonnade that functioned as a chapel in which the family and friends could leave offerings for the deceased.

The colonnade consisted of a large gathering area and a small statue chamber at the rear. A shaft located cut into the floor of the chapel led to the burial chamber beneath. The walls of these tombs are elaborately decorated with painted scenes of daily life, military training, battles, and hunting scenes.

If it's not nailed down . . .

Like the pyramids of the Old Kingdom, these elaborate Middle Kingdom rock-cut tombs were security risks. Unattended goods and offerings could easily be taken and sold on the open market.

The families that owned the tombs tried to limit the danger of robbery by regularly visiting the tombs to make offerings of food and drink. They also restricted the number of times the tomb was opened for the interment of additional family members. The mummified deceased were therefore stored in houses until an annual, bi-annual, or five-yearly opening of the tomb was due. Families then conducted group funerals for all members of the family who had died during a specific period.

The practice of waiting to inter bodies continued throughout pharaonic history. People were more concerned about robberies than the hygiene issues resulting from a collection of dead bodies in the basement. Today you would be investigated by the police and possibly a psychiatrist for similar behaviour.

Continuing the trend

The concern with security, however large, did not deter the Egyptians from using rock-cut tombs well into the New Kingdom.

A number of the Theban noble tombs – at the Valley of the Nobles (Sheikh abd-el Gourna), Deir el Bahri, and the Assasif – have elaborate façades, which were prominent on the landscape.

A number of these rock-cut tombs were also surmounted by a small pyramid, which had no function other than acting as a status symbol – and serving as a beacon to tomb robbers!

Getting completely shafted: Shaft tombs

In response to the security threat, as well as financial concerns, a number of Middle and New Kingdom officials were buried in shaft tombs. These tombs were dug directly out of the desert floor and consisted of a vertical shaft, which opened into a subterranean burial chamber. If the deceased was wealthy, the subterranean burial chamber was elaborately decorated or consisted of a suite of rooms.

Eternal rest for provincial governors

The site of Beni Hasan in Middle Egypt has the best collection of Middle Kingdom rock-cut tombs. There are 39 tombs here, all carved into the rock face of the cliff. At least four of the tombs belonged to local governors of the region from the end of the 11th and early 12th dynasties, and were impressive statements of their wealth and status.

Most of the tombs follow a similar construction of an outer portico and a larger inner chamber with at least two pillars and a statue niche. The scenes on the tomb walls focus on military training, including wrestling, stick fighting, and weight lifting using sand bags. There are also scenes of warfare, with the Egyptian army laying siege to fortified buildings. Some researchers believe that these scenes depict the civil war between northern and southern Egypt during the early 11th-dynasty unification battles of King Mentuhotep II.

The tomb of Khnumhotep II includes a particularly interesting scene in which a trading party from Syria-Palestine is bringing eye-paint to Egypt. The party leader Absha is titled *heka haswt*, from which the term Hyksos developed (see Chapter 3). The depiction is one of the earliest images of the people known as the Hyksos.

The advantage of a shaft tomb was that after the burial had taken place and the shaft filled with desert rubble, it was impossible to locate, because no superstructure advertised the tomb's location.

Shaft tombs were used for the rest of the pharaonic period. Today, these tombs are often discovered intact, because even well-trained robbers couldn't find them.

Sinking to their level: New Kingdom tombs

From the start of Egyptian history, tombs evolved architecturally and ideologically – and did much more than simply provide a place to dispose of the dead.

The ideological significance of the tombs was never more apparent than in the sophisticated New Kingdom. The New Kingdom tombs were divided into three parts

- ✔ **The upper level** or superstructure represented the realm of the sun god. This level was represented by a small niche, a *stela* (a stone slab with a curved top and an inscription), or a small pyramid.

- ✔ **The middle level** included the internal offering chapels and represented the juxtaposition between the realm of the living and that of the dead.

- ✔ **The lower level** included the burial chambers and represented the realm of the dead.

The kings of the New Kingdom, however, chose to build tombs that had no visible superstructure, as a means of preventing robberies. During this period, the construction of upper levels was only applicable to non-royal tombs. The royal offering chapel (middle level) was situated some distance from the tomb in the desert on the edge of the cultivated land closer to the Nile, while the royal burials (lower level) took place in the Valley of the Kings.

Interring the Divine

The Valley of the Kings on the west bank of the Nile at Thebes (Luxor) is separated into two valleys:

- ✔ **The Eastern Valley,** which contains 63 tombs numbered in the order in which they were discovered. KV (for King's Valley) 63 was discovered in February 2006.
- ✔ **The Western Valley,** which contains five tombs.

The development of the Valley of the Kings in the New Kingdom brought about a number of innovations in tomb design. All the tombs in the Valley of the Kings are rock cut, but rather than being built into the sides of cliffs with elaborate façades, the entrances are carved directly into the floor of the Valley – or, if the entrances are carved into cliffs, they are inaccessible and hidden.

Each individual tomb is different due to a number of design features:

- ✔ The **bent axis tomb** was introduced by Amenhotep II and consisted of a long corridor that turned 90 degrees before reaching the burial chamber. This style was used for 130 years.
- ✔ The **jogged axis tomb** was introduced by Horemheb and consisted of a long corridor that ended in the burial chamber. However, the axis was not entirely straight and jogged to one side after the first hall.
- ✔ The **straight axis tomb** was introduced by Ramses IV and was a long, straight corridor cut into the floor of the valley, which ended in the burial chamber.
- ✔ The **oval burial chamber** was introduced by Thutmosis III and was representative of a *cartouche*, an oval that surrounded the royal name. Surrounding the royal burial with the same shape offered the same protection in death as the ruler received in life.
- ✔ The **shaft burial** was used throughout the period of use of the Valley of the Kings and consisted of a vertical shaft that opened out into the burial chamber at the bottom. See 'Getting completely shafted: Shaft tombs', earlier in this chapter, for more information.

Would you like a flake with your cone?

An architectural feature used in the upper level of New Kingdom non-royal tombs was a frieze of funerary cones. Funerary cones were about 15 centimetres long and made of pottery. They were rounded at one end and pointed at the other. The round end was stamped with the tomb owner's name and titles, as well as those of his wife and family.

The frieze was constructed using up to 300 identical cones in a tomb, embedded into the external wall with the stamped, rounded end visible and flush with the wall. (Archaeologists use these cones to identify any missing tombs; if the cones exist today, then the tomb must have also existed at some point.)

Funerary cones were first introduced in the 11th dynasty and continued to be used until the 25th dynasty, although they were most popular in the 18th dynasty of the New Kingdom. There has been some debate as to their ritual function, including the suggestion that they represented loaves of bread to nourish the deceased in the afterlife.

Not one of the tombs in the Valley of the Kings is actually finished. Indeed, no tomb in Egypt is complete. Some are carved completely out of the rock and are waiting to be decorated, whereas others have the outlines drawn, ready for carving. Some tombs appear to be complete, but have missing inscriptions, or the painting of the images isn't complete. The most likely reason for this is the death of the intended recipient, forcing the workmen to halt their work. Also, to finish a tomb would be to admit perfection, and that the tomb was suitable to house a god. What architect could ever seriously make that claim?

The number of incomplete tombs is, to a certain extent, useful, because it allows archaeologists to record the methods of carving and decorating the tombs.

Taking a trip to the King's Valley

The Valley of the Kings is one of the most visited sites in Egypt, and consists of 63 elaborately decorated tombs. However, the name Valley of the Kings is somewhat misleading, because not all the 63 tombs in the Eastern Valley are royal. In fact, only 23 of the 63 tombs in the Eastern Valley are tombs of kings – all the New Kingdom kings from Thutmosis I to Ramses XI (see the nearby sidebar for the complete list).

The other 40 tombs are of unknown and named princes, officials, pets, and unknown individuals.

Officials

Some revered officials were also buried at the site, both in rock-cut and shaft burials. Burial in the Valley of Kings was a great honour for any official. At least seven tombs were built for officials:

- KV13 belongs to the Chancellor, Bay, from the reign of Sety II and Siptah.

- KV36 belongs to Maiherperi, a Nubian fan-bearer from the 18th dynasty. The title of fan-bearer was one of great status, because it enabled the individual to be in the king's company and privy to all his secrets.

- KV45 belonged originally to an official called Userhet from the 18th dynasty, although it was reused in the 22nd dynasty.

- KV46 was the intact tomb of Yuya and Thuya, the parents of Queen Tiye, who was the husband of Amenhotep III and mother of Akhenaten.

- KV48 belongs to an official called Amenemopet, commonly known as Pairy, from the reign of Amenhotep II.

- KV60 belongs to Sitre-in, the wet nurse of Queen Hatshepsut, and contained a female body that has been identified as either Sitre-in or Hatshepsut.

Those who would be king

The Valley of the Kings also accommodated the tombs of some queens and princes – some kings wanted their entire family close by.

- KV3 was the tomb of an unnamed son of Ramses III.

- KV5 is the biggest tomb in the Valley of the Kings and was intended for the burials of the sons of Ramses II.

- KV14 was originally built by Queen Tawosret for her and her husband Sety II, but this was usurped by King Setnakht, who extended the tomb and removed her body.

- KV19 was built for Montuherkhepshef, a prince who later became Ramses VIII.

- KV42 was constructed for Hatshepsut Merytre, a wife of Thutmosis III.

Even though these tombs were for the royal family, being buried in the Valley of the Kings was still a privilege, because the closer someone was buried to the king, the higher status he or she held. These burials show that these wives and children were highly praised by their husbands or fathers. In the 19th and 20th dynasty, the Valley of the Queens, south of the Valley of the Kings, was constructed as a place solely for members of the royal family and contains 75–80 tombs.

Who's who in the Valley of the Kings

The Valley of the Kings may be chock full of tombs, but who's who in this upmarket resting place?

- KV38: Thutmosis I, father of Hatshepsut

- KV20: Hatshepsut (refer to Chapter 3 for more on the life of Hatshepsut)

- KV34: Thutmosis III (Chapter 4 has more details of Thutmosis III)

- KV35: Amenhotep II

- KV43: Thutmosis IV, who set up the Dream Stela at the sphinx at Giza (see Chapter 14)

- WV (Western Valley) 22: Amenhotep III, the father of Akhenaten

- WV25: Akhenaten (Chapter 4 has more about Akhenaten)

- KV55: Smenkhkare – Akhenaten's successor

- KV62: Tutankhamun, the famous boy king (see Chapter 4)

- WV23: Ay, the uncle and successor of Tutankhamun

- KV57: Horemheb, Ay's successor

- KV16: Ramses I, a general of Horemheb who ruled for a short period

- KV17: Sety I, the father of Ramses II

- KV7: Ramses II (refer to Chapter 4)

- KV8: Merenptah, the 13th son and successor of Ramses II

- KV10: Amenmesse, possibly the son of a daughter of Ramses II

- KV15: Sety II, husband of Tawosret and father of Siptah

- KV47: Siptah, who ruled alongside his mother until he became an adult

- KV14: Tawosret and Setnakht – the tomb was started by Tawosret and then completed by Setnakht and is one of the only tombs with two burial chambers

- KV11: Ramses III (refer to Chapter 4)

- KV2: Ramses IV, son of Ramses III

- KV9: Ramses VI, son of Ramses III

- KV1: Ramses VII, son of Ramses VI

- KV6: Ramses IX, who reigned Egypt for 18 years

- KV18: Ramses X, who reigned for between three and nine years

Furry and feathered friends

Like many pet owners today, the Egyptians loved their pets. A few tombs in the Valley were constructed solely for the burial of these beloved family members.

- KV50 housed the pets of Amenhotep II, including the mummified remains of a dog and a monkey.

- KV51 contained the burial of three monkeys, one baboon, three ducks, and an ibis; however, the owner of this menagerie of animals is a mystery.

- KV52 contained the mummified remains of a monkey, although again the owner is unknown.

These burials and others discovered in other cemeteries tell us what types of pets were kept by the Egyptian kings – primarily monkeys, dogs, cats, and ducks. Many of these burials consisted of a mummified animal within a coffin, and some even contained funerary goods as well. The burial of pets was not exclusive to royals, and a number of pet mummies have been discovered, including horses, cats, and birds.

Considering unknown owners

Details of the ownership of 20 of the 63 Eastern Valley tombs have not survived, and the ownership of one of the Western Valley tombs is unknown.

Based on tomb style, researchers can sometimes identify the period when a tomb was built. All the tombs were robbed in antiquity, and priests moved a number of bodies to a store in the 21st dynasty to protect them from further violation, so many of the tombs do not contain bodies or grave goods. The priests re-wrapped the bodies before placing them in the store, but they may have confiscated the riches wrapped against the body as a means of boosting the flagging economy.

Still not exhausted

As the recent discovery of KV63 suggests, the Valley of the Kings still has discoveries to offer. In February 2006, an American team discovered a tomb shaft 5 metres from the tomb of Tutankhamun. This tomb had been identified using sonar survey by the British-run Amarna Royal Tomb Project in 2000, although it took six years for the tomb to be uncovered.

The tomb was approached by a 5-metre-deep shaft, which then leads into a rectangular, undecorated burial chamber measuring approximately 4 metres by 5 metres. The tomb contained seven wooden sarcophagi and 27 large storage jars dated to the reign of Tutankhamun, identified by a seal bearing the name of his wife Ankhesenamun.

Before the tomb was cleared, a lot of publicity and speculation focused on who the tomb belonged to – suggestions included Nefertiti, Kiya, and Ankhesenamun (the stepmother, mother, and wife of Tutankhamun, respectively). Imagine everyone's disappointment when the coffins and storage jars contained only the remains of an embalmer's workshop – a lot of linen, natron, pillows, miniature vessels, resin, chaff, and floral collars. Of course, these materials raise a number of questions, as embalmers' caches are normally remains from a burial. Whose burial does this cache belong to?

In July 2006, the Amarna Royal Tomb Project announced results of further sonar surveys that indicate another possible tomb in the same region as KV63 and KV62 (Tutankhamun). Perhaps the embalmer's cache in KV63 is the remains of the burial in KV64. Who knows?

A tomb fit for kings

The largest tomb in the Valley of the Kings – and indeed the whole of Egypt – is KV5, built by Ramses II for the burial of his numerous sons (for more on Ramses II, see Chapter 4). The tomb was originally discovered prior to 1799 and then recorded in the 1820s, although only the first court was entered and deemed not worthy of excavation.

However, in 1987, Kent Weeks, while working on the Theban Mapping Project (see Chapter 15 for details of the project and Chapter 19 for the low-down on Dr Weeks), entered the tomb to assess the damage of a leaking sewage pipe and discovered the potential of KV5. Due to numerous flash floods over the centuries, the tomb was filled to the ceiling with compacted desert rubble, which sets to the consistency of concrete. Weeks and his team have systematically removed rubble and revealed more than 120 chambers and corridors on three levels. More chambers are uncovered each season, and the total number of chambers is likely to exceed 150 over the coming years.

So far, six of Ramses's sons have been discovered buried here. However, the wall decoration depicts more then 20 sons, so many more may be awaiting discovery. There are many years of work still left on this tomb, and no doubt other surprises await Weeks and his team.

A couple of these mystery tombs have stood out from the rest due to remains that were discovered within them. Although these details bring researchers no closer to identifying the tombs' owners, the remains are fascinating none the less:

- ✔ KV56 is referred to as the 'Gold Tomb' because a collection of 19th-dynasty gold jewellery was discovered within it.
- ✔ KV58 is known as the 'Chariot Tomb' because a number of chariot fragments were discovered here. The chariot or chariots were most likely moved from King Ay's tomb in the Western Valley and dumped here, probably by ancient robbers.
- ✔ KV63 was discovered in 2006 and was an embalmer's cache – although which burial this cache is connected to is unknown.

Other houses for the royal afterlife

Although the Valley of the Kings is the most famous burial site, kings of other periods favoured different cemeteries:

- ✔ The early Old Kingdom kings favoured burial at Abydos, the mythical burial place of the god Osiris.

- The late Old Kingdom kings favoured the Cairo region (Saqqara, Memphis, and Giza).

- The Middle Kingdom kings favoured the Faiyum (Hawara, Lahun, and Dashur).

- The earlier New Kingdom kings were buried at Dra Abu el Naga on the West Bank at Thebes.

- Akhenaten was buried at Amarna in Middle Egypt.

- Amenhotep III and Ay were buried in the Western Valley of the Valley of the Kings, and Akhenaten started building a tomb here before he moved the capital city to Amarna (see Chapter 4).

- Those in the Tanite (22nd) dynasty were buried at Tanis in the Delta.

Embellishing Tombs: Decoration to Die For

Many burial places from the pre-dynastic period onwards contain decorative paintings that have some function in the afterlife and are supposed to make the eternal survival of the tomb owner more bearable.

Entertaining the robbers

The burial of a baboon and a dog in KV50 is not in itself remarkable. However, when the archaeologists were excavating the tomb in 1906, the placement of these animals caused some amusement, which was attributed to an ancient robber with a sense of humour!

Theodore Davis, the excavator, describes the scene:

I went down the shaft and entered the chamber, which proved to be extremely hot and too low for comfort. I was startled by seeing very near me a yellow dog of ordinary size standing on his feet, his short tail curved over his back and his eyes open.

Within a few inches of his nose sat a monkey in quite perfect condition; for an instant I thought that they were alive, but I soon saw that they had been mummified, and unwrapped in ancient times by robbers. Evidently they had taken a fragment of the wooden monkey box on which they seated the monkey to keep him upright, and then they stood the dog on his feet so near the monkey that his nose almost touched him ... I am quite sure the robbers arranged the group for their amusement. However this may be, it can fairly be said to be a joke 3,000 years old.

Well, they say the old ones are the best.

The earliest decorated tomb was Tomb 100 from Hierakonpolis, built around 3685 BC, which is the only decorated tomb from this period. There was a gap of 1,000 years or so before the next decorated tombs, which appeared in the third dynasty in the non-royal mastaba tombs, and the fourth dynasty pyramid of King Unas, which contained the Pyramid Texts. (See Chapter 14 for more on the pyramid and Chapter 10 for more on the texts.)

Even during the early Old Kingdom, which was the beginning of the tomb-decorating trend, artisans relied on certain themes that remained popular throughout the pharaonic period for both royal and non-royal tombs. Only the artistic representation of these themes changed (see Chapter 11).

Decorating for the plebs

From the Old Kingdom mastabas to the New Kingdom rock-cut tombs, the non-royal themes in paintings focused on

- Nourishment
- Daily life
- Banquets
- Funerals

These themes were in use for hundreds of years, and never lost their meaning and importance. Only the artistic style changed – but the main purpose was consistent.

Nourishment

Scenes showing rows of servants carrying piles of food to offering tables before the tomb owner provided the deceased with nourishment for the afterlife. Agricultural scenes showing food production include animal husbandry, sowing, harvesting, winnowing, vineyard tending, fishing, and bird hunting. Some New Kingdom examples of agricultural scenes show the tomb owner actively participating in farming, indicating that the deceased will always be able to provide themselves with food.

Other scenes show the deceased residing in the *Field of Reeds*, the ancient equivalent to paradise. The Field of Reeds was an exact copy of Egypt, but Egypt at its best, with abundant crops, lots of water, and beautiful flora and fauna peppering the landscape. The deceased are often seen in their best frocks, tending the land and harvesting the constant crops.

Daily life

Scenes showing the life of the tomb owner are based on the deceased's occupation:

- For a vizier, whose role was to oversee all the workshops attached to the palace, scenes show detailed images of a number of these crafts, including jewellery making, carpentry, stone masonry, brick making, and metal crafts.
- For a military individual, the tomb included images of battles, campaigns, and training.
- For an agricultural overseer, many of the agricultural scenes described in the previous section were used.

By the New Kingdom, these everyday life scenes, especially those dealing with agriculture, are associated with the cycle of life and rebirth.

Banquets

Banquets are often depicted in non-royal tombs and show the tomb owner and his wife seated before a heavily laden offering table with a number of guests, segregated by sex, being served by servants. The servants adorn the guests' necks with floral collars and their heads with perfume cones, and keep their food and wine topped up. Singers, musicians, and dancers are often shown entertaining guests.

These banquets can represent one of two things – a depiction of the funerary feast that occurred after the funeral, or the *Beautiful Festival of the Valley*, a Theban funerary festival at which the dead were remembered. (During this festival, processions on the West Bank were followed by people visiting their ancestors' tombs to participate in a feast with the dead.)

Funerals

Images of funerals show the procession into the tomb, consisting of a number of servants carrying boxes of goods. The contents of the boxes include jewellery, clothes, weapons, statues, and furniture.

The procession is often accompanied by a group of professional mourners – a group of women hired to wail and throw dirt over their faces in an open display of grief.

The funerary rituals are also often depicted, including the *opening of the mouth ceremony* (see Chapter 10), which enabled the deceased to breathe, speak, and eat in the afterlife, as well as the *ceremony of the breaking of the red pots*, an ancient ritual of unknown meaning or origin.

Decorating for the royals

The themes of royal tomb decoration are not as flexible or diverse as the non-royal tombs. Instead, royal tomb art focuses on religious rather than personal scenes. These religious themes do, however, vary from tomb to tomb and include

- Scenes from funerary texts (see Chapter 10), which primarily focus on the 12-hour nocturnal journey of the sun god. The king accompanied the sun god on this journey and faced the same dangers. These funerary texts protected the king and the god until dawn and rebirth.

- Scenes of the king making offerings to various gods, including Re-Horakhty, Osiris, Ptah, and Hathor – all deities associated with death and rebirth.

- Scenes of the gods embracing the king and welcoming him to the afterlife. Often the gods are seen holding the king's hand, leading him to the realm of the dead.

  One variant on this theme can be found in the tombs of the sons of Ramses III, where the king is shown leading his sons into the afterlife and introducing him to the gods.

Although kings, queens, and princes had little room to deviate from these themes, they could choose from a number of funerary texts with a large canon of images. Additionally, royals were able to change artistic representations, colours, and techniques, which allows each royal tomb to be unique despite the simple themes available. It seems that all people, ancient or modern, manage to work within the boundaries and still express their individuality!

Chapter 14

Probing the Pyramids

. . . .

In This Chapter

▶ Developing more impressive burials

▶ Clarifying the pyramid complex

▶ Outfitting pyramids with items for the afterlife

▶ Expanding the popularity of pyramids to non-royals

. . . .

Pyramids are synonymous with ancient Egypt. Over the years, these structures have been the topic of many discussions and books – some of a somewhat dubious nature.

The function of pyramids changed over the years, with the Old and Middle Kingdom pyramids acting as tombs designed as imposing declarations of wealth and status, and the smaller New Kingdom pyramids used to surmount a tomb, but not functioning as burial places themselves.

The history of the development of pyramids is a long one, peppered by mistakes and miscalculations before the 'true pyramid' was achieved. Even after the Great Pyramid was built, pyramid structure did not remain static. New innovations appeared in an attempt to build a perfect monument, one that was better than the ancestors' pyramids.

This chapter focuses on the development of these amazing structures during the course of more than 3,000 years of Egyptian history.

Defining the Shape

The shape of the pyramid had religious significance long before the pyramid structure itself.

So what exactly are they?

Researchers and historians now know that pyramids were tombs, even though some authors still dispute the fact. But for many centuries, people debated the function of these great monuments.

✔ Prior to the fifth century AD, the writer Julius Honorius believed the pyramids were granaries built by the biblical Joseph. This idea was also adopted by later Renaissance scholars.

✔ The Duc de Persigny (1808–1872 AD) tried to prove that the pyramids were screens against the desert sand to stop the Nile from silting up, although logically many more barriers would have been needed to create an effective barrier. Along the same lines, Arab writers of a similar period thought the pyramids were built as places where people could seek protection from natural disasters.

✔ Charles Piazzi Smyth (1819–1900) wrote two books about the pyramids, which he believed enshrined God's plan for the universe. Through mathematical measurements, Smyth believed this divine plan would be revealed and spent a great deal of time trying to decipher it. Whether he succeeded is unknown, but people are still looking for the deeper meaning to these funerary monuments.

Piles of desert rubble were initially used to cover pit burials during the pre-dynastic period. Over time, these mounds became more elaborate and developed into superstructures (see Chapter 13) and eventually step pyramids. These heaps were believed to represent of the mound of creation, from which all life began. All life started on this mound, so it obviously possessed creative powers and helped the rebirth of the deceased (see Chapter 9 for further information on Egyptian religion).

The pyramidal shape is just a stylisation of the mound of creation and was called a *benben*. As time progressed, the benben became closely associated with the sun god. The solar connection of the pyramids can't be denied – the shape was thought to resemble the rays of the sun, and the Pyramid Texts even refer to the pyramid as a ramp leading to the sky, enabling the dead king to join his ancestors, who became stars upon death.

Filling in the Gaps: Achieving the True Pyramid Shape

After the development of step pyramids (see Chapter 13), the next, um, step necessary to create a true pyramid was for the Egyptians to fill in the steps with masonry. There were, however, a few errors in the process, resulting in some interesting-looking monuments.

Indiana Jones and the temple of Meidum

The first attempt at a true pyramid was at Meidum, just south of Cairo. You can visit and explore inside this pyramid today. The pyramid of Meidum was built by Sneferu, the first king of the fourth dynasty. The pyramid was originally built as a step pyramid with seven steps, but before the fifth step was completed, the whole structure was enlarged to eight steps.

All that is visible today are the top three steps, because the casing stones have been removed. It was initially believed that this pyramid collapsed during construction, but recent excavations have uncovered no evidence of bodies, tools, or ropes, which would all indicate that the structure was indeed completed.

 The burial chamber of this pyramid is at desert level and is reached via an entrance in the centre of the north face, nearly 17 metres above the ground. The entrance passage descends into the pyramid, ending in a horizontal passage that then leads to a vertical shaft, which ascends to the burial chamber. Cedar beams embedded in the walls leading to this chamber may have been used to haul the sarcophagus up to the chamber, although the sarcophagus is no longer there. This shaft is ascended today by a rather rickety wooden staircase.

The burial chamber is not complete, and it seems that a burial did not take place here – although fragments of a wooden coffin were discovered in the burial chamber. Sneferu built another two pyramids at Dahshur and may have been buried in one of these.

Gotta Dahshur

Sneferu's two pyramids at Dahshur are known as the Bent Pyramid and the Red or North Pyramid, which is only exceeded in size by the Great Pyramid at Giza. You can still visit these pyramids today.

Getting bent

 The Bent Pyramid was built before the Red Pyramid and got its name from a bend half way up the structure, which was caused by a change in design that went wrong. The structure was initially built with an angle of 60 degrees (the true pyramid angle ranges from 72 to 78 degrees). While workers were building the pyramid, there was a problem with subsidence – the weight of the stone caused the foundations to sink into the ground. To counteract this, a girdle was built around the base, changing the slope at the base to 55 degrees. The top of the pyramid was completed with a 44-degree slope, creating a distinct bend in the centre, as you can see in Figure 14-1.

Figure 14-1:
The Bent Pyramid at Dahshur.

The Bent Pyramid is also unusual because it features two entrances, one in the north face and one in the south:

- The northern passage leads to a narrow chamber with a corbelled roof. The burial chamber, also with a corbelled roof, was directly above, probably reached by a ladder.

- The western passage leads through a series of portcullis blocking systems (vertical sliding blocks sealing the tunnel) to a second corbelled burial chamber.

Both of these burial chambers were for Sneferu as the king of Upper and Lower Egypt, with a chamber for each role. At a later date, the two chambers were connected by a passageway cut through the masonry, clearly by someone who knew the location of the two chambers – perhaps by some very sharp robbers.

The Bent Pyramid was abandoned because of weaknesses in the structure caused by the unsuitability of the desert plateau that the pyramid was built on. Sneferu was not to be put off though, and started the construction of the Red Pyramid.

In the red

The Red Pyramid is second in size only to the Great Pyramid of Khufu at Giza and was the first successful true pyramid. It gained its name from the colour of the exposed granite under the casing stones of limestone used to encase the pyramid. The capstone (also called the *pyramidion* or *benben*) was representative of the mound of creation from which all creation started, and was made of a single block of limestone, which archaeologists discovered on the site. You can still visit this pyramid at the site of Dahshur.

The entrance to the pyramid is in the north face and leads to a 63-metre descending corridor, which ends in two corbelled antechambers. High up in the wall of the second chamber is a short, horizontal corridor, which leads to the 15-metre-tall corbelled burial chamber. This burial chamber is not subterranean and is almost in the centre of the superstructure. Some human remains were discovered in the burial chamber, although whether these belong to Sneferu is unknown.

Middle Kingdom Kings at Dahshur

Kings of the Middle Kingdom continued to use Dahshur as a royal burial ground. Senwosret III and Amenemhat III of the 12th dynasty built their pyramids here.

Senwosret III's pyramid was built to the north-east of the Red or North Pyramid of Sneferu. The quality of construction had declined by this period (1878–1841 BC), and Senwosret III's pyramid was made of irregular-sized mud bricks in stepped courses, which were then covered in limestone casing stones. The entrance to the pyramid is at ground level on the west side of the pyramid and leads to a sloping passageway, ending in a store room. The antechamber lies at a 90-degree angle to the store, which then leads to a burial chamber constructed of granite. There is a granite sarcophagus in the burial chamber. Despite the discovery of a few objects in the pyramid, researchers doubt whether Senwosret was buried here.

As with all pyramids, Senwosret III's was part of a wider complex consisting of

- Seven pyramids for royal women
- A mortuary temple and causeway
- A further temple in the south

Senwosret III's son and successor, Amenemhat III, followed in his father's footsteps and built his pyramid at the same site. He also built his pyramid of mud brick with limestone casing blocks, all of which have since been removed for reuse. The son's pyramid stood 75 metres high. There are two entrances to this pyramid on the east and west sides, and the pyramid is entered via staircases rather than ramps. These staircases lead to a combination of corridors and chambers, a layout more complicated than that of any other pyramid. The complex includes

- Three burial chambers within the pyramid, one of which contains canopic equipment (see Chapter 10) of a queen named Aat, indicating she was buried here.

  The burial chamber situated just east of the central axis housed a sarcophagus, although Amenemhat III was probably not buried here.

- Several nearby underground chambers that feature a number of small chapels and a shrine.

Package tour – ancient style

One of the statue rooms of the funerary complex of Djoser at Saqqara contains graffiti showing the site was visited in later (but still ancient) periods as a tourist site. One of the inscriptions dates to the winter of year 47 of the reign of Ramses II. Two scribes of the treasury, the vizier and two brothers called Hednakht and Panakht, record their visit to the site.

The Great Pyramid of Giza was also visited as an ancient monument from the New Kingdom onwards, as attested by graffiti. Records note that Cleopatra took Mark Antony to the pyramids at Giza (they were already nearly 2,000 years old during her reign) on a romantic tour.

This structure was abandoned before completion because of unstable clay foundations and instability within the pyramid structure caused by the huge number of rooms it contains.

The Great Pyramid: Finalising the details

After the true pyramid was perfected by Sneferu at Dahshur, the next stage was to enlarge the structure, which is what Khufu did at the virgin site at Giza. The three main pyramids at Giza belong to Khufu, Khafra, and Menkaura, all of the fourth dynasty (2613–2494 BC).

The Great Pyramid of Khufu (shown in Figure 14-2) – Khufu is the son of Sneferu – is 146 metres high and was originally encased in limestone blocks, each weighing 16 tonnes. The entrance is in the north face of the pyramid and was entered via a descending passage, which led to a subterranean chamber. Near the beginning of the passage is another passage that ascended to the grand gallery, which led to the burial chamber.

The burial chamber is constructed of red granite and has five stress-relieving chambers above it that take the weight of the pyramid. Exactly placed on the central axis of the pyramid is the red granite sarcophagus, which was put in the chamber before completion because the doorway is too narrow to take the large block of stone. The burial chamber is sealed by a series of portcullis-type blocks and plugging stones that block the entrance to the grand gallery.

At the base of the grand gallery is a horizontal passage, which leads to the so-called queen's chamber and may have been a *serdab* (a chamber with a hole in the wall so that the statue can see out) designed to house the *ka* statue of the king (see Chapter 10). The burials of the bodies of the queens of Khufu took place in the three satellite pyramids to the east of the pyramid.

The pyramid complex was surrounded by a limestone wall standing 8 metres tall, enclosing a courtyard that could only be reached via the valley temple, causeway, and mortuary temple – all standard elements of the pyramid complex.

Following up one of the greats: Khafra's pyramid

The Great Pyramid was one of the seven wonders of the ancient world – indeed, it is the only one still standing.

Khafra, the son of Khufu, had a difficult act to follow, but he still decided to build his pyramid alongside that of his father. Because he was unable to beat the monumental splendour of the Great Pyramid, Khafra built his pyramid on a higher area of the Giza plateau, giving it the appearance of being larger, although it is in fact smaller. Cunning, eh?

There are two entrances to the pyramid, one at ground level and the other 11.5 metres (38 feet) above ground level on the northern side of the pyramid. The lower passage descends to a small chamber (which may have functioned as a serdab) and a horizontal passage, which gradually ascends to meet the descending passage of the upper entrance. This horizontal passage then leads to the burial chamber.

The sarcophagus in the burial chamber is made of black granite. The sarcophagus did contain bones, which were later identified as those of a bull. The bones are thought to have been given as an offering to the king's *ka* at a later date, after the body had been removed by robbers.

What a way to build a pyramid!

Herodotus records that Khufu was a bit of a tyrant, a reputation that the king has maintained for 4,000 years. While building his own pyramid, Khufu was also constructing pyramids for burying his queens. However, due to the expense of such huge construction works, he forced his daughter to pay for her own pyramid. According to Herodotus:

Cheops (Khufu) moreover came, they said, to such a pitch of wickedness, that being in want of money he caused his own daughter to sit in the brothels, and ordered her to obtain from those who came a certain amount of money (how much it was they

did not tell me): and she not only obtained the sum appointed by her father, but also she formed a design for herself privately to leave behind her a memorial, and she requested each man who came in to give her one stone upon her building: and of these stones, they told me, the pyramid was built which stands in front of the great pyramid in the middle of the three, each side being one hundred and fifty feet in length.

At one stone per sexual encounter, she would have been a very busy lady because there are probably more than 50,000 blocks used to build her pyramid!

Bringing up the rear: Menkaura's pyramid

The pyramid of Menkaura is the smallest of the three pyramids at Giza. The bottom courses are cased with granite, and limestone was used for the top. Granite was considered a superior building material, and clearly at this time size was not the primary concern. Although his pyramid was small, Menkaura increased the size of his mortuary and valley temples.

The internal structure of the pyramid is a complicated collection of descending ramps and chambers sealed by portcullis blocks. There were two burial chambers, one of which may be a serdab, and a sarcophagus was in the larger burial chamber. Within the sarcophagus was a wooden coffin with Menkaura's name, although the coffin dates from the late period and the bones date to the Christian period, indicating that the sarcophagus had been reused at a later date.

Accessorising the Pyramids at Giza

Like any great outfit, a pyramid wasn't complete without suitable accessories. Each Giza pyramid was part of a complex consisting of a number of buildings and elements, including

  ✔ Valley temple

  ✔ Mortuary temple

  ✔ Queens' tombs

  ✔ Burial chambers – three for Khufu, one for Khafra, and three for Menkaura

Khufu also went further and included boat pits, a sphinx, and a sphinx temple. The following sections examine the boat pits and sphinx; see Chapter 12 for more on the temple.

Sailing for eternity

Five full-size boat pits were constructed near the pyramid of Khufu, two of which definitely contained boats. One has been opened and consisted of a 31-metre-long by 8-metre or so deep and 7-metre-wide pit covered with large stone blocks. A 43.5-metre-long boat, dismantled into 1,224 pieces, was placed within one of the pits. Luckily, because the pit remained watertight over the centuries, the boat survived and has been reconstructed and is now on display in the boat museum at Giza (see Figure 14-3).

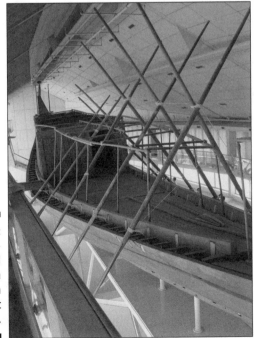

Figure 14-3:
Reconstructed boat from remains in the boat pit, Giza.

Dreams of the sun god

The stela (curved top stone monument) between the feet of the sphinx is known as the Dream Stela and was set up by Thutmosis IV. Thutmosis IV slept near the sphinx and dreamt that the solar god spoke to him, legitimising his claim to the throne. The voice in the dream instructed Thutmosis IV to remove the sand that had covered the sphinx up to the neck. He recorded this on the stela between the sphinx's paws;

On one of these days it came to pass, that the king's son Tuthmosis, came, coursing at the time of mid-day, and he rested in the shadow of this great god. A vision of sleep seized him at the hour when the sun was at the zenith, and he found the majesty of this revered god speaking with his own mouth, as a father speaks with his son, saying; 'Behold me, see me, you, my son Thutmosis. I am your father Harmakhis-Kheperi-Ra-Atum who will give

to you my kingdom on earth at the head of the living. You shall wear the white crown [of Upper Egypt] and the red crown [of Lower Egypt] on the throne of the earth-god Geb . . . The land shall be yours in its length and in its breadth, that which the eye of the All-Lord [sun god] shines upon. The food of the two lands shall be yours, the great tribute from all countries, the duration of a long period of years. My face is yours, my desire is towards you. You shall be to me a protector for my manner is as if I were ailing in all my limbs. The sand of this desert upon which I am, has reached me; turn to me, to have that done which I have desired.'

Thutmosis IV removed the sand as the god requested and then ruled on the throne, indicating that he had pleased the sun god.

The entire boat was constructed using wooden pegs and ropes only. (The boat currently on display has a number of gaps between the planks of wood. The wood expanded when wet and sealed the holes, making the vessel watertight.)

Evidence suggests that the boat was used at least once, probably during the funeral of Khufu, as his body sailed from the east to the west bank of the Nile. The boat had ten oars, five down each side, a covered chamber that may have held the body of the dead king at the rear, and an open shrine at the front that may have displayed a *ka* statue of the king as part of the funerary procession.

Khufu, however, wasn't the first king to include boat pits in the burial complex:

- ✔ King Khasekhemwy of the second dynasty had 12 boat pits surrounding his Abydos tomb. Each pit contained a boat.

- ✔ Unas of the fifth dynasty had boat pits, although these pits probably never contained any boats.

✔ Senwosret III had six boat pits at his pyramid at Dahshur. These boats were believed to have a solar connection. The sun god sailed in his solar bark through the afterlife, accompanied by the king.

Phew – what a sphinx!

The sphinx is another prominent feature of the Giza plateau and is an enduring symbol of ancient Egypt (shown in Figure 14-4). Although smaller sphinxes exist, the sphinx at Giza is the only one of this size and prominence in Egypt. It is situated at the end of the causeway leading to Khufu's pyramid and was carved from the natural bedrock, which was of the right proportions and approximate shape (although, saying that, the body is in fact too long). The sphinx consists of a lion's body with a human head, wearing the *nemes headdress* (the blue and gold headcloth) in place of the mane.

The lion was both a solar symbol and a symbol of the might and strength of the king. Having a human head on a lion's body indicates that the power of the lion is governed by the intelligence and wisdom of the king. The position of the sphinx at the end of the causeway to the great pyramid suggests its function is that of guardian, as well as being a large monument representing the importance of the king.

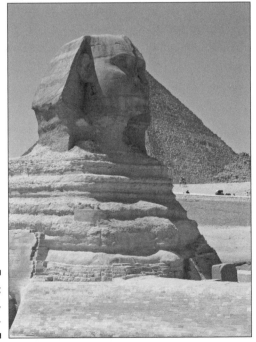

Figure 14-4:
The Sphinx, Giza.

Evolving Further: Later Pyramids and Complexes

Over the centuries, kings continued to construct pyramids and surrounding complexes of tombs and temples.

Making up for shoddy workmanship: Unas at Saqqara

The fifth-dynasty pyramid complex of Unas at Saqqara is not as well preserved as the pyramid of Djoser at the same site. Unas built his pyramid of mud brick, but it is still a perfect example of a fully developed Old Kingdom pyramid complex. The complex included all the elements that the king needed in the next life:

- ✔ A valley temple
- ✔ A causeway
- ✔ A pyramid
- ✔ Boat pits

This pyramid at Saqqara is the first to house the *Pyramid Texts*, carved on the walls of the burial chamber and antechamber. These texts described the following:

- ✔ Creation myths
- ✔ Myth of Osiris and Isis
- ✔ Myth of Horus and Seth
- ✔ How to survive death in the afterlife

The Pyramid Texts formed the basis for the Middle Kingdom *Coffin Texts* and the New Kingdom *Book of the Dead*. See Chapter 10 for information on these funerary texts.

The causeway of Unas leading to the mortuary temple is particularly noteworthy. It shows unusual depictions of a famine, with graphic images of emaciated men, a woman rummaging in her hair for head lice in the vain attempt to find something to eat, and a child with a distended stomach begging for food. This famine may not have taken place in Egypt, as such an event was unsuitable to record for eternity. Rather, the paintings depict a famine that affected the nomadic tribes in the surrounding desert. The appearance of some of the people is very un-Egyptian, and Egypt is represented as a wealthy and generous nation, coming the aid of these earliest refugees.

Jumping on the bandwagon: More Middle Kingdom pyramids

Pyramids continued to be used as tombs well into the Middle Kingdom. All the kings of the 12th dynasty had one, with complexes at Dahshur, El Lahun, and Hawara. Some kings of the Middle Kingdom had both a pyramid and a rock-cut tomb (see Chapter 13).

In the Middle Kingdom, the Faiyum region was very popular with royalty and nobles alike for the hunting of birds and other marshland wildlife. The popularity of the site saw the construction of a number of pyramid complexes situated at

- ✔ **Lisht:** Amenemhat I and Senwosret I of the 12th dynasty built pyramids here. Amenemhat's complex includes a number of tomb shafts for the burials of the royal women. Senwosret's complex also houses nine subsidiary pyramids of his queens.

- ✔ **Lahun:** A pyramid complex built by Senwosret II of the 12th dynasty. The foundation is built of a natural outcrop of limestone and the upper part is made of mud brick. There is a double enclosure wall around the pyramid with a number of queens' shaft burials between the walls.

- ✔ **Hawara:** The pyramid here was built by Amenemhat III of the 12th dynasty and was part of a complex containing a labyrinthine building with lots of interconnecting winding corridors and dark chambers.

Growing popularity: Small pointed things

By the start of the New Kingdom (approximately 1540 BC), pyramids were no longer being used by the royal family, who were now buried in secretive rock-cut tombs. Pyramids were adopted for non-royal burials of wealthy people, albeit on a much smaller scale.

At Deir el Medina, the workmen constructed small, hollow, mud-brick pyramids over the tops of their subterranean tombs, which limited the weight that the tomb roof needed to support. The pyramidia at the top of these structures were made of limestone and were carved with images of the tomb owner.

From the 19th dynasty onwards in Nubia, small pyramids were attached to mortuary chapels built over a shaft burial beneath, combining the pyramid and the practical cult of making offerings of food and drink to the deceased. These pyramids have small bases and are tall, narrow structures.

The 26th dynasty (664–525 BC) saw the last development in pyramid evolution at Abydos and Thebes. These mud-brick pyramids have a domed interior and are similar to granaries or ovens. Attached to the side of the pyramid was a rectangular chamber, which led to the shaft burial beneath and was the focus of the funerary cult.

By this period, the 3,000-year evolution of the pyramid came to an end. These structures have remained a symbol of all things Egyptian, even though they were only a small aspect of the wider funerary beliefs.

Part V
The Part of Tens

In this part . . .

*T*his part helps you to impress your friends and family (as well as anyone within earshot) with a whole bunch of useless but interesting facts about loads of things to do with Egyptology. You can wax lyrical about the top ten turning points in Egyptology, as well as the best ancient Egyptian achievements. Not only can you discuss ten famous Egyptologists, but also ten ancient Egyptian personalities, almost as if you knew them personally.

Then why not travel to Egypt and impress everyone in your hotel with the top ten places to visit, some off the beaten track? Start your journey here.

Chapter 15

Top Ten Breakthroughs in Egyptology

In This Chapter

▶ Celebrating the highlights of Egyptology

▶ Appreciating early and modern excavations

▶ Looking towards possible new discoveries

Archaeological discoveries and academic breakthroughs punctuate the history of Egyptology, which makes this discipline one that is constantly changing.

Egyptology is bit like a jigsaw with an unknown number of pieces, no picture, and half the bits missing, which may make you wonder why anyone bothers with it! Egyptologists continue in their research because so many questions still need answers. Each fresh discovery opens up a whole new area of study and provides further insights into the lives of the ancients.

The greatest breakthroughs and discoveries of persevering Egyptologists – from the 18th century onwards – are the focus of this chapter.

Deciphering Hieroglyphs

All the excavations in Egypt in the early 19th century weren't half as exciting as they could have been, because archaeologists were unable to read the hieroglyphic language inscribed on walls and coffins and thus were unable even to identify who had built the tombs and temples.

This frustrating state of affairs changed in 1826 when Jean-François Champollion published the first dictionary on ancient Egyptian hieroglyphs. At last the meaning of the inscriptions on architecture and objects could be deciphered. Egyptologists haven't looked back since!

This amazing breakthrough comes down to the discovery and translation of the Rosetta Stone (see Chapter 11), a stela written in three languages: ancient Greek, Egyptian hieroglyphs and demotic (a late cursive form of hieroglyphs).

Most historians could read ancient Greek, so with a lot of hard work and logical thinking, they gradually deciphered the other two languages and established a basic alphabet and list of common words. These linguistic tools were applied *ad infinitum* to any Egyptian inscription Egyptologists could get their hands on. Finally, researchers were able to identify who built certain tombs and temples, as well as identify the gods depicted on the walls.

Only later did grammar became an important focus of hieroglyphic studies. Even now, nearly 200 years later, dictionaries, grammar, and inscriptions are being reworked to provide ever more accurate translations of this ancient language. Find out more about translating hieroglyphs yourself in Chapter 11.

Petrie's Seriation Dating System

William Matthew Finders Petrie was a remarkable archaeologist and Egyptologist (see Chapter 19) in the 19th century. Not only did he excavate some of the most interesting sites in Egypt, he also devised a relative dating system that archaeologists the world over still use.

Seriation dating assigns dates to whole assemblages of items or locations, rather than isolated objects from a specific site.

Petrie devised the system while working at Diospolis Parva, where he had excavated a number of pre-dynastic graves that he couldn't link or match to king lists to provide a chronological date. Petrie wanted to put sites and contents into chronological order, so he wrote the contents of each tomb on a slip of paper and placed the slips in a long column. He kept rearranging the sheets until he believed he had a true chronological order based on the style and decoration of the artefacts in each burial.

Although a very simple system, seriation dating is very useful because researchers can create a relative date for the tomb assemblage by stating that one object is earlier or later than another one. The system is useful for arranging sites into some form of order when no written texts or datable objects are available. However, the problem with seriation dating is that it isn't always clear how this sequence fits into the wider chronology of an area.

The Temples at Abu Simbel

Two temples stand at the site of Abu Simbel, 250 kilometres southeast of Aswan. Ramses II built both temples – one in honour of the sun god and the other in honour of Ramses' wife, Nefertari (see Chapter 18 for more information).

Traveller Jean-Louis Burckhardt discovered the temples in 1813, although all that was visible was a colossal head of one of the statues on the façade. Wind-blown sand covered the rest of the three colossi.

In 1817, Giovanni Belzoni – an engineer, turned circus strongman, turned Egyptologist (see Chapter 19) – started to clear away the sand. Unable to find workers willing or strong enough to help with the task, Belzoni, who was 6 feet 7 inches tall, was able to do a lot of the work himself. Unfortunately, every time he cleared the temple façade, the sand built up again, making the process time-consuming and frustrating. Belzoni had to leave without locating the entrance.

In 1871, when his benefactor Henry Salt financed another trip to Nubia to collect antiquities, Belzoni briefly excavated in the Valley of the Kings and then returned to Abu Simbel, where he managed to locate the entrance. Belzoni was the first modern man to enter the temple – a great achievement for anyone – where he saw the towering images of Ramses II on the pillars and the barbaric scenes of the battle of Kadesh. This must have been (and still is) an amazing sight, albeit one tinged with mystery, because, at this point in history, no one could read hieroglyphs and so Belzoni was unable to identify who built the temple.

The Royal Cache of 1881

If it wasn't for the discovery of the Royal Mummy Caches, the only New Kingdom royal mummy recovered today would be Tutankhamun. The mummies in the Royal Cache helped to fill in the jigsaw of Egyptology, providing insights into royal burial practices, diseases, and age of death. In the future, with the help of DNA testing, researchers hope to clarify family relationships among the mummies.

The caches were created in the 21st dynasty as a means of protecting the royal mummies from robberies. The priests moved the bodies from their tombs in the Valley of the Kings, re-wrapped them, and placed them together in a safe, secure place.

The discovery of the first Royal Cache was a combination of luck and detective work – and could very well never have happened at all. As early as 1874, rumours suggested that a wonderful tomb had been discovered in western Luxor, full of fabulous treasure. No one had seen this tomb, but papyri and other artefacts began to appear on the black market, clearly from a new royal tomb. Eventually the Egyptian Antiquities Service, under the leadership of Frenchman Gaston Maspero, started to investigate. By 1881, Ahmed Abd er-Rassul, from a notorious tomb-robbing family from Gourna (the village on the Valley of the Nobles), was brought in for questioning.

Maspero questioned er-Rassul vigorously, but the Egyptian denied all knowledge of a tomb; Maspero eventually let him go. He was later arrested again with his brother Hussein by the Egyptian police, who were not as gentle in their questioning as the Frenchman. Still er-Rassul and his brother denied all knowledge and were allowed to return to their village. Once they returned, disagreement reigned in the Rassul household.

The eldest Rassul brother, Mohammed, was the culprit who had discovered the tomb. Ahmed and Hussein felt they should be rewarded for their unpleasant time with the authorities, as well as enjoy a larger share of the loot from the tomb. After much arguing that eventually involved the whole village, Mohammed went to the authorities and confessed. After receiving assurance that no one would be prosecuted, he revealed the location of the tomb, secreted in the Deir el Bahri Valley, close to the temple of Hatshepsut.

Inside the tomb, the authorities discovered many New Kingdom royal mummies, including

- Ahmose
- Amenhotep I
- Thutmose III
- Sety I
- Ramses II
- Ramses III

These kings were all taken to Cairo where they are currently on display (except Ahmose, who in 2004 was moved to the Luxor Museum). In 1898, another mummy cache was discovered in the Valley of the Kings, which provided an additional ten royal mummies.

In order to get the full set of royal mummies of the New Kingdom, Egyptologists still need to find the remains of

> ✔ Horemheb
>
> ✔ Ramses I (The second body in Luxor Museum is believed by some to be this king, although this is not proven.)
>
> ✔ Sethnakht
>
> ✔ Ramses VII
>
> ✔ Ramses X
>
> ✔ Ramses XI

Perhaps another cache of mummies is waiting to be found, one that will uncover the secrets of these pharaohs and give Egyptologists a 'full house'.

KV55: The Desecrated Tomb

KV55, or Tomb 55 in the Valley of the Kings, has for many years caused much discussion in the Egyptological world. Edward Ayrton and his benefactor Theodore Davis discovered it in the Valley of the Kings in 1907.

A panel from a large wooden shrine that was originally used in the burial of Queen Tiye, Akhenaten's mother, blocked the entrance corridor to the tomb. This led many Egyptologists at the time to believe the tomb was Tiye's. When they later entered the burial chamber, they discovered a coffin containing a body. While some assumed the body was Tiye's, all the names on the coffin had been erased, rendering the inhabitant unidentifiable. The body was sent to Grafton Elliot-Smith (an expert in Egyptian mummies) for analysis. Rather than being the bones of an elderly woman, they were from a young man. The plot thickened!

Egyptologists began debating whether the bones were Akhenaten's or his successor Smenkhkare's. Even now people do not agree, although due to similarities in head shape, the body is often stated and widely agreed to be the brother of Tutankhamun, and therefore probably Smenkhkare. DNA testing may make this identification clearer, but testing will not be carried out until results involving ancient DNA are more accurate.

Tomb 55 was thought to have provided the missing king of the Amarna period, an era that has intrigued Egyptologists for many years. Many bodies are missing from this period (Akhenaten, Nefertiti, and their six daughters; Smenkhkare; and Ay), so any tomb from this time takes Egyptologists one step closer to a complete picture.

Tutankhamun's Tomb

Tutankhamun's tomb is one of the most famous and monumental finds in the history of Egyptology, because it is the only undisturbed royal tomb found in Egypt. All the other royal tombs were robbed in antiquity, and indeed so was Tutankhamun's. Luckily, these burglaries were small, and the majority of Tutankhamun's goods were found intact.

In 1914, Egyptologist Howard Carter and his benefactor Lord Carnarvon started excavating in the Valley of the Kings, just after another excavator, Theodore Davis, who had worked in the area for some time, claimed that 'The Valley of the Tombs is now exhausted.' How wrong can one man be?

Carter and his team did uncover a number of tombs in the Valley, and in 1917 Carter began to search for the missing tomb of Tutankhamun (a number of objects had been discovered showing the existence of a tomb in the area). However, by 1921 the team still had not discovered the tomb, and Lord Carnarvon considered withdrawing his funding. After much debate, Carter convinced him to fund one final season.

Luckily for Carter this final season was a cracker. On 4 November 1922 his team uncovered the first stone step of Tutankhamun's tomb. The next day they cleared the steps to reveal the door, complete with ancient seals showing the tomb was intact. The first doorway was opened on 23 November 1922, and the second doorway within the tomb on 26 November. At the opening of this door, Carter and Carnarvon saw for the first time the wonderful objects hidden for three millennia. These include solid gold coffins, gilded shrines, scores of pieces of golden jewellery, and the famous solid gold death mask (see Chapter 4 for a photograph of the death mask).

The first chamber was officially opened on 29 November, and the burial chamber on 17 February 1923. The cataloguing of the objects started, and on 28 October 1925 the team finally opened the coffin and gazed at the face of the king who lived and died so long ago. Cataloguing and recording all the artefacts in the tomb was finally completed on 10 November 1930, eight years after the discovery.

KV5: The Tomb of the Sons of Ramses II

The existence of KV5 in the Valley of the Kings has been recorded since the early 19th century, but the entrance had long since been lost. When early explorers entered KV5, it was filled with rubble and debris almost to the ceiling, making progress difficult. In fact the tomb was abandoned as a lost cause. If only they knew what lay beyond the rubble.

In 1989, Kent Weeks, working for the Theban Mapping Project (see Chapter 19 and www.thebanmappingproject.com), entered this long-lost tomb. Rather than seeing golden treasure like Howard Carter did on entering Tutankhamun's tomb, Weeks was faced with raw sewage, the result of a leaky pipe that had been pumping waste into the tomb for decades. Coupled with the extreme heat of the Valley, it was not a nice experience! After the sewage was cleared away, the team started the job of removing the rubble and debris and revealing the tomb beyond.

And what a tomb it was – the largest tomb complex in the Valley of the Kings and indeed the whole of Egypt. Built by Ramses II for the burial of his numerous sons, the tomb (so far) includes more than 120 corridors and chambers spread over two levels. The number of corridors is expected eventually to be more than 150.

At least six sons of Ramses II were buried in the tomb complex, and their skeletal remains have been discovered. They were originally mummified, but flash floods over the centuries aided the decaying process, reducing their soft tissues to gunk.

Every wall of the tomb was carved and painted, but over the centuries this decoration has fallen off, creating an amazing puzzle for Egyptologists to piece together. Tomb depictions on the walls show more than 20 sons, including their funerary rites, so probably more than the six discovered mummies were buried here. Many years of work remain on KV5 – along with many more discoveries to be revealed.

Akhenaten's Talatat Blocks

During the reign of Akhenaten, a new building block was introduced, called a *talatat*. This word comes from the Arabic for 'three', which is appropriate, because the blocks were two hand widths long and one hand width high. Talatats could be handled by one individual, making building work easier and quicker to execute.

Akhenaten used these blocks when building a number of temples at the complex of Karnak in Luxor. During the reigns of Tutankhamun, Ay, and Horemheb, these temples were dismantled and the blocks reused for other building projects, as a means of destroying all evidence of Akhenaten (to find out why go to Chapter 4).

However, Horemheb decided to use talatat blocks to fill the hollow areas of his pylon gateways at Karnak to give these structures more stability. He was quite methodical in his work, and as he removed the block from the temple, he placed it directly into the pylon, creating a reverse order of many of the images originally carved onto the blocks. (Little did Horemheb realise he was in fact preserving, not destroying, the memory of Akhenaten.)

Since the first excavations of the pylons at the start of the 20th century, more than 35,000 talatat blocks have been discovered. They are being kept in a number of storehouses in the Karnak complex until they can be reconstructed.

All 35,000 blocks are decorated, including some on two sides, and reconstruction has been a monumental task. In Luxor Museum, a small wall of talatat have been reconstructed and researchers are continually adding to the display as work progresses.

From the reconstructions already made by the Akhenaten Temple Project, Egyptologists, using a high-tech computer program, are about to get an idea of the buildings that Akhenaten originally constructed, including

- A temple belonging to Nefertiti, Akhenaten's wife, which had a pillared courtyard with up to 30 pillars, all bearing images of the queen.

- A temple belonging to Akhenaten, which housed colossal statues of the king.

- A possible ceremonial palace where the royal couple stayed before performing ceremonies or rituals in the temple. Images from the talatat show a *window of appearances* (see Chapter 4) at this palace, where the king and queen stood to reward their favoured officials. Sadly this window hasn't yet been discovered, but you never know.

Palace of Cleopatra

In 1997, a French team in the Mediterranean discovered the sunken harbour of Alexandria and the two cities of Herakleion and Canopus just off the coast of Alexandria. This discovery started the underwater excavations of what was the city of Cleopatra. A devastating tidal wave caused by an earthquake flooded this area some 1,200 years ago.

The ongoing excavations have uncovered hundreds of artefacts, including colossal statues of kings and queens and of Hapi, the god of the Nile flood. These remnants, as well as smaller statues and architectural fragments including pillars and architraves, hint that the royal palace and gardens were situated close to the harbour.

As excavations have progressed, the position of Cleopatra's palace, Antony's palace, and a temple have been located. Just think, the setting of their romantic story and tragic demise has been identified.

In 2006, a proposal was put forward regarding an offshore underwater museum to display the city of Cleopatra. Many of the objects found underwater are left there in order to preserve them; when removed and dried, these items could disintegrate. The proposed museum includes a plexi-glass tunnel allowing the visitor to walk underwater in the footsteps of Cleopatra, Mark Antony, and Julius Caesar. Rather like the seal or the shark tunnel at the zoo – except no seals or sharks, just the eerily silent remains of a lost city.

Smaller articles like jewellery and coins have already been removed to prevent theft, and these will be displayed separately in an on-shore building.

KV63

On 10 February 2006, an American archaeological team discovered an 18th dynasty royal tomb, 5 metres from the tomb of Tutankhamun in the Valley of the Kings – long after the Valley was said to be exhausted.

The American team was working on a nearby tomb when its members discovered a number of New Kingdom workman's huts, built for those men who created the tombs in the Valley. Beneath these huts, they found the hidden entrance to the shaft of KV63. Some of the hut floors had never been disturbed, indicating that the tomb beneath was also undisturbed. The shaft is approximately 5 metres deep and leads through a 1.5-metre-high doorway to an undecorated 4 by 5 metre burial chamber. The blocking stones in the doorway were not original, which suggests that the doorway had been opened and closed a few times in antiquity.

The chamber contained seven wooden sarcophagi piled on top of each other and 27 large pots. A few of the jars had been opened and contained a number of items, including miniature vessels, natron (salt), scraps of material, seeds, wood, carbon, chaff, resin, and minerals – all items left over from a mummification (see Chapter 10). Researchers do not yet know whose mummification took place, although considerable evidence suggests the deceased was from the 18th dynasty, at the time of Tutankhamun.

By the end of May 2006, the sarcophagi had also been emptied and much to everyone's great disappointment no bodies were found within them. Instead, researchers found a number of items, similar to those from the jars. One sarcophagus was full of linen pillows, and another contained a small golden coffinette, perhaps for the burial of a servant figure.

The whole tomb was probably used as an embalmer's store and was entered frequently. Embalmer's stores were common, and many royal burials included a cache of materials left over from mummification. If KV63 was such a store, at least one more tomb may yet be discovered. Perhaps it's the elusive tomb of Akhenaten, Nefertiti, Tutankhamun's wife Ankhesenamun, or his grandmother Tiye. Who knows? Watch this space at www.kv63.com for developments.

Chapter 16

Ten Egyptians Worth Knowing

In This Chapter

▶ Meeting victorious kings and mysterious queens

▶ Working at Deir el Medina

▶ Getting to know members of the royal administration

*H*istory is made up of people, not events. Fortunately, the archaeological evidence from Egypt provides lots of information about these ancient people. Unfortunately, this evidence only relates to the upper classes, including royalty and the elite, who formed only a small percentage of society (see Chapter 1). The majority of the population – the farmers and labourers – are completely lost to modern historians.

Although the elite are very interesting – ten of the most intriguing are the focus of this chapter – the unknown lower classes were almost certainly interesting as well, adding another dimension to the history of ancient Egypt. If you want to find out more about the individuals of ancient Egypt, see *People of Ancient Egypt* by yours truly (Tempus Publishing, 2005), and John Romer's *Ancient Lives* (Phoenix Press, 2003).

Thutmosis III: The Egyptian Napoleon

Many of the kings of the 18th and 19th dynasties were military kings, but none more so than Thutmosis III. He didn't start out his rule in the most conventional way, though, and he is lucky he was able to make his mark on the military history of Egypt.

Thutmosis III was the son of Thutmosis II and a secondary queen called Isis. On the death of his father, Thutmosis III became king at the tender age of 2 or 3 years old. Because he was clearly too young to rule, he was married to his stepmother Hatshepsut, the widowed Great Royal Wife of Thutmosis II. After a few short years, Hatshepsut took over the throne as a king in her own right (see Chapter 5 for details), shoving Thutmosis III to the side. When Hatshepsut died, Thutmosis III was still only 24 or 25 years old and took over the rule of Egypt as the rightful king.

At the beginning of his sole rule, Thutmosis III started re-establishing the borders and control that Egypt had over the Near East, starting with a great campaign to Megiddo (a city in modern Israel), territory of the Hittites. With great bravery, Thutmosis marched into Megiddo via the most difficult route, catching the Hittites off guard. The Egyptians, however, lost their advantage when they stopped to loot the Hittite camp. The Hittites were able to resist the Egyptians for more than seven months, and the Egyptians eventually returned home. Refer to Chapter 4 for more on this campaign.

Thutmosis didn't give up though. During his 50 years or so of sole rule, he made 17 additional campaigns into Syria, as well as further campaigns into Nubia – some when he was in his 80s. Through his efforts, he firmly re-established Egypt as a power to be reckoned with.

Horemheb: The Maintainer of Order

Horemheb is a particularly appealing character in Egyptian history because his life is a true rags-to-riches story. He was born in a small town near the Faiyum, to a local middle-class family. He excelled at his studies and became a military scribe during the reign of Akhenaten in the 18th dynasty.

Horemheb slowly and carefully proceeded in his career and rose through the military ranks until he was a general – a powerful and influential position. But the story gets better: By the time the boy-king Tutankhamun was on the throne, Horemheb was a very prominent figure in the royal court. He is recorded as being the only person who could calm the young king down when he was having a tantrum, and he may even have taught Tutankhamun his military skills. Tutankhamun rewarded this general with the title of deputy king, meaning that Horemheb stood in for the king in some royal appointments and ceremonies.

At the death of Tutankhamun, Horemheb didn't push his right as deputy king and take over the throne. Instead he allowed the elderly vizier Ay to occupy the throne. Four years later, Ay died and Horemheb became king. A far cry from the middle-class family of his upbringing!

As king, Horemheb started the full-scale restoration of Egypt to the glory of the reign of Amenhotep III, before Akhenaten and his religious revolution (see Chapter 4). This set the standard for the 19th dynasty that was to follow, started by Horemheb's army general Ramses I. The 19th dynasty was to be an empire-building, military-based, incredibly disciplined and yet religious period of Egyptian history.

Ramses II even built a shrine at the tomb of Horemheb at Saqqara to worship him as a god. From rags to riches to divinity – can anyone hope for more?

Nefertiti: The Beautiful One Has Come

Nefertiti, the wife of Akhenaten, is one of the most famous queens from ancient Egypt, which is strange because remarkably little is known about her. Although she is mentioned frequently during the reign of Akhenaten (see Chapter 4), no record of her parents, family, or background exists.

Some Egyptologists think Nefertiti was a Mittannian (from an empire that spread from western Iran to the Mediterranean) princess sent to Egypt for a diplomatic marriage. Her name means 'the beautiful one has come', which may show that she travelled to Egypt and was given the name when she arrived. However, the wife of Ay holds the title 'wet nurse' of Nefertiti, indicating Nefertiti was in Egypt as a young infant and was therefore unlikely to be a foreign princess sent for marriage. Egyptologists now widely accept that Nefertiti was the daughter of Ay, and his wife was her stepmother, indicating perhaps that Nefertiti's own mother had died.

Nefertiti lived at Amarna and followed the religion of her husband; she is often depicted worshipping the sun disc alongside him. The most famous image of Nefertiti is a painted limestone bust. However, the bust does not have any identifying inscriptions; the identification as Nefertiti is based on the bust's crown, a design that only she is ever shown wearing.

Nefertiti and Akhenaten had six daughters but no sons, as far as the records show, and one of Nefertiti's daughters married Tutankhamun. Nefertiti disappeared from the records in year 13 of her husband's reign when she was in her 30s. Whether she died or was disgraced and banished from the king's palace to be replaced by another consort is unknown.

Although Nefertiti's life and death is shrouded in mystery, people are intrigued by Nefertiti, probably because of the lovely bust of Nefertiti in the Berlin Museum, and because she is associated with one of the most written-about kings in Egyptian history. However, we know very little, and until a body is clearly attributed to her we'll never really know who she was.

Ramose: The Honest Scribe

Ramose was a scribe from Deir el Medina, the village that housed the workmen who built the Valley of the Kings (see Chapter 2). He moved to the village as scribe during the reign of Sety I of the 19th dynasty and worked there for more than 40 years. Ramose was one of the richest and most popular men in the village. He spent a great deal of his wealth on religious shrines and temples and was particularly pious.

Unlike some of the other characters who lived in the village (see the following sections on Kenhirkhepshef, Naunakhte, and Paneb), Ramose was very honest. Available records include no accusations of corruption, bribery, or general naughtiness. He was a goody-two-shoes through and through.

Sadly, the one thing Ramose wanted more than anything was a child, and he and his wife Mutemwia tried for many years, unfortunately without success. A stela was found at Deir el Medina begging the goddess Hathor to grant them a child in reward for all their piety. This also didn't work, and Ramose and Mutemwia ended up adopting a new arrival to the village, a scribe called Kenhirkhepshef.

Kenhirkhepshef: An Ancient Historian

Kenhirkhepshef was also scribe at Deir el Medina during the fourth decade of the reign of Ramses II, and he held the position for more than 50 years. Various accusations of corruption were levelled against him, so he was not as honest as his adopted father Ramose.

Kenhirkhepshef is accused of taking bribes to cover up the misdeeds of others and forcing a number of workmen to work for him without pay:

> *The Draftsman Prahotep salutes his superior . . . Kenhirkhepshef: What does this bad way mean in which you treat me? I am to you like a donkey. If there is some work, bring the donkey, and if there is some food, bring the ox. If there is some beer, you do not look for me, but if there is work, you do look for me.*

Corruption aside, Kenhirkhepshef has other intriguing facets. He had an extensive library with papyri on various topics. These papyri contained medical texts, religious spells and hymns, letters, poetry, household hints, and dream interpretations.

Kenhirkhepshef was an early historian and had a particular interest in the history of Egyptian kings. He liked to make long lists, and one of these records the kings of the 18th and 19th dynasty in chronological order. Kenhirkhepshef also had a copy of the Battle of Kadesh report, the famous battle of Ramses II, which shows that Kenhirkhepshef had an interest in current affairs.

Kenhirkhepshef, as an elder of the village, was very firm in his beliefs and didn't seem to mind voicing them. He was particularly against alcohol, and a text from his library admonishes

> *Do not indulge in drinking beer for fear of uttering evil speech. If you fall no one will hold out a hand to you. Your companions will say 'out with the drunk', you lie on the ground like a little child.*

Naunakhte: The Property Owner

Naunakhte lived at Deir el Medina during the reign of Ramses II, and she was married to Kenhirkhepshef, the scribe. At the time of their marriage, she was as young as 12 years old while he was between 54 and 70 years old. Naunakhte and Kenhirkhepshef were married for eight to ten years, although they did not have any children. Kenhirkhepshef was more of a father figure than a husband. He probably married Naunakhte as a means of caring for her and ensuring that she inherited his possessions. As a childless widow when she was only in her 20s, Naunakhte married a workman called Khaemnum from Deir el Medina, and they were married for 30 years. She had eight children with him – four boys and four girls.

Although little has survived about the life of Naunakhte, she left four papyri recording her last will, in which she disinherits four of her children. This meant they would inherit only their father's and not her personal wealth. The reason she disinherits these children is neglect:

> *As for me I am a free woman of the land of Pharaoh. I brought up these eight servants of yours, and gave them an outfit of everything as is usually made for those in their station. But see I am grown old, and they are not looking after me in my turn. Whoever of them has aided me, to him I will give of my property but he who has not given to me; to him I will not give any of my property.*

Two of the papyri list, item by item, all the objects she owns and which of her children she leaves them to. These documents show that women were in complete control of their own property; but they also show her rather petty and pedantic nature, because each bowl or dish is listed. Ironic, considering the most valuable item today is the papyrus itself.

Paneb: The Loveable Rogue

Paneb was one of the most colourful characters from Deir el Medina. He lived there during the reign of Ramses II and probably knew Kenhirkhepshef in later life. Kenhirkhepshef was not keen on alcohol, so some friction may have existed between the two because Paneb was notorious for getting drunk and disorderly. Despite this behaviour, Kenhirkhepshef stood up for Paneb and covered some of his misdeeds.

Throughout his career at Deir el Medina, numerous accusations were made against Paneb of criminal deeds and adultery (for which he was punished). All accusations were recorded on a document known as the Papyrus Salt (because it was purchased by archaeologist Henry Salt) by a man called Amenakht, who greatly resented the position that Paneb held. The accusations were numerous and varied, including

- Bribing the vizier to gain the position of foreman
- Forcing many workmen and their wives to work for him without payment, including making a relation of Amenakht's feed his (Paneb's) ox
- Using government tools to build his own tomb
- Stealing cut stones from the tomb of Merenptah and using them in his own tomb
- Threatening to kill his father, Neferhotep, while he was drunk
- Threatening to kill another Deir el Medina foreman, Hay
- Murdering some men who were to deliver a message to the king

Despite the slowly increasing severity of these accusations, none was proven, and therefore Paneb went unpunished. The accusation of murder, in fact, seems to be hearsay, because Amenakht doesn't even bother to mention the victims' names, indicating perhaps he didn't know who they were.

However, some robbery accusations appear to be based in fact and may have resulted in punishment:

- **Tomb robbery 1:** A list of items stolen from the tomb of Sety II, includes tomb doors, chariot coverings, incense, wine, and statues. The case was brought before the vizier, and Paneb swore an oath saying 'Should the vizier hear my name again I shall be dismissed from my office and become a stone mason once more'. This oath was enough to acquit him on this occasion.

✔ **Tomb robbery 2:** According to records, Paneb 'went to the tomb of the workman Nakhmin and stole the bed which was under him. He carried off the objects which one gives to a dead man and stole them.' No punishment for this, so perhaps the accusation was false.

✔ **Tomb robbery 3:** Paneb was accused of taking a model goose from the tomb of a wife of Ramses II, Henutmire. Paneb swore he didn't take the goose, but the authorities found it in his house. This accusation was shortly followed by Paneb's disappearance from the records, so perhaps this was enough to get him executed, which was the punishment for tomb robbery.

Bearing in mind he was in his 60s when he died, Paneb lived an active and interesting life. Even at 60 he was clearly a bit of a lad, ducking and diving until the day he got caught – or died.

Mereruka: The Princess's Husband

Mereruka was a very prominent official during the reign of King Teti in the fifth dynasty. Mereruka's mother was 'the royal acquaintance', Nedjetempet, which means Mereruka came from a prominent noble family before his promotion. Mereruka held a number of important titles including

✔ Overseer of the house of weapons

✔ Overseer of the king's harem

✔ Vizier

✔ High priest of Re

These important titles show that Teti held Mereruka in high esteem, a fact the king reinforced by allowing Mereruka to marry his daughter Sesheshat. In addition to becoming son-in-law to the king, Mereruka was made 'foster child of the king', indicating that the king favoured him a great deal. So much in fact that Mereruka took the place of the eldest son, acting as Teti's funerary priest during his funeral.

Mereruka had three children with Sesheshat, and he was also privileged enough to have a secondary wife with whom he had five sons. Mereruka led a busy and varied life, and as vizier he was responsible for much of the state administration (Chapter 1). He also supervised the construction of the pyramid complex of Teti at Saqqara, and in fact he had his own huge mastaba tomb (see Chapter 13) with 32 chambers very close to the pyramid of his king.

Mereruka's is the largest tomb in the cemetery and is decorated with elaborately and beautifully carved decoration, showing that he was wealthy, prominent, and held the favour of the king. All in all a very privileged young man.

Asru: Chantress of Amun

Asru was a chantress of Amun at the temple of Karnak at Luxor in the third intermediate period. She was of noble birth and inherited the position of *chantress*, a priestly title, from her mother. Her mummified body was encased in two highly decorated coffins, and her remains tell us a lot about her life.

Fingerprints and footprints taken of the mummy show she was neither a dancer nor a musician, rather a singer who sang prayers and incantations for the worship of the god Amun. In her later years, Asru probably found singing difficult because of breathing difficulties.

Asru suffered from a number of parasitic worms, which caused nausea, dizziness, and anaemia. She probably saw blood and worms in her stools and urine. Her lungs showed evidence of sand pneumoconiosis, which was caused by breathing in sand and led to major respiratory problems. She also had a 20-centimetre cyst on her lung at the time of her death, caused by one of her worms.

When she died, Asru was 60–70 years old – elderly for an ancient Egyptian. She suffered from osteoarthritis and chronic arthritis throughout her body, which damaged the joints of her fingers. At some point in her life, she had a nasty fall that damaged her lower back, sending sciatica pains down her left leg. Her last years were painful, and walking and sitting were difficult, but as a full-time priestess she may have spent her last days in the temple teaching the younger priestesses how to continue their roles.

Nesperenub: The Priest of Khonsu

Nesperenub was a priest of Khonsu at Karnak in the third intermediate period. The temple at the time was very rich because the high priests of Amun had taken over the throne and were ruling the Theban region. This meant the priests at Karnak were well paid and well fed. But poor Nesperenub did not always have such a wealthy lifestyle. His body shows that when he was young he suffered a growth interruption, perhaps caused by poverty or disease.

As was traditional, Nesperenub inherited his position from his father; in fact generations of his family all held the same titles. He also held the title of fan bearer, and he probably fanned the god and ensured he did not overheat in the hot desert sun during processions (see Chapters 9 and 12). Nesperenub was the 'fan bearer on the right of the king', showing that he was also responsible for keeping the king cool – another very privileged position to hold.

Nesperenub was approximately 40 when he died, and a CT scan has shown he may have died from a brain tumour. A small hole on the inside of his skull may be the result of the fluids from the tumour eating into the skull. Imagine the headaches – and no ibuprofen to deal with it. The added pain and stink of the abscesses in his mouth and the wear on his teeth mean that Nesperenub was probably quite ratty.

CT scans of Nesperenub's mummy also show a rather strange object on the back of his head – a small clay bowl used by the embalmers to catch excess resin when sticking the bandages in place. Clearly the embalmers forgot about the bowl, which allowed the resin to set solid and stick the bowl to the back of his head. Damage around the bowl indicates that the embalmers tried to chisel it off. Their efforts didn't work, and they must have figured if they wrapped up the body, no one would ever know. Poor Nesperenub, destined to wander eternity with a bowl on his head.

Chapter 17

Ten Ancient Egyptian Achievements

*T*he ancient Egyptians were a very civilised nation and had many achievements to their name, including monumental buildings and extensive trade networks. They were a very busy society – constantly improving and progressing in their lifestyle and technology.

While the Greeks are attributed with most academic, scientific, and philosophical achievements, evidence shows that the Egyptians were not lacking in these departments; they just had a different approach. Everything the ancient Egyptians did had a practical purpose. They did not believe in researching for research's sake or contemplating unusable theories. Theirs was a practical rather than academic society. This chapter showcases ten of their greatest successes.

Scientific Method

As very practical people, the ancient Egyptians liked to solve problems with the least amount of fuss and general theorising. Therefore science as a discipline and as a word did not exist, because the ancient Egyptians no doubt believed they were only ever doing the necessary to continue with their work. Research for the sake of research did not seem to be carried out.

However, the Edwin Smith Medical Papyrus and the Ebers Papyrus show that the Egyptians conducted themselves according to scientific rules – they were willing to experiment within the frame of their daily work.

For example, when examining a medical patient (see Chapter 8 for details), scientific method was strictly used and included

- An interview with the patient
- Examination of bodily discharges
- Study of reflexes
- A diagnosis of the illness

Doctors then went about curing the ailment and recorded the results for future reference.

A similar scientific method was applied to building monuments, with many mathematical calculations (see the following section, 'Mathematics') being taken into account before work commenced. Sadly, little of this process has survived, but from the evidence available, the Egyptians clearly relied on multiple disciplines – such as mathematics, astronomy, geography, and surveying – when designing and planning the pyramids, temples, and tombs.

Mathematics

A few mathematical papyri have been discovered that give some indication of the advanced mathematical knowledge the Egyptians possessed.

While the Greeks are well known for their mathematical formulae, the Egyptians didn't really see the point. Instead they had a more practical collection of small calculations that produced the same answers.

This practical use of mathematical calculations can be identified in Egyptian building works – the pyramids in particular. Archaeologist William Matthew Finders Petrie (see Chapter 15) was the first to record and measure the pyramids systematically. The work of Petrie and others clearly shows that these structures were very well planned mathematically.

The Egyptians were among the first to consistently and correctly combine and utilise these techniques:

- ✔ The use of fractions (½, ¼, ⅓, and so on)
- ✔ Calculating the area of a rectangle by multiplying the length by the width
- ✔ Calculating the area of a triangle by turning it into a rectangle and then halving that area
- ✔ Calculating the area of a circle using the length of the diameter and an approximation of pi (3.16)
- ✔ Finding the volume of cylinders and pyramids based on knowledge of areas

The Egyptians were in fact more advanced in their mathematical knowledge than they are given credit for. The reason for this underrating seems to be that the ancient Egyptians' concerns were practical rather than theoretical.

Astronomy

The Egyptians were very knowledgeable about the stars and constellations. From the Middle Kingdom, constellations were often depicted on coffins as star clocks, showing the length of time stars were visible or invisible. From the New Kingdom, ceilings of tombs and temples often displayed the constellation of stars. These constellations were the same as the ones we see today, but represented differently. For example:

- ✔ Orion was represented as a man turning his head.
- ✔ Ursa Major was represented as a bull's foreleg.

Like mathematics (see the preceding section), astronomy was used by the Egyptians for many different practical uses including

- ✔ Scheduling temple-building ceremonies, which relied on the visibility of the constellations we refer to now as the Great Bear and Orion
- ✔ Setting the cardinal points for the orientation of the pyramids by observing the North Star
- ✔ Setting the New Year always to coincide with the rising of Sirius in mid-July and the annual flooding of the Nile

From the Middle Kingdom, the Egyptians were able to recognise five planets, known as stars that know no rest, which were often associated with Horus, the Egyptian god of the sky:

- ✔ Jupiter, known as Horus who limits the two lands
- ✔ Mars, known as Horus the red
- ✔ Mercury, known as Sebegu (a god associated with Seth)
- ✔ Saturn, known as Horus, bull of the sky
- ✔ Venus, known as god of the morning

The stars were not used to predict the fate of humans in Egypt until the Ptolemaic period when the Greeks introduced astrology. The most famous zodiac in Egypt is on the ceiling at Denderah and dates to the first century AD. This zodiac displays all the familiar zodiac signs, including Leo, Aries, and Taurus.

Understanding of the Human Body

The ancient Egyptians had a remarkable understanding of the human body, primarily gained through their observations during mummification. They probably didn't perform live internal surgery, but their greatest anatomical achievement was the near-discovery of circulation.

The Greeks were credited with discovering circulation in the fifth century BC, the but the Egyptians clearly understood a lot more about the workings of the human body than they're often given credit for.

The Edwin Smith Medical Papyrus, which dates back to approximately 1550 BC, discusses blood circulation through observation of the pulse, making clear that these two concepts were connected in the minds of the Egyptians. Pulse-related observations include:

- ✔ 'It is there that the heart speaks.'
- ✔ 'It is there that every physician and every priest of Sekhmet places his fingers . . . he feels something from the heart.'

Additionally, this papyrus indicates that the Egyptians knew that the blood supply ran from the heart to all organs:

- ✔ 'There are vessels in him for every part of the body.'
- ✔ 'It speaks forth in the vessels of every body part.'

Even the creation story of the ram-headed god, Khnum, who fashioned humans on a potter's wheel, reads a little like an anatomical record. For example, Khnum:

- Oriented the bloodstream to flow over the bones and attached the skin to the skeletal frame
- Installed a respiratory system, vertebrae to support it, and the digestive system
- Designed sexual organs for comfort and ease of use during intercourse
- Organised conception in the womb and the stages of labour

Not only did Khnum create Egyptians this way, his creation extended to foreigners, as well as animals, birds, fish, and reptiles. He was truly a universal creator – and a very talented potter!

Irrigation

Egypt is situated in the desert with the Nile as the only source of water. Using a complicated system of irrigation canals and water dykes, the Egyptians were able to make the most of the water available. Canals were directed to dry areas and were deep enough that they were still full when the flood waters receded.

Evidence suggests that in the Middle Kingdom the natural lake in the Faiyum was used as a reservoir. Water filled the lake during the annual inundation (flood) and was stored to be used in the drier times of the year. In addition to this lake was a canal leading directly from the Nile, which would provide a constant supply of water to the area.

In order to irrigate the land artificially, channels needed to be dug during the inundation to direct the water to areas of land in desperate need. To get water into the channels:

- In the Old and Middle Kingdoms, water was transported by hand in large vessels and then physically poured into the irrigation channels.
- In the New Kingdom, the *shaduf* was introduced. The shaduf is a wooden pole with a jar on one end and a weight on the other, which can easily lift and direct water.
- During the Ptolemaic period, the *sakkia* was introduced. The sakkia is an animal-powered water wheel that moves more water – which meant more land could be irrigated, resulting in more agricultural land and ultimately more food production.

Artificial irrigation was a necessity, and it was a major achievement. Even today, with only one water source and still situated in the desert, the Egyptian people never have hosepipe bans and water shortages!

Stone Buildings

The third-dynasty King Djoser is credited with building the first stone building in the world. This was his pyramid complex at Saqqara, dominated by the step pyramid that still towers over the landscape.

The step pyramid started from much humbler origins, however – as a pit burial and mastaba tomb (see Chapter 13), which covered a total of eleven burial shafts. Djoser's structure was gradually extended outwards and upwards until the step pyramid was created, standing 60 metres high and consisting of six steps.

Most impressively, the step pyramid was built of stone instead of the mud bricks normally used at this period. To maintain a traditional appearance, the stone blocks were of the same dimensions as the mud bricks. The outside was then completely encased in limestone blocks, giving the finished pyramid a smooth look.

The use of stone was a great achievement, particularly considering that other buildings were made of perishable materials. This pyramid complex was designed to last for eternity – and it looks like it is well on its way. After the third dynasty, buildings were built of stone more often. However, stone was only ever used for buildings that were intended to last for centuries, such as temples and tombs. All other buildings (houses, palaces, and even some shrines) were built using mud brick. We have to be thankful to Djoser – if he didn't want such an impressive monument, we might not have the stone structures in such abundance today.

A Surviving Wonder

Egypt has the only surviving Wonder of the Ancient World – the Great Pyramid of Giza (see Chapter 14). King Khufu of the fourth dynasty built this pyramid. It stands proud on a natural rock plateau and towers 146 metres into the sky. Even with modern Cairo encroaching, the Great Pyramid is visible for miles around.

The outside of the pyramid is encased in limestone blocks, which give it a beautiful white, shining appearance. The pyramid incorporates two burial chambers, one of which contains the red granite sarcophagus designed for the burial of the king. However, no royal burial seems to have happened in this pyramid; it is likely that Khufu was buried elsewhere.

The Great Pyramid has been visited for many years as a tourist attraction, with Cleopatra VII and Julius Caesar among the earliest celebrity visitors. Even Tutankhamun, Ramses II, and Ramses III almost certainly travelled to Giza to marvel at these monuments, which were ancient even then.

Glass Production

Glass was not introduced until the early New Kingdom, probably brought from Syria by Thutmosis III. The Egyptians gradually became proficient in

- ✔ Glass making from raw materials (including silica, alkali, and lime)
- ✔ Glass working from imported ready-made blocks of glass

Glass was used in clear or coloured form from the reign of Hatshepsut. Egyptians even fashioned vessels by making a core of clay in the required shape and then dipping it in molten glass. Removing the clay core was quite difficult, especially in vessels with narrow necks, so vessels crafted this way have an opaque quality.

Other methods of manufacture include

- ✔ **Moulding:** Molten glass is poured into moulds of clay.
- ✔ **Cold cutting:** Pre-moulded glass is carved as if it were stone using stone, bronze, or copper tools.
- ✔ **Core moulding:** A clay or sand core in the shape of the cavity in a vessel is dipped in molten glass and moved around until it is completely covered. Once cold, the core is scraped out.

Archaeologist William Matthew Finders Petrie (see Chapter 15) discovered a great deal of waste from glass production at Amarna, the city of Akhenaten. Other production sites were at the palace of Amenhotep III at Malkata in Luxor and the site of el-Lisht in the north of Egypt.

A more recent glass-related discovery was at the site of Pi-Rameses, the city of Ramses II in the Delta. In 2005, excavations uncovered a glass factory, showing that glass was produced in great quantity at this site. Enough of the equipment was unearthed to reconstruct the manufacturing process:

- ✔ The raw materials were heated in used beer jars up to temperatures of 750 degrees Celsius and then again in crucibles to as high as 1,000 degrees Celsius.

- ✔ The glass was coloured using natural pigments added to the raw ingredients. Sometimes a coil of coloured glass was draped around the completed vessel while soft and then blended to create waves, marble effects, garlands, and arches of feathered patterns.

Glass was a prestige item, under royal control, and was often given to foreign dignitaries as a diplomatic gift. This prestige is due to the extensive skills needed to produce quality items, and glass is used with some frequency in the artefacts from Tutankhamun's tomb. It was such a sought-after commodity that those who couldn't afford glass made replicas from wood or stone.

Female Leadership

The female pharaoh Hatshepsut is famous for many things, and many achievements punctuate her reign. The most spectacular achievement is that as a woman she took over the role of king, pushing Thutmosis III (her husband, step-son, and co-ruler) aside. This is the first time that a woman had ruled Egypt as a king rather than a queen or co-ruler. Check out Chapter 5 for more on the role of women.

Hatshepsut ruled in relative peace and spent her 20-odd years on the throne building monuments. Her funerary temple at Deir el Bahri records the transportation of two red granite obelisks – even showing the massive structures tied on Nile barges – and their erection at Karnak. These obelisks were completely covered in gold.

Other records on the walls of Deir el Bahri detail Hatshepsut's expedition to Punt. No one really knows where Punt is, and Egyptologists have never agreed on this issue. Even Hatshepsut wasn't sure, and she appealed to the oracle of Amun to give the direct route to this 'god's land'. It's a pity she didn't draw a map.

When Hatshepsut returned from Punt, she brought a number of incense trees carried in baskets on a carrying pole. She planted the trees along the approach to her temple and aspired to make incense a local product, thus eliminating the need for trade. The expedition also returned with incense bundles, animal hides, and exotic woods. These items boosted the Egyptian economy and made a number of exotic items available.

Although Hatshepsut did plant incense trees, historians do not know whether she was able to produce enough incense to prevent the need for trade. A self-contained Egyptian incense industry is unlikely; incense is often a prominent feature of later booty and trade lists.

Continuing Civilisation

The most spectacular achievement of the ancient Egyptians is the continuance of their civilisation for more than 3,000 years. The Roman Empire lasted just over 500 years and the ancient Greek civilisation was at its height for about 400 years. Ancient Egyptian society was fully developed in 3100 BC when King Narmer united Upper and Lower Egypt for the first time. From this time until the death of Cleopatra in 30 BC, the culture's religion, practices, and lifestyle did not change a great deal, making Egypt a civilisation to be reckoned with.

Even after the death of Cleopatra, the Romans did not totally destroy Egyptian culture straight away. Indeed, the religious practices continued at the temple of Philae until the fourth century AD.

Although Egyptian culture may appear to be static for 3,000 years or so, it was in fact ever changing, and this is the secret of its success. The Egyptians were ever so accommodating. They were more than happy to absorb aspects of foreign culture and religion into their own, which enabled an immigrant community to thrive in Egypt. Their religion and culture had a something-for-everyone policy; if something was missing, they simply added it.

Problems occurred when the influx of foreigners was so great that Egyptian culture could not easily accommodate the new culture or cultures. This was why Egyptian culture died a slow death with the infiltration of the Greeks from the time that Alexander the Great entered Egypt, followed by the Romans in 30 BC.

These newcomers were unprepared to adopt Egyptian culture completely, and a Hellenistic society slowly formed. After Alexander the Great and the Romans, came the Christians and the Muslims, which eventually resulted in a total loss of ancient traditions – until archaeologists started to reconstruct a portrait of this great civilisation.

Chapter 18

Top Ten Places to Visit in Egypt

*E*gypt continues to be a marvellous travel destination, but the number of temples, tombs, and museums can be overwhelming. You may be tempted to plump for a package tour with all your trips planned for you, but they have tight schedules and often spend longer at alabaster, papyrus, and perfume shops than at the ancient monuments.

Why not plan your Egyptian trek on your own? This chapter features the top ten places to visit – some on the tourist trail and others a little off the beaten track. For locations, have a peek at the Cheat Sheet map. Armed with a guide book, camera, and taxi driver, the sky's the limit. You never know, you may even discover other sites to add to this list as must-goes.

Hundreds of guidebooks are on the market, but the best are Jill Kamil's guides (although they can be tricky to get hold of) and those published by Lonely Planet or Rough Guides. Also take a look at the Egyptian Monuments Web site at www.egyptsites.co.uk which outlines all the sites in Egypt with directions on how to get to them.

The following recommended sites are listed in geographical order, starting in the north and working your way south.

All the sites require tickets – normally costing less than LE.30 (£3 or $6) per site, with many costing as little as LE.10 (£1 or $2). You can buy tickets at each site.

Giza Plateau, Cairo

Although the prominent pyramids dominate the skyline, the Giza plateau in Cairo is teeming with places to visit. An average tour spends about an hour here, but to see everything you need at least three hours – maybe longer if you like to wander off the beaten track.

The three main pyramids were built by Khufu, Khafra, and Menkaure, and each is accompanied by satellite pyramids belonging to the kings' wives – for a grand total of nine pyramids. At least three are open to the public.

Only 200 or so tickets for the Great Pyramid are sold daily, so you must be at the ticket office when it opens at approximately 8 a.m. (check the opening time before going there, arrive early, and be prepared to sprint up the hill to beat the coaches). After purchasing your ticket, wait a couple of hours before entering the pyramid, after the crowds have lessened. The pyramid is worth the wait!

Alongside the Great Pyramid of Khufu, be sure to visit the empty boat pits (see Chapter 14) and the modern boat museum (for which you need a separate ticket), which features a reconstructed vessel from the pits. This boat was used in the funeral of Khufu and has been reconstructed according to ancient techniques. Walkways at different levels enable visitors to view the boat from all angles.

The causeway of Khafra leads from the Great Pyramid to the sphinx (made of solid rock and so only viewed from the outside), the sphinx temple (closed to the public, but you can see it from a short distance away), and the valley temple. (You can visit the valley temple, although it bears no decoration.) Between the paws of the sphinx is the Dream Stela erected by Thutmosis IV after the sun god appeared to him in a dream (refer to Chapter 14). On both sides of the causeway is the mastaba cemetery with a number of beautifully decorated structures, three of which are open to the public. The mastaba of Seregemib (which includes a lovely scene of driving donkeys) and that of Khnumenty (a two-level structure with an Indiana-Jones-type ladder to climb) are worth visiting.

Saqqara, Cairo

Saqqara is the site of the oldest stone building in the world – a step pyramid – as well as a 'dummy complex' of shrines, temples, and ritual areas designed for King Djoser to rule in the afterlife.

The site also has a number of other pyramids, including the pyramid of Unas, which appears to be nothing but a pile of rubble. Sadly the pyramid of Unas is closed to the public because it is structurally unsafe, but you can see the Pyramid Texts from Unas's pyramid in the burial chambers of the pyramid of Teti nearby.

Close to Teti's pyramid are the mastaba tombs of Mereruka (with the image of his wife on the bed playing the harp), Ankhmahor (with an image of the earliest circumcision scene), and Ti (with elaborate farming scenes and a *serdab* and statue). For more information on mastabas and serdabs, go to Chapter 13.

A short distance away stand the large underground catacomb known as the *Serapeum*, constructed for the burials of the sacred Apis bulls, which were worshipped at Saqqara. The bulls were mummified, according to tradition, and then buried with huge stone sarcophagi and canopic jars. Their mothers also received elaborate burials complete with a burial suite of their own.

The Imhotep Museum has also opened on the site and showcases archaeological finds from the Saqqara region. Highlights include a beautiful reconstruction of the wall tiles that decorated some of the chambers of the Djoser complex, as well as the infamous famine scene from the causeway of Unas, depicting emaciated people entering Egypt looking for help. This scene is very graphic and even shows one chap pulling lice from his hair and eating them.

To see everything at Saqqara takes all day, so negotiate with your driver to wait for you. Take some food with you, because there's no café at the site.

Museum of Egyptian Antiquities, Cairo

The Museum of Egyptian Antiquities (commonly known as the Cairo Museum) is soon to be replaced by the Grand Egyptian Museum and relocated near Giza, where it will be centred around the colossal statue of Ramses (moved in 2006 from Ramses Square in Cairo). The new museum is scheduled to open by 2010.

The museum as it now stands is spectacular and is bursting at the seams with hundreds of objects from 3,000 years of Egyptian history. Most package tours spend a couple of hours here but you could spend an entire day – the morning upstairs and the afternoon downstairs. The café does quite nice sandwiches and cold drinks.

Unusual objects are tucked away in every corner, from the sarcophagus of Akhenaten (in the garden to the left of the main building) to the beautiful wooden coffin of Ramses (who oversees the goings-on of the first floor). Close by is the only human-shaped shroud in Egypt, two real wigs, which are very close to a classic 'mullet' style, and a leather military kilt.

Wonder at the weight of the gold jewellery awarded to favoured officials and stare into the eyes of long-dead animal mummies. Marvel over the statue of the dwarf Seneb, seated with his wife and children, as well as the statue of Ramses III with Horus and the little-represented Seth. Spend hours discussing the anomalies of the Amarna art style on the ground floor. If you have any time left, be sure to visit the Tutankhamun exhibition and gaze on the face of the boy-king.

If you'd like to know more, take a look at the official Web site at www. egyptianmuseum.gov.eg.

Tell el Amarna, Al Minya

Tell el Amarna was the city Akhenaten established for the worship of the sun disc, the Aten. The city is situated in Al Minya in Middle Egypt about half way between Cairo and Luxor. Very little of the actual city is exposed because of the fragility of the remains, but British archaeologists have reconstructed some buildings. These structures include the small temple to the Aten, the north palace where Nefertiti and Tutankhamun lived, a city house that is typical of many from the site, and the bridge that joins two temples over the so-called King's Road. The King's Road would have seen the daily processions of Akhenaten, Nefertiti, and their children in their sparkling chariots. This bridge on the King's Road is also believed to be the site of the *window of appearances*, from which the royal family bestowed golden jewellery on their favoured courtiers. Visit Chapter 2 for more details on the town.

The real reason to visit Amarna, however, is to tour the two sets of tombs (the north and the south tombs) and the royal tomb. Many of these tombs are open to the public. These tombs are some of the only places where you can see classic Amarna-style art outside a museum.

Most of tombs include images of Akhenaten and Nefertiti standing at the window of appearances along with the princesses, riding in a chariot, or worshipping the Aten. A classic image of Ay can be found in his tomb here, showing him boasting to his friends about his new red leather gloves, a rare commodity in Egypt. The royal tomb is badly damaged, but trying to make out the images on the walls is interesting, and this monument once probably held the secrets to the Amarna period, which continue to elude Egyptologists today.

To make the most of Amarna and Beni Hasan (see the following section) you need to stay overnight at Al Minya. Only a couple of hotels are here – and don't be surprised if you're the only people there. You can't drive to Al Minya alone and need to organise with your driver to travel with the military convoy that leaves daily. You can travel there by train, but first check the safety issues. Your hotel in Cairo or Luxor may be able to help.

Beni Hasan, Al Minya

Near Al Minya is the Middle Kingdom burial site known as Beni Hasan. This site is formed by an outcrop of rock, high up in the cliff face. The site includes 39 rock-cut tombs (see Chapter 13) built by local *nomarchs*, or governors.

Of the 39 tombs, 5 or so are open to the public. Each tomb has an entrance consisting of a pillared courtyard. A central door leads into the tomb itself, and images and inscriptions decorate some tombs. All tombs have large open rooms with supporting pillars, and statue rooms at the rear of the chambers that housed statues of the deceased individuals. The family of each deceased individual laid offerings of food and drink at the statue to nourish the departed's spirit. (Actual burials took place at the end of a long shaft that opens out into the burial chamber under the main room; these rooms are not open to the public.)

The decoration in these tombs features lots of action. Notable images include:

- ✔ **Military training activities,** such as wrestling, stick fighting, and weight lifting with sandbags.

- ✔ **Siege warfare,** including the earliest image in Egypt of the wheel and an image of foreign diplomats travelling to Egypt to participate in trade.

  The most important of these siege scenes is in the tomb of Khnumhotep II and features the earliest depiction of the Hyksos, a rather colourful group of people bringing eye paint to trade with the Egyptians.

- ✔ **Elaborate fishing and fowling scenes,** awash with colour and detailed renderings of marsh flora and fauna.

Karnak Temple, Luxor

Karnak temple in Luxor is the largest temple ever built. Because it took more than 2,000 years to construct, Karnak temple includes a number of different shrines, temples, statues, and chapels dedicated to many different kings and gods. It covers 247 acres and many hours can be required to walk around the various monuments. Most package tours spend about two hours here, but you need at least a morning to do it justice – although even a morning won't allow time for the open air museum and the temples of Khonsu and Opet. The complex includes a coffee shop, and the Tutankhamun restaurant outside does a lovely lunch. Check with the guards when leaving the temple, because they often let you come back in after lunch on the same ticket. The temple can easily provide a couple of days' entertainment to any Egyptophile tourist!

The main temple has ten entrance pylons, each decorated with elaborate images and texts, as well as the largest hypostyle hall, consisting of 134 columns. These columns, which stand up to 21 metres (69 feet) tall, create a stone version of the primeval marshes – a most impressive sight. And if you can tear yourself away from the pillars, the surrounding walls feature images of the coronations of Sety I and Ramses II in great detail.

The Karnak complex also has two sacred lakes – a rectangular one built by Thutmosis III and a horseshoe-shaped lake built by Amenhotep III (although the latter is closed to the public and forms part of the complex of Mut outside the present enclosure walls). Within the enclosure walls are a number of small temples worth going to see, including the temple of Ptah (with a beautiful statue of Sekhmet enhanced by ancient lighting techniques), the temple of Khonsu (built with re-used blocks, many of which retain their original images), and the Chapels of the God's Wives of Amun (some of the only chapels built by and depicting women).

The complex also has an open air museum displaying a number of decorated blocks as well as a large-scale temple of Thutmosis III and three reconstructed chapels – the Alabaster Chapel of Amenhotep I, the White Chapel of Senusret I, and the Red Chapel of Hatshepsut, which includes some lovely scenes of her coronation. Don't miss a reconstructed temple gateway of Akhenaten's temple to the Aten, which surprisingly shows him in a traditional manner, smiting foreign prisoners with a large mace head. Compared with later images, this depiction of Akhenaten is completely unrecognisable.

Medinet Habu, Luxor

When in Luxor, you must visit the spectacular mortuary temple of Ramses III at Medinet Habu on the west bank of the Nile. This temple is a copy of the temple of Ramses II at the Ramesseum (which is situated further north and is also open to the public). Some of the scenes on the walls have been directly copied without any thought for reality; for example, Ramses II recorded battles with the Nubians, whereas Ramses III didn't, but copied the Nubian battle scenes as his own victory! The temple is a good means of seeing what the Ramesseum looked like, because now the Ramesseum is in a ruined condition.

The pylons at Medinet Habu depict the many battles of Ramses III, including his Libyan wars. An external wall shows the battle of the Sea People. Although these scenes are difficult to make out, it is worth the effort because they show the first naval battle in history. Don't miss the image of the world's first crows' nest, which enabled sailors to see for great distances and shoot fire arrows into the enemy ships.

To the left of the entrance pylon is a palace with a window of appearances that looks into the first court of the temple. No doubt the king himself stood in this area, so why not stand in the footsteps of the pharaohs.

The palace itself was for women. A number of three-room suites – perhaps a sleeping area, dressing room, and lounge area – are at the rear of the structure. You can also see an audience chamber complete with throne dais, a pillared court, and even two showers – the drain is still visible.

The main gate to the temple is an amazing structure – a copy of a Syrian *migdol*, or ceremonial gateway. The hollow gateway, which, sadly, isn't open to the public, contains images of the king and his royal women. Although historians once thought the site was a harem, many now believe it was a visiting place for royal women. Evidence shows patio gardens on various levels of the gateway where women sat and sunned themselves. From the windows in the gateway, the women viewed processions and activities happening outside the temple or entering into the temple itself. The decoration on the gateway retains a lot of colour. In fact, this temple is one of the most colourful in Egypt and gives visitors an idea of what it must have looked like new.

Put aside a morning for this temple. Cafés opposite the entrance provide lovely food and cold drinks – you can re-enter the temple feeling refreshed.

Deir el Medina, Luxor

The village of Deir el Medina, which housed the workmen who created the royal tombs in the Valley of the Kings, is situated on the west bank at Luxor. This site offers much to see and is well worth the trip – set aside a morning or an afternoon for this site. Check out Chapter 2 for all the details on this village.

The entire village is extant, with the foundations up to a metre high, giving a clear view of the village layout. Each house consists of four or five rooms, and many include staircases (the bottom few steps are still visible), which led to flat roofs.

Some in-built furniture, such as couches and box beds, can be seen in many houses, as well as sunken pots used for storage, and even bread ovens in some of the kitchens. In a couple of the houses, religious shrines are still standing, and you can almost imagine the incense burning and ancient Egyptians praying to their household gods.

The tombs of the workmen surround the village in the cliffs. Three of them are open to the public: those belonging to Sennedjem (with lovely farming scenes), Pashedu (showing one of the few scenes of salt-and-pepper-and white-haired ancestors), and Inherkhau (with an image of the deceased playing senet).

If the preceding isn't enough, you can also visit a number of temples built and used by the inhabitants of the village. These include a small temple to Ramses II, a terraced temple to Amenhotep of the Garden (Amenhotep I, the original builder of the village), and a large Ptolemaic temple dedicated to Hathor, built by and for tourists on the way to the Valley of the Kings. Even tourism isn't new!

Luxor Museum

The Luxor Museum has recently undergone an extension, which has improved it no end. Although it is a small museum, there is plenty to see, and the low lighting creates a great atmosphere for viewing the objects inside.

Highlights include the Kamose stela describing the expulsion of the Hyksos, and the mummy of Ahmose, the brother of Kamose, who finally *did* expel the Hyksos. Gaze into the beautiful carved face of Thutmosis III and wonder why Senwosret III looks so unhappy. Follow the Tutankhamun trail, which begins as you enter the museum with a statue of Tutankhamun as the god Amun and includes shabti figures on the first floor, each of which bears his youthful chubby face.

The reconstructed wall from the temple of Akhenaten at Karnak is still being worked on, so if your timing is right, you may be able to see archaeologists making additions. There is also a case of large ostraca (limestone flakes) used to draw the plan of a tomb and a house. The grid system is marked out on another wall to practise illustration. If all this isn't interesting enough, don't miss a number of weapons, a chariot, and a stela showing Amenhotep I in his chariot shooting arrows at a copper target.

The Luxor cache wing of the museum includes numerous royal statues discovered in the courtyard at Luxor temple, including Horemheb kneeling before the creator god Atum, a lovely red statue of Amenhotep III with rather slinky cat's eyes, and a large statue of Amun and Mut built by Ramses II. Although this last statue is damaged, many historians believe that the face of Mut is the true face of Nefertari, Ramses's beloved wife.

Visit the museum after 5 p.m. when it reopens for the evening, and plan to spend a couple of hours here.

Abu Simbel, Aswan

Ramses II built the temples of Abu Simbel at Aswan at the southernmost reaches of the Egyptian borders. The project may have taken more than 30 years to build, although the smaller of the temples is not complete. Ramses built two temples out of the cliff face, oriented to the east to meet the rising sun – one to the sun god Re-Horakhty and the other to Hathor and Nefertari. The façade of the Re-Horakhty temple is constructed of four colossal seated figures of Ramses, standing 21 metres (69 feet) high, carved directly from the rock face.

On entering the temple, a hall confronts you featuring pillars carved into *Osirid* (wrapped like a mummy) figures of the king. At the rear of the temple is a statue room with figures of Ramses, Re-Horakhty, Ptah, and Amun-Ra creating the focus of the worship in the temple. In February and October, sunlight enters this sanctuary and illuminates the faces of the gods.

Temple decoration shows Ramses II at his battle of Kadesh against the Hittites, as well as his Libyan, Syrian, and Nubian wars. The scenes are lively, brutal, and colourful, with much of the original paint still vibrant.

The smaller temple to Hathor and Nefertari has colossal figures of Ramses II and Nefertari on the façade, standing 10 metres (33 feet) tall. There are only two statues of the queen and four of the king, demonstrating that the building of this temple glorified the king as much as the queen. Within the temple, the first pillared court has Hathor-headed columns, and the sanctuary at the rear has a carved image of Hathor as a cow emerging from the marshes. Again the king is present and is standing beneath the head of the cow. Nefertari is shown throughout the temple carrying out rituals in worship of the gods, which was unusual, because queens normally played a more passive role.

Both temples were moved to higher ground in the 1960s when the Aswan dam was built and Lake Nasser submerged many of the Nubian temples. While visiting Abu Simbel, you can take a tour of the concrete support structure within the cliff face that stabilised these newly placed temples – itself a feat of modern engineering.

You can fly or drive to Abu Simbel. The drive from Luxor takes about four hours, but the road is often closed for security reasons. You can fly from Aswan, but the return flight is such that you only have an hour or so from the arrival time. I recommend staying overnight at Aswan and arranging transport with a local driver to really make the most of this site.

Chapter 19

Ten Key Egyptologists

During more than 200 years of Egyptian archaeology, hundreds of important archaeologists, scholars, and historians have contributed in one way or another to the discipline of Egyptology. This chapter looks at ten people who have made Egyptology what it is today, although many others made equally important discoveries and contributions and continue to do so – so this list is by no means conclusive.

Giovanni Belzoni (1778–1823)

The Italian Giovanni Belzoni was a tall man – 6 foot, 7 inches – which cut a fine figure in Egypt where the average height was at the time about 5 foot, 8 inches. His earliest career was as a circus strongman, touring Europe, before he turned his attention to Egypt.

Initially, Belzoni travelled to Egypt to sell a new type of water wheel (nothing to do with his strongman career). When this endeavour proved unsuccessful, he turned to the more lucrative work of excavating and transporting ancient monuments. In 1816, he started working for Henry Salt; one of his first jobs was to move the top half of a colossal statue from the Ramesseum, near Luxor. The statue today forms part of the Egyptian collection at the British Museum.

Belzoni carried out extensive excavation work and discovered, among other things, the tomb of Sety I and the temple of Ramses II at Abu Simbel in Nubia. Although his techniques of excavation were scandalous by modern standards – he often used dynamite when a trowel would have sufficed, and he had a habit of carving his name into objects – Belzoni did a lot to promote Egyptology through the exhibition of his objects.

He excavated for more than eight years. He died of dysentery in 1823 on an expedition to locate the source of the river Niger.

Jean-François Champollion (1790–1832)

Egyptologists will always remember Jean-François Champollion as the linguist who made the final breakthrough in deciphering hieroglyphs. His discovery changed Egyptology and enabled the world finally to read the ancient Egyptian language.

Champollion was always interested in language, and by 1807 (when he was 17) he had delivered his first paper on the language of ancient Egypt at the Lyceum. He spoke many languages, including Hebrew, Coptic, Arabic, Syriac, and Chaldean, when he embarked on deciphering the Rosetta Stone, a stela from Rosetta in the Delta written in three languages: hieroglyphs, demotic, and ancient Greek (see Chapter 11).

Champollion consulted with the English physician Thomas Young and compared notes until Young's death in 1817, after which Champollion continued the work. By 1822, he had worked out the key to hieroglyphs, although it wasn't until the completion of his grammar book in 1832 that he was able to read hieroglyphs with any certainty.

Between 1828 and 1829, Champollion and Ippolito Rosellini travelled to Egypt to record and survey further monuments, no doubt bringing back detailed copies of inscriptions to decipher. Champollion died from a stroke in 1832; not until shortly after were his books *Egyptian Grammar* and then *Egyptian Dictionary* published, so he never got to see the difference his work made.

Karl Lepsius (1819–84)

Karl Lepsius, a German Egyptologist, gained his doctorate in 1833 and then used the newly published *Egyptian Grammar* by Champollion to learn to read hieroglyphs. He made his first trip to Egypt in 1842 with the aim of recording the monuments and collecting antiquities, which was the norm at the time. In his career he collected more than 15,000 artefacts, which formed the basis for the Egyptian Museum in Berlin.

Between 1842 and 1845, Lepsius led the Prussian expedition to Egypt and Nubia and recorded its work in 12 volumes entitled *Denkmaeler aus Aegypten und Aethiopien*. This publication is still valuable for modern Egyptologists because many of the monuments recorded have since deteriorated, and these volumes provide clear images and descriptions of their appearance more than 150 years ago.

Lepsius founded the study programme of Egyptology at the University of Berlin and was appointed the keeper of the Egyptian collection at the Berlin Museum, which housed his growing collection from the expeditions. The Berlin Museum still thrives today and houses some of the most famous images in the world, including the painted limestone bust of Nefertiti.

Amelia Edwards (1831–92)

Amelia Edwards, an English Egyptologist, journalist, and novelist, went to Egypt in 1873 and was hooked. This trip inspired her to write *A Thousand Miles up the Nile*, a travelogue of her adventures.

Writing, however, wasn't new to Edwards: Her first poem was published at 7 years old, her first short story at 12. She was home educated and was clearly a promising student. She had written a number of travelogues prior to her Egyptian trip, recording her adventures with her female travel companion.

On her first trip to Egypt, she spent six weeks excavating at the site of Abu Simbel. In 1880, she set up an informal group to deal with the conservation and excavation issues of Egypt. In 1882, the organisation was officially named the Egypt Exploration Fund (now the Egypt Exploration Society). The society's goal, then and now, is to excavate and record the monuments of Egypt. You can visit the society's Web site at www.ees.ac.uk.

On her death, Edwards bequeathed a number of artefacts, her books, photographs, and other Egypt-related documents to University College, London, to be used as teaching aids for Egyptology students. As a supporter of the Suffrage movement, she chose University College because it was the first college to admit women as students. She also bequeathed enough money to set up the United Kingdom's first professorship in Egyptian archaeology and philology at University College, which went to W. M. Flinders Petrie.

W. M. Flinders Petrie (1853–1942)

Flinders Petrie was an archaeologist for more than 70 years. He started his Egyptological career in the 1880s when he went to measure the Great Pyramid at Giza. He then directed excavations at a number of important sites around Egypt at a time when there were still lots of things to be discovered.

Petrie was not only a famous Egyptologist but also a great archaeologist. His *seriation dating technique* is still used worldwide. This technique creates relative dates for any site through the arrangement of items into an evolutionary sequence. (See Chapter 15 for more on this technique.) Petrie also had a great interest in the less glamorous side of archaeology and collected all the bits – mostly hundreds of potsherds – that most archaeologists left behind because they weren't gold and shiny.

Over his many years excavating, Petrie collected thousands of Egyptian artefacts, some of great interest, which he sold to University College, London, in 1913, creating the Petrie Museum of Egyptian Archaeology. Petrie retired from his position as Edwards Professor at University College in 1933. He then excavated for a few years near Gaza before his death in Jerusalem in 1942.

Howard Carter (1874–1939)

English Egyptologist Howard Carter was born in Kensington in London and is famous for his discovery of the tomb of Tutankhamun in 1922.

However, Carter had a rich career *prior* to this discovery. He started life as an artist and was sent to Egypt to record the tomb decoration at Beni Hasan (see Chapter 18). He then tried his hand at archaeology alongside Petrie at Amarna, although Petrie didn't think Carter would be a great archaeologist. Just goes to show what an impressive find can do.

Carter was appointed inspector general of Upper Egypt in 1899 and was responsible for putting electric lights in the Valley of the Kings. He resigned his position in 1903 after a dispute with some drunk and disorderly French tourists. He worked as a draftsman and antiquities dealer until Lord Carnarvon offered to finance excavations, employing Carter as director. They worked for many years around Luxor and the Valley of the Kings, making many discoveries until by accident in the last year of excavating they found KV62, the tomb of Tutankhamun.

The remainder of Carter's life was filled with recording and analysing Tutankhamun's artefacts, as well as writing excavation reports and giving lecture tours around the world.

Alan Gardiner (1879–1963)

Sir Alan Gardiner was an amazing linguist and made great advances regarding the language of the ancient Egyptians. He was an expert in *hieratic*, the cursive form of hieroglyphic script that the Egyptians used for everyday writing. Egyptology students the world over are familiar with Gardiner's *Egyptian Grammar*, a comprehensive guide to Egyptian hieroglyphs with a dictionary that is still used regularly. During his career, Gardiner made trips to Paris and Turin to copy hieratic manuscripts; many translations being used today are the result of his work.

Gardiner was born in Eltham and was interested in Egypt from a young age, which resulted in his being sent to Gaston Maspero in Paris for a year to study. He then returned to The Queen's College, Oxford. From a wealthy family, Gardiner never needed to work and spent his time teaching himself all he wanted about Egypt and Egyptology and pursuing his own goals. From 1912 to 1914 he held a readership at Manchester University, after which he continued his linguistic work.

Jac Janssen (born 1922)

Professor Jac Janssen, a Dutch Egyptologist now in his 80s, has been fundamental in the work at Deir el Medina (see Chapter 2). He has held the emeritus professorship of Egyptology, University of Leiden, Netherlands, for many years and is now living in the United Kingdom where he still works to further enlighten students and historians on the workmen's village of Deir el Medina.

As a New Kingdom hieratic expert, Janssen has worked on many of the inscriptions from Deir el Medina, which has provided invaluable information regarding the day-to-day lives of everyday Egyptians.

Janssen has worked primarily on the economic side of history, publishing important books such as *Commodity Prices from the Ramessid Period: An Economic Study of the Village of Necropolis Workmen at Thebes*, which gives all the prices for various household goods. In 2006, he published a book on the economic use of the donkey at Deir el Medina called, not surprisingly, *Donkeys at Deir el Medina.*

Kent Weeks (born 1941)

Dr Kent Weeks, an American Egyptologist, is best known for his current work in the Valley of the Kings on the Theban Mapping Project, which resulted in the rediscovery of KV5, the tomb of the sons of Ramses II. The discovery of KV5 is a major achievement. The Theban Mapping Project began in 1978 with the goal of recording the locations of tombs, temples, and other archaeological sites and structures on the Theban west bank. This is a monumental task that will take many more years to complete.

Weeks has worked in Egyptology from the 1960s, and from 1972 taught at the American University in Cairo. Between 1977 and 1988 he returned to the United States as the assistant and then associate professor of Egyptian Archaeology at the University of California, Berkeley, before returning to the American University in Cairo for the professorship in Egyptology that he still holds.

Rosalie David (born 1947)

Professor Rosalie David OBE holds numerous titles, including:

- Director of the Manchester Mummy Project
- Director of the KNH Centre for Biological and Forensic Studies in Egyptology at the University of Manchester. The project was set up in 2003 to enable the unique opportunity for university training in biomedical Egyptology
- Director of the International Mummy Database (University of Manchester)
- Director of the Schistosomiasis Investigation Project (University of Manchester)

Professor David set up the Manchester Mummy Project in order to study the 24 human and 34 animal mummies in the Manchester Museum collection. Before the project was set up, mummies were X-rayed using portable equipment in galleries or in situ at the find site. Manchester now provides permanent facilities for ongoing mummy-related research. Recent successes include discovering the DNA of a schistosomiasis (bilharzia) worm found inside one of the mummies.

Manchester is also home to a tissue bank, which includes a collection of Egyptian mummified tissue from mummies held in various international museums. The tissue bank is a modern resource for DNA, which can provide information about these Egyptians of the past, and a real pioneering project.

Professor David is the first female Egyptology professor in the United Kingdom and has taught Egyptology for more than 25 years. She received an OBE from the Queen in recognition of her services to Egyptology in the New Year Honours List of 2003.

Index

• N •

Notes

Notes

Notes

Notes

Notes

Notes

FOR

DUMMIES®

Do Anything. Just Add Dummies

PROPERTY

UK editions

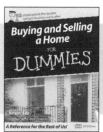

978-0-7645-7027-8

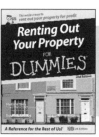

978-0-470-02921-3

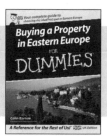

978-0-7645-7047-6

PERSONAL FINANCE

978-0-7645-7023-0

978-0-470-51510-5

978-0-470-05815-2

BUSINESS

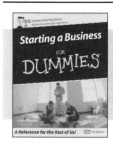

978-0-7645-7018-6

978-0-7645-7056-8

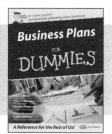

978-0-7645-7026-1

Answering Tough Interview Questions For Dummies (978-0-470-01903-0)

Arthritis For Dummies (978-0-470-02582-6)

Being the Best Man For Dummies (978-0-470-02657-1)

British History For Dummies (978-0-470-03536-8)

Building Self-Confidence For Dummies (978-0-470-01669-5)

Buying a Home on a Budget For Dummies (978-0-7645-7035-3)

Children's Health For Dummies (978-0-470-02735-6)

Cognitive Behavioural Therapy For Dummies (978-0-470-01838-5)

Cricket For Dummies (978-0-470-03454-5)

CVs For Dummies (978-0-7645-7017-9)

Detox For Dummies (978-0-470-01908-5)

Diabetes For Dummies (978-0-470-05810-7)

Divorce For Dummies (978-0-7645-7030-8)

DJing For Dummies (978-0-470-03275-6)

eBay.co.uk For Dummies (978-0-7645-7059-9)

English Grammar For Dummies (978-0-470-05752-0)

Gardening For Dummies (978-0-470-01843-9)

Genealogy Online For Dummies (978-0-7645-7061-2)

Green Living For Dummies (978-0-470-06038-4)

Hypnotherapy For Dummies (978-0-470-01930-6)

Life Coaching For Dummies (978-0-470-03135-3)

Neuro-linguistic Programming For Dummies (978-0-7645-7028-5)

Nutrition For Dummies (978-0-7645-7058-2)

Parenting For Dummies (978-0-470-02714-1)

Pregnancy For Dummies (978-0-7645-7042-1)

Rugby Union For Dummies (978-0-470-03537-5)

Self Build and Renovation For Dummies (978-0-470-02586-4)

Starting a Business on eBay.co.uk For Dummies (978-0-470-02666-3)

Starting and Running an Online Business For Dummies (978-0-470-05768-1)

The GL Diet For Dummies (978-0-470-02753-0)

The Romans For Dummies (978-0-470-03077-6)

Thyroid For Dummies (978-0-470-03172-8)

UK Law and Your Rights For Dummies (978-0-470-02796-7)

Writing a Novel & Getting Published For Dummies (978-0-470-05910-4)

FOR DUMMIES®

Do Anything. Just Add Dummies

HOBBIES

978-0-7645-5232-8

978-0-7645-6847-3

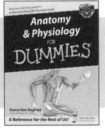

978-0-7645-5476-6

Also available:

Art For Dummies
(978-0-7645-5104-8)

Aromatherapy For Dummies
(978-0-7645-5171-0)

Bridge For Dummies
(978-0-471-92426-5)

Card Games For Dummies
(978-0-7645-9910-1)

Chess For Dummies
(978-0-7645-8404-6)

Improving Your Memory
For Dummies
(978-0-7645-5435-3)

Massage For Dummies
(978-0-7645-5172-7)

Meditation For Dummies
(978-0-471-77774-8)

Photography For Dummies
(978-0-7645-4116-2)

Quilting For Dummies
(978-0-7645-9799-2)

EDUCATION

978-0-7645-7206-7

978-0-7645-5581-7

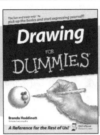

978-0-7645-5422-3

Also available:

Algebra For Dummies
(978-0-7645-5325-7)

Algebra II For Dummies
(978-0-471-77581-2)

Astronomy For Dummies
(978-0-7645-8465-7)

Buddhism For Dummies
(978-0-7645-5359-2)

Calculus For Dummies
(978-0-7645-2498-1)

Forensics For Dummies
(978-0-7645-5580-0)

Islam For Dummies
(978-0-7645-5503-9)

Philosophy For Dummies
(978-0-7645-5153-6)

Religion For Dummies
(978-0-7645-5264-9)

Trigonometry For Dummies
(978-0-7645-6903-6)

PETS

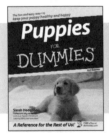

978-0-470-03717-1

978-0-7645-8418-3

978-0-7645-5275-5

Also available:

Labrador Retrievers
For Dummies
(978-0-7645-5281-6)

Aquariums For Dummies
(978-0-7645-5156-7)

Birds For Dummies
(978-0-7645-5139-0)

Dogs For Dummies
(978-0-7645-5274-8)

Ferrets For Dummies
(978-0-7645-5259-5)

Golden Retrievers
For Dummies
(978-0-7645-5267-0)

Horses For Dummies
(978-0-7645-9797-8)

Jack Russell Terriers
For Dummies
(978-0-7645-5268-7)

Puppies Raising & Training
Diary For Dummies
(978-0-7645-0876-9)
